Colorado's High
THIRTEENERS

A CLIMBING & HIKING GUIDE

Third Edition

Mike Garratt and Bob Martin
With a Foreword by Walter R. Borneman

D0111182

JOHNSON BOOKS
Boulder

Copyright © 1989, 1992 by Mike Garratt and Bob Martin

All rights reserved. No part of this publication may be reproduced, stored in a retrieval system, or transmitted, in any form or by any means, electronic, mechanical, photocopying, recording, or otherwise, without the prior written permission of the Publisher.

Library of Congress Cataloging in Publication Data

Garratt, Mike.
    Colorado's high thirteeners.

    Includes index.
    1. Mountaineering—Colorado—Guide-books.
2. Colorado—Description and travel—1981-
Guide-books. I. Martin, Bob, 1920-   . II. Title.
GV199.42.C6G37   1984   796.5'22'09788   84-27436

Third Edition
    2   3   4   5   6   7   8   9

Printed in the United States of America

ISBN: 0-917895-39-8

Cover photo of the Weminuche Wilderness courtesy of Gary Koontz.

All photographs by the authors.

Contents

Foreword

Mountain men traveling the breadth of Colorado more than a century ago carried with them a leather pouch referred to as a "possibles" bag. From it, these hardened voyageurs might produce just about anything. In **Colorado's High Thirteeners**, Mike Garratt and Bob Martin have honored the mountain man tradition and produced an extraordinary "possibles" bag for climbers of all interests and abilities.

Garratt and Martin, unlike the rest of us who were climbing Fourteeners, each became interested in climbing Colorado's other mountains, seeking out lower, but less-traveled and frequently more interesting peaks. Independent of one another, each worked to refine a comprehensive list of Colorado's 13,000-foot summits. Mike and Bob became acquainted by finding each other's name on obscure summit registers long before they finally met in 1981. Combining their talents, they worked to produce what is both an informative guide to the one hundred sixty-nine highest Thirteeners and— if that isn't enough of a possibles bag—a complete listing of the 740 Colorado summits which rise above 13,000 feet.

Garratt and Martin have climbed these mountains independently, often by different routes, and their partnership in this guide gives the reader a unique consensus on the best route to each summit, as well as good alternatives on some mountains.

I plan on stuffing this book in my pack and heading out— under the guise of checking these guys out, you understand— with a whole new "possibles" bag. Mike and Bob have reminded us that the mountains are there—the times we have to make ourselves. See you on the trail!

Walter R. Borneman
September 10, 1984

To Judy, Mike's companion
on many mountain adventures.

Introduction

Compiling the Lists

This book provides a systematic listing of all Colorado mountains thirteen thousand feet and above and gives route descriptions for the highest 169 Thirteeners. This includes all Thirteeners 13,580 feet and above. With the existing guidebooks to the Fourteeners, detailed route descriptions are now available for more than two hundred of the highest summits in the state.

While many of Colorado's mountains were climbed prior to this century, it wasn't until the 1920s that the state's highest peaks were climbed on a systematic basis. In 1923, Carl Blaurock and William Ervin became the first to climb all of the Fourteeners, which then numbered forty-six summits. Since then (according to Colorado Mountain Club records), over six hundred others have climbed all of the Fourteeners.

Over the years, the list of Colorado Fourteeners has changed, both from remeasurement of elevations by the United States Geological Survey and by changes in the concept of what constitutes a mountain. In recent years, the list has stabilized at fifty-four summits, the ones listed in various publications of the Colorado Mountain Club. The list evolved without use of rigid criteria, more according to what certain people "thought" should constitute a mountain. (A detailed treatment of the current procedures for classifying mountains precedes the tables at the end of the book.)

Bill Graves was one who attempted to establish some definitive criteria for the recognition of mountains as separate summits. His article in the February 1968 **Trail and Timberline** (a Colorado Mountain Club publication) proposed that a summit be recognized as a separate mountain if it rises at least three hundred feet above all saddles between it and higher peaks. This proposal was reasonable because it nearly fit the then-current list of recognized Fourteeners. Only

North Maroon Peak and El Diente failed to meet the 300-foot test, while Ellingwood Point was the only known summit not recognized by the Colorado Mountain Club as a Fourteener that did meet the test. There were several interesting comments regarding the Graves proposal reported in **Trail and Timberline**, but no further action was taken.

Since Bill Graves proposed the 300-foot criterion in 1968, it has come into general acceptance as the measure of a separate mountain. The list of recognized Fourteeners continues to include North Maroon Peak and El Diente, while omitting other summits that fail the 300-foot criterion, such as Mount Cameron, Conundrum Peak, and North Eolus. Ellingwood Point is included on most lists of Fourteeners, so whether or not it is officially "accepted" as a Fourteener by the Colorado Mountain Club may be a moot question.

While the systematic climbing of the Fourteeners began early in this century, the systematic climbing of the Thirteeners is a much more recent development. The first impetus to such an effort was the publication of "100 Highest Summits in Colorado," by Bill Graves, in the May 1968 **Trail and Timberline**. The Graves list was compiled using the 300-foot criterion as the measure of a separate summit. Using this same criterion, R.D. (Bob) Martin prepared two listings of summits in different Colorado areas. "Mountains of Rocky Mountain National Park" appeared in the July 1969 **Trail and Timberline** and "Mountains of the Southern Sawatch" was published in the March 1971 issue.

In **Trail and Timberline** of May 1978, Bill Graves presented a revised list of the hundred highest summits in Colorado. The revisions were due to new data from the USGS and the addition of mountains overlooked in the original compilation that were "found" by others poring over topographic maps.

Another effort to compile a list of highest mountains was by Evans and Ellen Winner. In 1977, they published a book entitled **Four Thousand Meters**. The book lists summits in the United States that are four thousand meters (approximately 13,123 feet) and above. The Winner requirements for a separate summit are that it rise at least one hundred meters above saddles between it and higher summits and that it meet certain distance requirements from higher summits. This results in a quite complicated and difficult-to-understand set of qualifications. The fact that their tables list the elevations of mountains in meters, while topographic map elevations are in feet, compounds the problem.

The pioneer work in compiling a list of Colorado summits 13,000 feet and above was done by Jim Hoerlein. Jim's first effort in compiling such an extensive list was based on the same criteria developed by Bill Graves. Jim also included the named summits that fail the 300-foot test, identifying them as named points that do not qualify as separate summits. Hoerlein also developed the technique of numerically ranking the mountains that qualify as separate summits and listing the named points that do not qualify as separate summits by elevation but without numerical rank.

Jim Hoerlein gave the authors the opportunity to comment on, add to, subtract from, and verify the data in his original list. The tabular listings presented at the end of this book evolved from the first list developed by Jim Hoerlein in 1977. The authors are grateful to Jim for his efforts in compiling the original data and for his help as the lists were refined.

Using This Guide

This guide includes directions for reaching all of the Colorado summits below the Fourteeners down to the 202nd highest ranked peak. In addition, we include directions to the named Thirteeners that do not qualify as separate summits and are 13,580 feet and above.

In the route descriptions, the mountains are grouped by areas generally running northeast to southwest across Colorado. In many cases, two or more summits can be reached on the same day hike or backpacking trip. Information is given to let you choose how to group the summits for your own trip.

In preparing the route descriptions, we assume that the reader will have at least some experience in hiking and climbing and will obtain and use other sources of information.

Besides a Colorado state highway map, minimum tools for most of these climbs are the applicable National Forest Service map and the United States Geological Survey topographic maps (available respectively from USDA Forest Service, P.O. Box 25127, Lakewood, Colorado 80225 and USGS, Box 25286, Federal Center, Denver, Colorado 80225).

In the heading for each hike and climb, the **general description** briefly summarizes the character of the trip. It is intended to help hikers and climbers select trips that fit their interests and levels of ability. **Hiking distance** in each route description is the approximate round-trip distance from the normal passenger-car trailhead. **Starting elevation** is the elevation at the trailhead. **Elevation gain** is the total amount of vertical ascent required in the course of the climb and the return to the trailhead. The elevation gain usually is greater than the difference between the starting elevation and the high point, due to descents along the route. The **maps** listed are the applicable USGS topographic map quadrangles and the national forest map.

The route descriptions assume you can find the trailhead with a minimum of direction and that on the easier peaks you can find your way along trails, ridges, and valleys using your own navigational skills. The descriptions also assume the reader has acquired or is familiar with the relevant maps listed in the heading for each route description.

On the more difficult summits, we try to give much more detail so that the preferred route can be followed most efficiently. Unlike many guidebooks, we don't say much about the sights you will see along the way to and from the top, but concentrate on describing a good route to the top. We do, however, guarantee the scenic values on the summits covered are at least as great as you would find on the Fourteeners. There is one big difference; you will find far fewer people on the routes to these summits.

We assume that you will be getting to the trailhead in a passenger car. In some cases the hike and climb can be shortened with a four-wheel-drive vehicle. To the extent possible, we have described a route that can be covered in a day hike. There are some summits that can be reached only by backpacking. In a few cases, we have suggested an approach by backpacking to avoid an extremely long day hike.

The 169 Thirteeners covered in the route descriptions are a diverse group. A few are harder than any of the Fourteeners. A number of summits are remote enough to require backpacking. Many are in scenic wilderness areas away from any of the Fourteeners. Others are easy day hikes that make good trips for those less experienced in mountain climbing. Because many of the Thirteeners are more remote than the Fourteeners and are not as frequently climbed, you need to be better prepared and more cautious while climbing them.

By accepted mountaineering standards, there are no really difficult ascents covered in this book. Proficient mountaineers can climb each of Colorado's two hundred highest summits without rope or other artificial aids when following the easiest route under good weather conditions. This does not mean, however, that any of these summits can be taken lightly. Rapidly deteriorating weather can turn a pleasant climb into a nightmare. Poor route selection can lead to much more difficult climbing than anticipated. By Colorado standards, many of these summits are in remote areas where other hikers and climbers might not be seen for weeks.

The loose rock danger on many of the more difficult Thirteeners is greater than on the Fourteeners since the number of ascents has been insufficient to "clean" the routes of debris. All footholds and handholds should be tested for security. A hard hat, rope, and some technical climbing gear occasionally may be required for safety. In addition, while climbing steeper snow slopes in spring and early summer, an ice axe and possibly crampons are advised.

The accompanying table entitled "Classification of Trips" is included to further assist you in selecting hikes and climbs that are convenient, safe, and within your ability. The duration of the hike and climb and the type of trip are listed down the left side of the page. "Half Day" hikes can be completed within five hours. Allow six to eight hours for the "Short Day" trips. "Long Day" trips might take nine to twelve hours. "Extremely Long Day or Backpack" trips might last even longer and most may prefer to backpack. A "Trail Backpack" is on established trails, paths, or easy-to-hike off-trail terrain. A "Climbing Backpack" has some off-trail backpacking on steep slopes or rocky terrain and may require route finding.

Across the top of the page, the table shows the most difficult climbing portion of the trip. The classifications range from trail hiking on the left to difficult climbing on the right. The "Easy Hiking" column includes hiking on trails, paths, and gentle off-trail routes. The "Harder Hiking" column includes rougher walking on steep slopes and over rocky terrain. The "Easy Climbing" column includes covering terrain that requires the use of the hands for balance. The column "Moderate Climbing" includes climbing on steep rocky slopes, perhaps with some exposure and rock fall danger. The "Difficult Climbing" column includes trips where technical climbing skills are essential and rope may be needed.

If a trip includes multiple-peak climbs of more than one level of difficulty, its number is shown in more than one box. The classifications assume hikers and climbers of average speed and proficiency. They assume good summer weather.

We take the responsibility for describing the routes to the summits to the best of our ability, based both on what we found when we climbed them and on any other information we have been able to find. **You will have to take the responsibility of using good judgment in following this guide.** Choose trips within your ability, allow sufficient time, turn back in case of mishap or bad weather, have the proper equipment, and select experienced companions to make a safe group. We hope you will enjoy reaching these summits as much as we have.

Classification of Trips

	Easy Hiking	Harder Hiking	Easy Climbing	Moderate Climbing	Difficult Climbing
Half Day	5	7, 14, 64, 87	16, 26	89	
Short Day	4, 19, 28, 49, 61	6, 8	3, 11, 12, 18, 22, 24, 25, 27, 30, 32, 33, 37, 43, 44, 46, 69, 71, 73, 95	15	
Long Day	40, 41, 54, 55, 68	39, 53, 66, 67, 74	9, 10, 17, 29, 38, 45, 57, 60, 75, 90, 91	1, 2, 23, 31, 85, 90, 92, 93, 94	34, 48, 50, 70, 76, 86, 88, 90
Extremely Long Day or Backpack		71	35, 36, 84	13, 21, 42, 58	52, 93
Trail Backpack		82	62, 65	20, 51, 56, 62, 63, 72, 77, 83, 90	47, 48, 59, 72, 82, 90
Climbing Backpack				78, 79, 80, 81	78, 79, 80, 81

Front Range and Gore Range

Mount Meeker, far right, with The Notch and Longs Peak center.

1. MOUNT MEEKER (13,911 feet)

General description:
A lengthy day hike with a trail approach and steep,
rough travel on the final portions of the ascent
Hiking distance: 12 miles
Starting elevation: 9,400 feet
Elevation gain: 4,600 feet
Maps:
7.5 minute Longs Peak
7.5 minute Allens Park
Roosevelt National Forest

Mount Meeker is in Rocky Mountain National Park just
southeast of Longs Peak. It is much less frequently visited than
Longs Peak and is considered harder to climb. Mount Meeker
can be climbed from the trailhead at Longs Peak Ranger
Station in a long day.

Midway between Estes Park and Allens Park, leave
Colorado 7 a mile and a half south of Wind River Pass. Turn
west and drive a mile to the trailhead parking area at the ranger
station.

Hike up the well-traveled trail to the Chasm Lake
emergency shelter house, which is located at 11,600 feet at
trail's end two hundred yards from the lake. The route to the
shelter house goes left at a trail junction a half mile from the
ranger station. It goes left again two miles farther at the Jims
Grove junction and left a third time another mile farther at a
junction on Mills Moraine. The shelter house is reached in
another mile, four and a half miles from the ranger station.

From the shelter house, climb south on grassy slopes up the
drainage. Stay left and on the east side of the spectacular
jutting prominence called Ships Prow. At 11,860 feet, continue
up the right-hand subsidiary drainage that descends directly
from the Longs Peak-Mount Meeker saddle. Traveling up the
east side of the drainage, the footing alternates between rock
slabs and boulders. Early in the summer occasional steep
snowfields may be encountered.

When the gully appears to end at a cliff face at 12,800 feet, follow a broad ramp that climbs south and to the left across the cliff face. This ramp allows access to the gentler slopes of The Loft, a broad flat saddle between Longs Peak and Mount Meeker.

The last four hundred feet of climbing over the boulder-strewn terrain leads to the west end of the narrow Mount Meeker ridge. Make a short scramble east along the ridge to the summit, a large flat boulder. The rugged climb of 2,300 feet above the shelter house is covered in less than one and a half miles.

Because of camping restrictions within Rocky Mountain National Park, it is best to do this climb as a lengthy day hike. Climbers may be tempted to combine the climb of Mount Meeker with Longs Peak. However, the seemingly straightforward traverse is complicated by The Notch, a deep gash in the ridge just below and southeast of Longs Peak. Though The Notch can be bypassed on the southwest side, a long day made even longer is best avoided by not attempting the two peaks on the same day.

Climbs of Mount Meeker are also possible from the south via Sandbeach Lake and up the southeast ridge. Any southeast ridge route requires a traverse of the Mount Meeker knife-edge ridge from the lower eastern summit to the main summit. The Sandbeach Lake route avoids this traverse by an ascent of the south ridge, but it is longer than the route via Chasm Lake. The main route described above is not obvious and may not be the one most frequently used, but it is straightforward and goes well.

2. MOUNT POWELL (13,580 feet)

General description:
An approach on trails of varying quality to a high alpine meadow for the rugged direct finish on talus and probably snow

Hiking distance: 12 miles

3

Starting elevation: 9,340 feet
Elevation gain: 4,500 feet
Maps:
7.5 minute Vail West (trail approach only)
7.5 minute Vail East
7.5 minute Mount Powell
White River National Forest

Mount Powell is the highest summit in the Gore Range. Its ascent requires a long hike into the Eagles Nest Wilderness. Some climbers may prefer to approach on a backpack trip. The climb of Mount Powell goes without great difficulty by the suggested route, though it can become quite difficult if you get off the best route.

From the Vail exit on Interstate 70, take the frontage road on the north side of the freeway. Drive one mile west to the Red Sandstone Creek road, Forest Service road 700. Follow this winding road north up Red Sandstone Creek and Indian Creek into the Piney River drainage. Just after the road crosses Piney River, turn right and drive another mile northeast and east toward Piney Lake. A fence and gate belonging to Piney River Ranch marks the end for car travel.

Forest Service trail 1885 gives access across private land through open meadows on the north side of Piney Lake. After a half mile, avoid a side trail that climbs out of the valley to the left. Continue east along the trail into the upper reaches of Piney River.

After three and a half miles the trail crosses a stream coming in from the north in a level stretch at 9,900 feet. Good campsites for backpackers can be found here. Shortly before the stream crossing, a rough unmarked trail splits off on the left. It climbs steeply north and then northeast up the drainage. When the trail fades out in a pastoral alpine meadow, continue up the grassy drainage toward the 12,260-foot saddle south of Mount Powell.

At the 11,900-foot level, bear left and climb north in a series of grassy couloirs to intersect the ridge at a minor saddle at

4

12,460 feet. Cross the saddle and climb fifty feet down the east side of the ridge. Climb north along the east side of the ridge over snowfields and talus to the summit.

3. BARD PEAK (13,641 feet)

General description:
   A short strenuous off-trail climb requiring bushwhacking
Hiking distance: 5 miles
Starting elevation: 9,800 feet
Elevation gain: 3,900 feet
Maps:
   7.5 minute Grays Peak
   Arapaho National Forest

The starting point for the climb is the Bakerville exit on Interstate 70 between Silver Plume and the Eisenhower Tunnel. Bard Peak is a high summit less than two miles from the interstate, but it is scarcely noticed by the thousands that pass each day. The ascent route follows the drainage from the saddle between Mount Parnassus and Bard Peak.

After parking at Bakerville, walk to the north side of the interstate on the exit bridge. Turn left and walk thirty yards west along the exit ramp to get beyond private property north of the exit bridge. Begin climbing north up the west side of the drainage.

The climb requires sixteen hundred feet of bushwhacking through dense tree cover. Traveling on the west side of the stream provides the best footing. It also avoids mistakenly ascending the subsidiary drainage branching off northeast at 11,100 feet. After passing tree line at 11,400 feet, the climbing becomes easier. Follow grassy and gravel slopes leading to the 13,037-foot saddle west of Bard Peak. From the saddle, the ridge walk east to the summit is a simple matter.

A much longer but more gradual approach uses the long trail up Bard Creek from the road end south and west of Empire. From trail's end an ascent can be made west up the valley to the 12,940-foot saddle north of Bard Peak. The finish is south along the ridge.

4. ARGENTINE PEAK (13,738 feet)
MOUNT EDWARDS (13,850 feet)
McCLELLAN MOUNTAIN (13,587 feet)

General description:
A pleasant walk on old roads and ridges
Hiking distance: 7 miles
Starting elevation: 11,600 feet
Elevation gain: 3,200 feet
Maps:
7.5 minute Grays Peak
7.5 minute Montezuma
Arapaho National Forest

These peaks frame Argentine Pass, the highest pass on the Continental Divide. The three peaks can readily be climbed on a day hike.

Drive south from Interstate 70 at Georgetown on the Guanella Pass road. After a sharp switchback to the northwest three miles from Georgetown, turn right onto a dirt road. This side road climbs a mile through a series of switchbacks to join an abandoned railroad grade coming up around Leavenworth Mountain from the town of Silver Plume. Follow the railroad grade another four and a half miles to the inactive Waldorf Mine. Shortly beyond the mine, the road becomes rough and may be closed to all vehicles. In any event, this is a good parking place for passenger cars.

Walk south up the old road a mile to a junction at 12,219 feet. Take the right fork another one and a half miles to

Argentine Pass at 13,207 feet. Turn left and hike south a mile up the gentle ridge on tundra and rocks to Argentine Peak. Return to Argentine Pass and climb gradually up the broad ridge a mile northwest to Mount Edwards.

McClellan Mountain is three-fourths of a mile along the ridge northeast of Mount Edwards, with a climb of less than two hundred vertical feet from the saddle. Descent from McClellan Mountain can be made directly east-southeast down grassy slopes to the trailhead at Waldorf. For a longer but more gradual return, follow the McClellan Mountain ridge northeast to find old mine roads that descend on switchbacks to Waldorf.

5. SQUARE TOP MOUNTAIN (13,794 feet)

General description:
   A comfortable hike on mostly grassy slopes above timberline
Hiking distance: 7 miles
Starting elevation: 11,669 feet
Elevation gain: 2,400 feet
Maps:
   7.5 minute Mount Evans
   7.5 minute Montezuma
   Arapaho National Forest

This pleasant hike begins at Guanella Pass on the county road between Grant on US 285 and Georgetown on Interstate 70. It is a good one for those who like gentle off-trail hiking at high altitude. The hike leads to the distinctive flat summit of Square Top Mountain. The road over Guanella Pass is kept passable for passenger cars year-round.

Hike west from Guanella Pass over marshy ground. After a slight descent the route begins to ascend the broad grassy ridge west of Guanella Pass. Follow this ridge through its gentle turns over two minor ridge points to the broad flat summit. Deciding on a high point can be difficult, so you may want to explore the entire summit area.

This climb can be made in any month of the year since Guanella Pass has easy access and the ridge route tends to accumulate little snow in winter.

6. GRAY WOLF MOUNTAIN (13,602 feet) MOUNT SPAULDING (13,842 feet)

General description:
  A moderate off-trail hike on easy terrain mostly above timberline
Hiking distance: 10 miles
Starting elevation: 11,600 feet
Elevation gain: 3,200 feet
Maps:
  7.5 minute Mount Evans
  Pike National Forest

These two summits are along the ridge northwest of Mount Evans. The route along the ridge from Mount Evans is rough, so we suggest an easier approach from the west.

The road over Guanella Pass from Grant on US 285 to Georgetown on Interstate 70 provides easy access to the starting point for this climb. Park cars at 11,600 feet at the east end of the first switchback a tenth mile north of Guanella Pass.

The trickiest part of this climb is navigating through the dense willows in the upper reaches of Scott Gomer Creek. The best route is to follow the high strip of land dividing the drainages of Scott Gomer Creek and South Clear Creek. From the parking place hike east, losing a hundred feet of elevation, and traverse north of a lake at 11,510 feet. Continue east over two minor ridge points. Then climb northeast through the last stand of trees to a small pond at 11,860 feet just west of the upper reaches of Scott Gomer Creek. At this point travel becomes much easier on the grassy slopes above timberline. Continue hiking northeast and north to the broad saddle at 12,740 feet west of Gray Wolf Mountain. Then climb the gentle west ridge to the summit of Gray Wolf Mountain.

The traverse to Mount Spaulding is over terrain strewn with large boulders. Head southeast from Gray Wolf to the large flat saddle at 13,020 feet. Continue up the north side of Mount Spaulding to the top.

The descent route uses the west ridge of Mount Spaulding until the ridge merges with Scott Gomer Creek at 12,200 feet. Bear left and make a descending traverse southwest to the 11,860-foot pond passed on the ascent. The rest is simply a matter of retracing the best route back through the willows to the road just north of Guanella Pass.

During the short summer season when the Mount Evans road is open to Summit Lake, Mount Spaulding and Gray Wolf Mountain can be climbed from Summit Lake via Mount Spaulding's east ridge.

7. BALD MOUNTAIN (13,684 feet)

General description:
An off-trail hike and rocky ridge walk from a scenic high pass
Hiking distance: 5 miles
Starting elevation: 11,360 feet
Elevation gain: 2,800 feet
Maps:
7.5 minute Boreas Pass
Arapaho National Forest

Bald Mountain is a high point along the Continental Divide east of Hoosier Pass. It is the prominent summit that can be seen to the southeast from Interstate 70 in the Frisco area.

Drive to Boreas Pass, either from Breckenridge on Colorado 9 or from Como on US 285. Park a half mile north of the pass at an elevation of 11,360 feet.

Walk up the grassy slope northeast to the Continental Divide ridge at 12,800 feet. Follow the ridge northwest over rocks and tundra to the summit of Bald Mountain. You cross over three ridge points before reaching the 13,684-foot summit. At the first ridge point, at 13,679 feet, the Continental Divide turns east. Leave the divide and continue northwest on the broad ridge to the summit of Bald Mountain.

8. MOUNT SILVERHEELS (13,822 feet)

General description:
An off-trail day hike over gentle terrain
Hiking distance: 6 miles
Starting elevation: 10,920 feet
Elevation gain: 3,400 feet
Maps:
    7.5 minute Alma
    Pike National Forest

Mount Silverheels is a broad-based mountain north of Fairplay that is visible from throughout South Park.

The starting point for the hike is on Colorado 9 between Breckenridge and Fairplay. The hike begins at 10,920 feet, one and three-quarter miles south of Hoosier Pass. This point is just over three miles north of the north edge of Alma. It is at the second major drainage on the east side of the highway south of Hoosier Pass. There is adequate parking on either side of the highway.

The climb proceeds east up the broad ridge on the south side of the drainage. Walk through an old burn area toward the 12,033-foot ridge point on the crest of Beaver Ridge. Shortly before reaching the ridge point, contour left on a jeep track to the 11,940-foot saddle just north of the ridge point. From this saddle, turn right and descend directly east, losing two hundred feet of elevation.

Cross the upper reaches of Beaver Creek. Climb the grassy slopes east of the creek to the broad western ridge of Mount Silverheels. The gentle slopes lead over a 12,984-foot ridge point to the summit, with its panoramic view of South Park.

For an even easier route, though a slightly longer one, continue northeast on the jeep track from the saddle north of the 12,033-foot point on Beaver Ridge. When the jeep track bends southeast and approaches a mine, turn right, head south across a drainage, and hike up the northwest ridge of Mount Silverheels. Ascend this gentle ridge southeast and join the west ridge near the summit.

*   *   *   *   *

The hike to Bard Peak on pages 5 and 6 offers the opportunity to also climb Mount Parnassus, which at 13,574 feet just misses being in Colorado's highest two hundred summits. From the 13,037-foot saddle, it is a simple ridge walk west to Mount Parnassus. Engelmann Peak and Robeson Peak look inviting to the north of Bard Peak. These peaks are best approached from the east up Bard Creek.

After climbing Bald Mountain as described on pages 9 and 10, you may be looking for other hiking objectives. You can descend south along the Continental Divide to 12,159-foot Black Powder Pass and continue south along the ridge crest to 13,082-foot Boreas Mountain. The Continental Divide turns westward at a 12,815-foot ridge point along the way.

Tenmile Range and
Mosquito Range

Horseshoe Mountain

9. PEAK 10 (13,633 feet)
CRYSTAL PEAK (13,852 feet)
FATHER DYER PEAK (13,615 feet)

General description:
A moderate hike partly on trails and almost entirely above timberline
Hiking distance: 8 miles
Starting elevation: 11,200 feet
Elevation gain: 3,300 feet
Maps:
   7.5 minute Breckenridge
   Arapaho National Forest

These peaks are southwest of Breckenridge. The hike provides high-altitude walking on the ridges between the peaks.

The trailhead is in the Crystal Creek drainage on the east side of the Tenmile Range. From Breckenridge drive south on Colorado 9 two and a half miles to a quarter mile south of Goose Pasture Tarn. This is seven miles north of Hoosier Pass on Colorado 9. Drive west on the Spruce Creek road, Summit County 800. Drive left on the dirt road at each of two forks at one-tenth and two-tenths mile. Continue southwest another two miles. The road becomes rockier as it begins to climb, though usually it is passable for passenger cars. At the road junction at 10,940 feet, switch back sharply to the right. Drive another half mile to the road end near Crystal Creek at 11,200 feet.

The trail crosses Crystal Creek immediately, turns left on a jeep track, and continues west up the north side of Crystal Creek. In a quarter mile the jeep track crosses the Wheeler Trail. Continue west on the jeep track past Lower Crystal Lake at 11,980 feet and through switchbacks to Upper Crystal Lake at 12,860 feet.

From Upper Crystal Lake it is a short scramble northwest over talus to the 13,260-foot Crystal Peak-Peak 10 saddle.

Turn right and climb north up the ridge to Peak 10.

Return south from Peak 10 to the saddle at 13,260 feet. Ascend Crystal Peak via its northeast ridge. Using Crystal Peak's east ridge, make the simple traverse to Father Dyer Peak, which rises only 115 feet from the low point along the ridge.

The name "Father Dyer Peak" was officially approved by the United States Board on Geographic Names in 1980. On the summit there is a plaque commemorating Father Dyer, one of the pioneers in the settlement of Breckenridge.

From Father Dyer Peak, descend on scree directly down the north face slopes. Bear left to the abandoned mine at the jeep track's end at 12,940 feet just above and southwest of Upper Crystal Lake. Finish by following the jeep track used in the ascent back to the trailhead.

10. PACIFIC PEAK (13,950 feet)
UNNAMED 13,841

General description:
   A moderate hike up a broad valley and along rocky ridges
Hiking distance: 9 miles
Starting elevation: 11,080 feet
Elevation gain: 3,500 feet
Maps:
   7.5 minute Breckenridge
   7.5 minute Copper Mountain
   Arapaho National Forest

Pacific Peak is the prominent pointed summit northwest of Fourteener Quandary Peak. It combines well with the unnamed 13,841-foot summit to make a fine all-day hike.

Drive on Colorado 9 fourteen miles north of Fairplay or seven and a half miles south of Breckenridge. At this point, two

Looking north along the ridge from unnamed 13,841 to Pacific Peak.

miles north of Hoosier Pass and just north of a sharp switchback, turn north on Summit County road 850. After 0.15 of a mile turn right at a junction. A little less than two miles farther choose the left fork and find a parking place within another half mile.

Walk west from the road end on a trail that takes you up McCullough Gulch beyond timberline. After the trail fades out, bear west-northwest past a lake at 12,695 feet. A steeper climb beyond the lake brings you to a broad saddle at 13,380 feet. Pacific Peak is to the north and the unnamed 13,841-foot summit is a short climb south along the rocky ridge.

Return to the saddle and climb north up the ridge toward Pacific Peak. The route takes you over a small ridge point southwest of an often-frozen lake at 13,420 feet. The final climb is north over rocky footing along the ridge to the summit. For a more difficult variation on either the ascent or the return you can make an interesting walk along the long narrow east ridge of Pacific Peak.

These peaks can also be approached from the west from Colorado 91 via Mayflower Creek and Pacific Creek. The unnamed 13,841-foot summit is climbed using its long west ridge. For Pacific Peak, a steep scramble up the southwest face and west ridge is best.

11. FLETCHER MOUNTAIN (13,951 feet)

General description:
    A moderate climb on trails and rocky ridges
Hiking distance: 6 miles
Starting elevation: 11,700 feet
Elevation gain: 2,400 feet
Maps:
    7.5 minute Breckenridge
    7.5 minute Copper Mountain
    Arapaho National Forest

Fletcher Mountain is a high summit that is hidden from the populated valleys by its higher eastern neighbor, Quandary Peak.

Drive to Summit County road 850 as in hike number 10. From Colorado 9, drive two miles west up Monte Cristo Creek to Blue Lakes Reservoir. Park at the base of the north end of the dam.

Climb to the north end of the dam and find an old unmarked trail that leads west well above the north side of the reservoir. This trail goes up the east side of a drainage that enters Blue Lakes Reservoir from the northwest. It ends near an abandoned mining cabin at 12,300 feet.

Climb west from the cabin up the nose of a ridge. Follow this ridge as it curves northwest to the summit.

This peak can also be climbed from the west from Colorado 91. From Mayflower Creek the route uses a gully, or the steep buttress to its left, which reaches the range crest one-quarter mile southwest of the summit.

12. NORTH STAR MOUNTAIN (13,614 feet)

General description:
    A walk on old roads and a climb along a rocky ridge
Hiking distance: 8 miles
Starting elevation: 11,539 feet
Elevation gain: 2,400 feet
Maps:
    7.5 minute Alma
    7.5 minute Breckenridge
    Arapaho National Forest

The hike starts at Hoosier Pass, twelve miles north of Fairplay and ten miles south of Breckenridge on Colorado 9. Park west of the highway at Hoosier Pass.

Walk west along an old road that sometimes can be driven part way with passenger cars. The road contours south of the ridge line and after a mile and a half it reaches a saddle at 12,100 feet. Leave the road on the right near this saddle and climb up the gentle slopes northwest and west. Follow the ridge west along the crest of the Continental Divide.

Climb west over ridge points of 13,460 feet and 13,500 feet with descents of 120 feet beyond each. Continue west to the 13,614-foot high point.

The second ridge point, at 13,500 feet, is near the name "North Star Mountain" on the 1987 photo revised Breckenridge topographic map, however, we elect to apply the name to the entire high ridge and consider the 13,614-foot high point to be the summit of North Star Mountain.

13. WHEELER MOUNTAIN (13,690 feet) CLINTON PEAK (13,857 feet) McNAMEE PEAK (13,780 feet) TRAVER PEAK (13,852 feet)

General description:
  A long trek over moderate terrain that can be shortened appreciably with a four-wheel-drive vehicle
Hiking distance: 13 miles
Starting elevation: 10,940 feet
Elevation gain: 3,800 feet
Maps:
  7.5 minute Alma
  7.5 minute Copper Mountain
  7.5 minute Climax
  Pike National Forest

Three of these four summits are located along the Continental Divide between Fremont Pass and Hoosier Pass. The fourth is just south of the divide. They are in an area of intense mining activity.

Drive eleven miles north of Fairplay or one mile south of Hoosier Pass on Colorado 9 to a dirt road that leads northwest. Drive this road northwest one and one half miles to the entrance to the Hoosier Pass water diversion tunnel above Montgomery Reservoir. This is the terminus for passenger car travel, though a rugged jeep track continues west up Middle Fork South Platte River to Wheeler Lake.

From the tunnel at 10,940 feet, it is a four-mile hike up the rocky jeep track to Wheeler Lake at 12,168 feet. Traverse north around the west side of Wheeler Lake and climb up the grassy slopes to a smaller lake at 12,500 feet. Hike north up the drainage above the lake two hundred vertical feet. Turn left and climb to a saddle at 13,340 feet on the ridge south of Wheeler Mountain. Turn right and climb north up the ridge to the top. Several steep cliffs are encountered that are best negotiated on the west side of the ridge. Wheeler Mountain has three small summits. The southern one is the highest.

To reach Clinton Peak, retrace your steps and descend south along the ridge. Climb south and then west from the saddle at 13,340 feet. Climb over two minor ridge points on the way to the summit of Clinton Peak. The summit provides a bird's eye view of the molybdenum mining operation near Fremont Pass.

McNamee Peak and Traver Peak are short ridge walks south along the rocky, gently contoured ridge crest. At McNamee Peak you leave the Continental Divide as it curves west down Ceresco Ridge to Fremont Pass.

To return from Traver Peak, descend northeast into the drainage east of McNamee Peak. Follow this stream down over grassy slopes to the point where it intersects the jeep track south of Wheeler Lake.

If the venture as described is too long for one day, the climbing day can be shortened with a backpack to a high camp on the tundra near Wheeler Lake. In addition, from this base Wheeler Mountain could be climbed on a day separate from the other three summits.

14. LOVELAND MOUNTAIN (13,692 feet) MOUNT BUCKSKIN (13,865 feet)

General description:
   A moderate hike over gentle terrain mostly above timberline
Hiking distance: 5 miles
Starting elevation: 11,340 feet
Elevation gain: 2,900 feet
Maps:
   7.5 minute Alma
   7.5 minute Climax
   Pike National Forest

These high summits are in the same area as three fourteen-thousand-foot peaks and thus are often overlooked as climbing objectives.

Drive to Alma on Colorado 9 between Fairplay and Hoosier Pass. Turn west and drive four miles up the Buckskin Creek road to the Sweet Home Mine at 11,340 feet.

To start the hike, cross Buckskin Creek and climb west up the grassy slopes. Bear slightly south. This route will lead you to intersect the east ridge of Loveland Mountain at 13,000 feet. Follow this ridge west to the summit.

Walk north and northwest along the gentle but rocky ridge to the summit of Mount Buckskin. Though a peak register has been located on the 13,860-foot northwest ridge point, the 13,865-foot southeast summit is the higher.

From Mount Buckskin descend the gradual northeast tundra slope until intersecting the Buckskin Creek road at the switchbacks at 11,800 feet. Walk down the road to the starting point.

15. MOUNT TWETO (13,672 feet)
MOUNT ARKANSAS (13,795 feet)

General description:
   A stiff hike above timberline with a rocky traverse
   between the two summits
Hiking distance: 7 miles
Starting elevation: 11,540 feet
Elevation gain: 2,900 feet
Maps:
   7.5 minute Climax
   Pike National Forest

Mount Arkansas is the prominent summit seen east of Colorado 91 between Leadville and Fremont Pass. Mount

Tweto, recently named, is a summit south of Mount Arkansas that is a survey point called "USLM Divide." The suggested approach is from the east.

From the south part of Alma on Colorado 9 or from Alma Junction five miles north of Fairplay, drive west through Park City. Two and a half miles west of Park City avoid the left fork to active mines along South Mosquito Creek. Continue on the right fork another two and a half miles toward Mosquito Pass. Park where the Mosquito Pass road makes a sharp left turn across Mosquito Creek to begin its steep climb to the pass.

Leave the Mosquito Pass road and hike north along a jeep track on the east bank of Mosquito Creek. Leave the jeep track after a half mile at 11,840 feet and continue on the tundra up the drainage. At 12,800 feet bear left and angle northwest to intersect the southwest ridge of Mount Tweto at 13,300 feet. From here it is a short hike northeast to the summit.

Follow the rough ridge north from Mount Tweto over two false summits to Mount Arkansas. The terrain on the traverse is quite slow as it involves a good deal of boulder-hopping. On the return it is possible to avoid climbing back over Mount Tweto. Make a traverse at the 13,300-foot level across the west face of Mount Tweto to intersect its southwest ridge. Descend east into the basin for the return.

These summits can be approached from the west off Colorado 91. Some private property must be skirted and a creek must be crossed before climbing the steep rocky west side of Mount Arkansas.

16. MOSQUITO PEAK (13,781 feet) TREASUREVAULT MOUNTAIN (13,701 feet)

General description:
An off-trail hike over gentle terrain above timberline
Hiking distance: 5½ miles
Starting elevation: 11,540 feet

Elevation gain: 2,600 feet
Maps:
    7.5 minute Climax
    Pike National Forest

Mosquito Pass is the highest pass in Colorado that is crossed by a road. These summits are along the ridge north of the pass. The hike uses the same starting point on the Mosquito Pass road as hike number 15.

Hike up the Mosquito Pass road three-fourths of a mile to 12,000 feet. Leave the road on the right and hike west over the tundra past Oliver Twist Lake to a small lake at 12,460 feet. Turn southwest and climb three hundred vertical feet to a bench that allows access to the east-southeast ridge of Mosquito Peak. Hike westward up the ridge to the summit. A short walk north along the talus-strewn ridge gives access to Treasurevault Mountain.

To return descend to the 13,420-foot saddle between the peaks. Walk east and southeast across the tundra to intersect the ascent route at the 12,460-foot lake.

If you want to visit Mosquito Pass, these peaks also make a pleasant ridge walk from the pass.

17. DYER MOUNTAIN (13,855 feet)

General description:
    A walk up a rough road to a high pass and a three-mile hike along a ridge
Hiking distance: 12 miles
Starting elevation: 11,540 feet
Elevation gain: 3,500 feet
Maps:
    7.5 minute Climax
    7.5 minute Mount Sherman
    Pike National Forest

Dyer Mountain is on the crest of the Mosquito Range between Mosquito Pass and Mount Sherman. It can be approached in several ways. One good approach is via Mosquito Pass. Start from the same trailhead as used for hike number 15.

From the parking area, walk up the rough road three miles to Mosquito Pass at 13,186 feet. Hike south from Mosquito Pass along the broad ridge. After a mile you will pass a series of buildings housing radio and television facilities for Leadville. The second rounded ridge point encountered, two miles south of Mosquito Pass, is 13,577-foot Mount Evans. The ridge becomes rougher in the next mile. Cross over or skirt west around a minor ridge point at 13,383 feet before the final climb to Dyer Mountain.

An alternate route, perhaps less interesting but shorter, is from the west via Iowa Gulch. Turn east from US 24 in the southern part of Leadville and find the road which leads into California Gulch and winds its way into Iowa Gulch. Park at 12,000 feet below the gate to the Continental Chief Mine. A steep scramble up talus leads one to the south ridge of Dyer Mountain.

18. MOUNT SHERIDAN (13,748 feet)
GEMINI PEAK (13,951 feet)
WHITE RIDGE (13,684 feet)

General description:
   A comfortable hike mostly on ridges above twelve thousand feet
Hiking distance: 8 miles
Starting elevation: 11,800 feet
Elevation gain: 3,300 feet
Maps:
   7.5 minute Mount Sherman
   Pike National Forest

These three summits surround Mount Sherman, one of the easier fourteen-thousand-foot peaks to climb. Most climbers ignore these other summits on their first trip to Mount Sherman.

From US 285 a mile and a half south of Fairplay and just south of the intersection of Colorado 9 to Hartsel, turn west on the Fourmile Creek road. Continue on the dirt road ten miles to the townsite of Leavick. Passenger cars can continue a mile and a quarter beyond Leavick until the road steepens at 11,800 feet.

Once parked, hike up the road another half mile to the Dauntless Mine. Above the mine follow any of various jeep tracks to the Hilltop Mine. Continue beyond to the Mount Sherman-Mount Sheridan saddle. Walk southwest up the broad ridge crest over talus to the summit of Mount Sheridan.

From Mount Sheridan retrace your steps to the saddle. Proceed north and northeast up the well-beaten path on the ridge to the summit of Mount Sherman. From Sherman it is a simple walk north across the broad plateau to Gemini Peak. The northeast summit, a large symmetrical rock pile, is the high point.

From Gemini Peak proceed south, bypassing the summit of Mount Sherman on the east side. Then descend to the long saddle at 13,500 feet southeast of Mount Sherman. A walk over the rolling terrain to the southeast end of White Ridge brings you to the high point at 13,684 feet.

To avoid the loose talus slopes on the south face of White Ridge, it is best to return to the northwest end of the Mount Sherman-White Ridge saddle. Descend south down the drainage to your vehicle.

It is possible to add Horseshoe Mountain and/or Dyer Mountain to the south and north ends, respectively, of this hike. This would lengthen the trip and increase the elevation gain significantly. We suggest separate ascents for these two mountains.

19. PTARMIGAN PEAK (13,739 feet)
HORSESHOE MOUNTAIN (13,898 feet)

General description:
  A long high-altitude ridge walk
Hiking distance: 9 miles
Starting elevation: 11,921 feet
Elevation gain: 2,800 feet
Maps:
  7.5 minute Mount Sherman
  Pike National Forest

Horseshoe Mountain merits its name for the vast rugged cirque visible from South Park. Ptarmigan Peak is south of Horseshoe Mountain along the crest of the Mosquito Range.

Drive to Weston Pass, either from US 285 south of Fairplay or from US 24 south of Leadville. Park at the pass.

Climb northeast from the pass up the long grassy slope. At the ridge crest at 13,360 feet, turn left and skirt left of a 13,525-foot ridge point. Follow the ridge north to Ptarmigan Peak.

Descend north from Ptarmigan Peak and follow the broad ridge two and a half miles to the summit of Horseshoe Mountain. There is just one obstacle, a 13,717-foot ridge point, along the way. There is an old cabin near the summit of Horseshoe Mountain.

A shorter approach to Horseshoe Mountain can be made from the north. Drive up the Fourmile Creek road as in hike number 18 to one mile west of Leavick. Use care in skirting private property southwest of the road before climbing to the north ridge of Horseshoe Mountain. Follow the ridge south to the summit.

Sawatch Range—Northern Area

Frasco benchmark

20. MOUNT JACKSON (13,670 feet)

General description:
A long scenic backpack approach on trail with a rugged bushwhack to timberline for the final climb
Hiking distance: 17 miles backpacking; 6 miles climbing
Starting elevation: 8,500 feet
Elevation gain: 1,500 feet backpacking; 3,900 feet climbing
Maps:
7.5 minute Minturn
7.5 minute Mount of the Holy Cross (small portion of the trail in corner)
7.5 minute Mount Jackson
White River National Forest

This remote peak is located deep within the Holy Cross Wilderness. The approach uses the scenic trail up Cross Creek for the first eight and a half miles. Climbers will find a two- or three-day backpack trip an enjoyable experience in a truly wilderness setting.

Drive on US 24 two miles south of Minturn or thirty-one miles north of Leadville. Turn west on the dirt road toward Half Moon Campground. After one and a half miles at the first sharp left turn, park at the trailhead for the Cross Creek trail.

Leaving the trailhead, the trail crosses Cross Creek after a mile and continues to climb southwest very gradually on the northwest side of the stream. Eight and a half miles from the parking area the trail recrosses to the southeast side of Cross Creek on a bridge at 9,880 feet. This area provides good camp sites and a fine base for the climb of Mount Jackson.

To begin the ascent return north along the trail two hundred yards to the first creek crossing north of the bridge. Leave the trail and bushwhack northwest through the alders. At 10,800 feet, begin contouring southwest. Intersect the drainage from the east side of Mount Jackson in a swampy area at 11,000 feet. Angle northwest up the main drainage to a small lake at 11,660 feet. Bypass left of a band of cliffs above the lake. Ascend the large cirque on the northeast side of Mount Jackson. In early summer this cirque is an easy snow climb and a fine glissade on the descent. Bear left and intersect the summit ridge at 13,400 feet. Turn left and walk south to the summit.

21. HOLY CROSS RIDGE (13,831 feet) UNNAMED 13,768

General description:
   A long trek on roads, scenic trail, and rocky terrain
Hiking distance: 14 miles
Starting elevation: 10,280 feet
Elevation gain: 4,000 feet
Maps:
   7.5 minute Mount of the Holy Cross
   White River National Forest

The Holy Cross Ridge is a rugged crest extending south from Mount of the Holy Cross in the Holy Cross Wilderness. These two summits are the most prominent high points on the ridge immediately south of Mount of the Holy Cross. The highest, at 13,831 feet, marks the high point of Holy Cross Ridge. The two summits can be climbed together in one long day. Of several possible approaches, we prefer the one from the south.

From US 24, halfway between Minturn and Tennessee Pass, take the road southwest along Homestake Creek. A little over a mile beyond the entrance to Gold Park Campground, turn right and ascend two miles to a "T". Turn right at the "T" and then right again at a junction after another mile. Park passenger cars in a flat area three-fourths of a mile farther, at 10,280 feet.

Hike north fifty yards to meet a road leading uphill to the left. This is the rugged jeep trail that starts southeast of Gold

Park Campground. Follow the rough road a mile and a half northwest to a large meadow. At 11,160 feet, where the road to Holy Cross City makes a sharp left turn up the hill, continue west to circle the flat meadow on the left. Follow the old road and then the trail past Hunky Dory Lake into the Seven Sisters Lakes area. After passing between two lakes at 12,160 feet, leave the trail and climb northwest.

The route goes past another lake at 12,750 feet. Climb west up the rocks to a 13,420-foot saddle between the 13,768-foot summit and a 13,618-foot ridge point south of it.

From the 13,420-foot saddle, it is a straightforward rocky ridge walk north to the 13,768-foot summit. Follow the rocky ridge north down to a 13,380-foot saddle. Then continue north up to the higher summit, the high point on Holy Cross Ridge at 13,831 feet.

On the return it is possible to traverse over boulders beneath the 13,768-foot summit on the west side of the ridge.

There are at least two other approaches to these two mountains. One is to follow the usual route to Mount of the Holy Cross from Half Moon Campground over Half Moon Pass. Then traverse the ridge south from Mount of the Holy Cross to the two summits. A second approach is to hike to the Seven Sisters Lakes area on trail from Half Moon Campground to Lake Constantine and over Fall Creek Pass. Then follow the route described from Seven Sisters Lakes to the summits. Each of these two approaches probably would require backpacking.

22. MOUNT OKLAHOMA (13,845 feet)

General description:
      A hike on old roads and a stiff climb on talus slopes
Hiking distance: 8 miles
Starting elevation: 10,260 feet
Elevation gain: 3,600 feet

Maps:
7.5 minute Mount Massive
7.5 minute Mount Champion
San Isabel National Forest

Mount Oklahoma is a summit named in 1967 that sits on the Continental Divide in the Mount Massive Wilderness. It is hidden from the main roads by Mount Massive and other mountains.

From US 24 south of Leadville, drive west on Colorado 300 and turn south toward Halfmoon Campground. Continue west beyond the campground along the north side of Halfmoon Creek three and a half miles. Park at a junction with a road that crosses Halfmoon Creek and goes south up South Halfmoon Creek.

Hike west on the road along Halfmoon Creek a half mile to a junction with an old road leading north. This road stays on the north side of Halfmoon Creek while the main road crosses the creek. Take the right fork and walk north and northwest up the old road. Continue on trail along the northeast side of Halfmoon Creek. Stay northeast of North Halfmoon Creek, which joins Halfmoon Creek a half mile west of the Mount Massive Wilderness boundary.

After two miles, approach the ridge that extends east from Mount Oklahoma between creek forks from valleys to the north and to the southwest. At 11,400 feet, head west up the timbered ridge. At tree line, stay left of a band of cliffs on the east end of the ridge. Continue west up a minor drainage south of the main ridge until beyond the cliffs. From a more level area at 12,600 feet, turn right and climb north to the main east ridge of Mount Oklahoma. Turn left and climb west to the summit.

30

23. FRENCH MOUNTAIN (13,940 feet)
FRASCO BENCHMARK (13,876 feet)
CASCO PEAK (13,908 feet)

General description:
  A lengthy hike on jeep trails with gradual off-trail
  climbing
Hiking distance: 12 miles
Starting elevation: 10,260 feet
Elevation gain: 4,700 feet
Maps:
  7.5 minute Mount Massive
  7.5 minute Mount Elbert
  San Isabel National Forest

French Mountain and Casco Peak are two seldom-climbed summits due to their proximity to their more-visible higher neighbors, Mount Elbert and Mount Massive. Frasco benchmark is a point on the ridge between French and Casco.

Drive to the same parking place used for hike number 22 to Mount Oklahoma. Hike up the left fork south across Halfmoon Creek. Walk up the jeep trail that follows South Halfmoon Creek. Continue into the vast basin south of French Mountain to Iron Mike Mine.

Turn right at the mine and climb the grassy slopes north to the 13,620-foot saddle west of French Mountain. Walk the ridge east on good footing to the summit of French Mountain.

Return west from French Mountain to the saddle at 13,620 feet. Then climb the ridge west to Frasco benchmark. The ridge walk continues south from Frasco benchmark to Casco Peak. Rough spots on the ridge descent from Frasco benchmark are best bypassed on the west side. After crossing the saddle, for the ascent of Casco Peak, difficult sections of the ridge crest are best avoided by staying left on the east side of the ridge.

To descend, follow the east ridge of Casco Peak to 13,400

feet. Contour and descend east off the left side of the ridge to intersect the road where it crosses South Halfmoon Creek below Iron Mike Mine.

24. DEER MOUNTAIN (13,761 feet)

General description:
    A medium hike on an obscure trail and a rocky ridge
Hiking distance: 9 miles
Starting elevation: 10,794 feet
Elevation gain: 3,000 feet
Maps:
    7.5 minute Independence Pass
    7.5 minute Mount Champion
    San Isabel National Forest

Deer Mountain is a high point on the Continental Divide north of Independence Pass. It is on the boundary of the Mount Massive Wilderness and the Hunter-Fryingpan Wilderness.

The trailhead is off Colorado 82 five miles east of Independence Pass and nineteen miles west of US 24. Park passenger cars at the beginning of the rough road that leaves the highway a hundred yards south of a hairpin curve at 10,794 feet.

The trail leads north into Mount Massive Wilderness from the end of the rough road. It stays on the west side of North Fork Lake Creek. The trail may become wet and difficult to follow in the willows. In any event, continue north on the west side of the creek. At 11,500 feet the drainage divides. Follow the northeast fork right to a small lake at 12,378 feet. Continue north to a 12,460-foot pass just beyond. Turn right and climb east a seemingly long 1,300 vertical feet up the rocky ridge to the summit.

Deer Mountain also can be combined with a trip to Mount

Oklahoma. Another possibility is to climb Deer Mountain as described and return on the ridge south over two more of the top two hundred summits. For this you would first climb the unnamed 13,736-foot summit and then continue south over Mount Champion for the return to the trailhead. Either of these possibilities would make a much longer day than the climb of Deer Mountain alone.

25. MOUNT CHAMPION (13,646 feet) UNNAMED 13,736

General description:
   A moderate rocky climb and ridge walk
Hiking distance: 6 miles
Starting elevation: 10,794 feet
Elevation gain: 3,400 feet
Maps:
   7.5 minute Independence Pass
   7.5 minute Mount Champion
   San Isabel National Forest

Mount Champion is a rugged summit east of the Continental Divide and north of the highway over Independence Pass. It has an old mine and mill on its south flank. The higher unnamed summit is farther from the highway and less noticeable than Mount Champion.

Drive to the same trailhead used for Deer Mountain, hike number 24. Hike north along the old road a quarter mile and look for a suitable crossing to the east side of North Fork Lake Creek. If the creek is too high, you can park a half mile south of the hairpin curve where the highway crosses the creek and hike north along the east side of the creek.

From the east side of North Fork Lake Creek, climb northeast through the timber. Continue up the steep, partly rocky southwest ridge of Mount Champion. Climb north to the summit.

Descend the north ridge of Mount Champion to a saddle at 13,340 feet. Continue north up the rocky ridge to the unnamed 13,736-foot summit.

Return south toward Mount Champion to the 13,340-foot saddle. Turn right and make a steep scree-slope descent to the west. Cross to the west side of North Fork Lake Creek, turn left, and pick up a trail that leads south back to the trailhead.

26. TWINING PEAK (13,711 feet)

General description:
   A short off-trail climb on gentle terrain
Hiking distance: 4 miles
Starting elevation: 12,093 feet
Elevation gain: 1,700 feet
Maps:
   7.5 minute Independence Pass
   7.5 minute Mount Champion
   White River National Forest

Of the peaks in Colorado's highest two hundred, Twining Peak is the shortest climb from a paved highway; however, it should not be attempted by the casual tourist inexperienced in mountain hiking who just happens to stop at the Independence Pass trailhead.

Twining Peak is not a well-known mountain, perhaps because it was named in 1975, too late for the name to appear on the latest topographic map. On the 1960 Mount Champion topographic map, Twining Peak is the summit on the Continental Divide identified by the benchmark "Blue."

Drive to Independence Pass, on Colorado 82 between US 24 and Aspen. From the parking area skirt east of the bogs and hike directly north. Keep left of the ridge leading northeast and contour north a mile, gaining elevation slightly.

After meeting a drainage that runs off southwest and west,

turn right and climb the tundra and rocky slopes northeast. Continue climbing east to a 13,140-foot saddle on the Continental Divide south of the peak. Follow the ridge left as it leads northwest and bends north to the summit.

27. UNNAMED 13,823

General description:
    A short steep off-trail climb with bushwhacking in the timber
Hiking distance: 5 miles
Starting elevation: 10,794 feet
Elevation gain: 3,200 feet
Maps:
    7.5 minute Independence Pass
    San Isabel National Forest

This unnamed summit directly east of Independence Pass is easily visible from the pass and from the highway east of the pass. Drive to the same trailhead used for Deer Mountain, hike number 24.

Cross North Fork Lake Creek to the east and ascend through the timber southeast. If the creek is high, you may prefer to start a half mile south as in hike number 25. Some old roads can be used for the first part of the climb southeast. It is a steep climb up through the timber, but the going becomes easier after you get above timberline. After leaving the timber, head right of a ridge point at 13,620 feet. Bypass this ridge point on the right. Descend to a 13,380-foot saddle for the final pleasant ridge walk southeast and south to the summit.

An alternative route is to leave the highway directly south of the peak, at an elevation of 10,360 feet. From here the climb is shorter but steeper, with a climb of 3,600 feet in a four-mile round trip.

28. BULL HILL (13,761 feet)

General description:
   A comfortable hike mostly on trail and old mine roads
Hiking distance: 8 miles
Starting elevation: 9,700 feet
Elevation gain: 4,100 feet
Maps:
   7.5 minute Mount Elbert
   San Isabel National Forest

Bull Hill is said to be the highest "hill" in the United States; however, although it is only a hill, it takes a climb of over four thousand feet to reach the top.

Drive west on Colorado 82 from US 24 ten and a half miles to Black Cloud Creek. This point is thirteen and a half miles east of Independence Pass.

Hike north on the trail that leaves the highway east of the Black Cloud Creek bridge at 9,700 feet. Climb steeply one mile to a trail junction at 11,000 feet. Take the left fork trail another mile toward Fidelity Mine. When you leave the last trees on the southeast ridge of Bull Hill at 12,000 feet, climb the grassy ridge northwest and then north to the summit.

Sawatch Range—Central Area

Judy Atwater on Mount Yale

29. GRIZZLY PEAK (13,988 feet)
GARFIELD PEAK (13,780 feet)

General description:
   A rugged hike and climb with steep slopes and rocky
   ridges
Hiking distance: 9 miles
Starting elevation: 10,740 feet
Elevation gain: 3,700 feet
Maps:
   7.5 minute Independence Pass
   San Isabel National Forest

There are six summits in Colorado above thirteen thousand feet named "Grizzly." Four of them are in the highest two hundred summits. This one was once rated a Fourteener, but new surveys demoted it so that it is now the highest Thirteener.

Drive on Colorado 82 fourteen and a half miles west of US 24 or nine and a half miles east of Independence Pass to the South Fork Lake Creek road. Drive southwest two and a half miles on this fair to poor road to a side road on the left at 10,560 feet leading south up Sayres Gulch. Continue straight ahead three-fourths of a mile to another intersection at 10,740 feet. Passenger cars should be parked here.

Walk up the road to the right into McNasser Gulch. Continue two miles to near mining operations at 12,000 feet. Skirt the mines and walk west up the basin to 12,500 feet in three-quarters of a mile. Turn right and head north up steep slopes to the 13,300-foot saddle east of Grizzly Peak. Turn left at the saddle for a gradual rocky ridge walk west and south to the summit.

Garfield Peak is reached by a ridge walk south along the Continental Divide from Grizzly Peak. There are some difficult-looking towers and spires that readily can be bypassed on the west side of the ridge. A scree-slope descent back into McNasser Gulch can be made either east from the saddle between Garfield and Grizzly or down the north slope from the ridge just east of Garfield Peak.

30. SAYRES BENCHMARK (13,738 feet)

General description:
   A long walk on mining roads and a short off-trail climb
Hiking distance: 10 miles
Starting elevation: 10,560 feet
Elevation gain: 3,500 feet
Maps:
   7.5 minute Independence Pass
   7.5 minute Mount Elbert
   San Isabel National Forest

Climbing Sayres benchmark, a prominent ridge point southwest of La Plata Peak, requires a long hike up a four-wheel drive roadbed.

Drive up the South Fork Lake Creek road as in hike number 29. This time stop and park after two and a half miles at the road intersection at 10,560 feet.

Take the left fork at the intersection and walk south. Cross South Fork Lake Creek after a tenth of a mile. Within a hundred yards, take the left fork at an intersection. The right fork continues south up Sayres Gulch on the west side of the drainage. The left fork that you should follow crosses to the east side of the drainage from Sayres Gulch and climbs south and east on many switchbacks. There is a locked gate closing this fork to vehicle travel.

Higher up the mountain there is a choice of routes. The aim is to follow roads toward the 13,020-foot saddle south of a 13,430-foot summit that is at the end of one of the road branches. As you approach the saddle, leave the road to climb to it. Follow the ridge southeast and east from the saddle to the summit where you will find the benchmark.

A southern approach to Sayres benchmark uses the Clear Creek road to Winfield and the old road up North Fork Clear Creek.

31. RINKER PEAK (13,783 feet)

General description:
A steep climb through the timber and along a rocky ridge
Hiking distance: 8 miles
Starting elevation: 9,280 feet
Elevation gain: 4,700 feet
Maps:
7.5 minute Mount Elbert
San Isabel National Forest

This hidden summit is on the ridge west of Twin Peaks, south of Colorado 82 and across the valley east of La Plata Peak. It sits back out of sight from the highway, unlike the more visible Twin Peaks on its northeast ridge.

Drive west from US 24 eight and a half miles to a point almost two miles beyond the village of Twin Lakes. From the west, this point is a little over a half mile east of Parry Peak Campground. Find a road leading southwest a hundred yards to a trailhead parking area.

Hike south across Lake Creek on a substantial bridge. Turn right on an old road and walk southwest a hundred yards to an obscure trail leaving the road on the left. Walk up this trail as it goes south through brush in a swampy area and then east up the hill. After a half mile on the trail, leave the path on the right and climb steeply through the timber.

Continue climbing southwest up the northeast ridge toward Twin Peaks. Either cross or bypass the two summits of Twin Peaks and several minor ridge points. From a saddle at 13,100 feet, follow the ridge on good footing southwest and west to the objective.

An alternate longer approach is up Willis Gulch. For this route, continue on the trail, taking a right fork that climbs to meet a level trail along Arlington Ditch at 9,900 feet. Turn left and walk east on the trail along the ditch. This trail crosses Willis Gulch to meet an old road that climbs south on the east side of the gulch. Climb a half mile south on this old road. At a junction at 10,300 feet, take the right forking trail. Continue on this trail two and a half miles toward Willis Lake. In open country at 11,600 feet leave the trail on the right and climb to the 13,100-foot saddle. Follow the ridge southwest and west to the summit.

32. UNNAMED 13,616

General description:
A steep climb through timber and along a ridge
Hiking distance: 6 miles
Starting elevation: 10,260 feet
Elevation gain: 3,700 feet
Maps:
7.5 minute Winfield
7.5 minute Mount Elbert
San Isabel National Forest

This little-known summit, on the long ridge between La Plata Peak and Mount Hope, is dwarfed by its higher neighbors. The most direct approach to this peak is from the south.

From US 24 fifteen miles north of Buena Vista or nineteen miles south of Leadville, drive west on the Clear Creek road, Chaffee County 390. Go twelve miles to Winfield. Park at a "T" junction where the main road turns south.

Walk the jeep track north and west a mile to a junction with a mine road that crosses the creek and leads south high on the slopes of Winfield Peak. Take the right fork. In less than a quarter mile turn right on another older mine road that goes up the hill. Here you are between Grey Copper Creek and Blackbear Creek. When the mine road turns east, leave the road and climb north.

Ascend the ridge between the two drainages in a tedious climb over varied terrain all the way to the summit. The last stretch goes northwest over several false summits to the northwest summit which is the highest.

This peak also has a northern access from Colorado 82. This access uses the long trail up Willis Gulch that is described in the alternate approach to Rinker Peak in hike number 31.

33. MOUNT HOPE (13,933 feet)

General description:
A short trail hike and a moderately steep climb
Hiking distance: 5 miles
Starting elevation: 9,850 feet
Elevation gain: 4,100 feet
Maps:
    7.5 minute Winfield
    7.5 minute Mount Elbert
    San Isabel National Forest

Mount Hope is a block-top summit in the central Sawatch Range. It is southwest of Twin Lakes Reservoir and is a dominant peak when viewed from that area.

Drive to the Clear Creek road, Chaffee County 390, that leads west from US 24 fifteen miles north of Buena Vista or nineteen miles south of Leadville. Drive west along Clear Creek eight miles to Vicksburg and one and a half miles farther to a narrow road leading north toward Sheep Gulch. Follow this road a tenth mile to a small parking area.

A good trail takes off left near the end of the road. It climbs steeply through the timber. In a mile and a half the trail crosses to the east side of Sheep Gulch at 11,300 feet. Leave the trail a half mile beyond this crossing and climb up the gulch.

After leaving the timber and passing some cliffs on the left, turn left at 12,100 feet and climb west up through a huge basin. Climb out of the basin onto the southeast ridge of Mount Hope at 13,600 feet. The walking is much more gradual from here northwest to the summit plateau.

An alternate route, and perhaps a better one when a lot of snow is present, follows the trail to the 12,540-foot pass between Mount Hope and Quail Mountain. The climb is then to the left up the east ridge of Mount Hope.

34. APOSTLE NORTH (13,860 feet)
ICE MOUNTAIN (13,951 feet)

General description:
   A long hike on highly varied terrain with one straightforward peak climb and one very difficult ascent
Hiking distance: 15 miles
Starting elevation: 10,250 feet
Elevation gain: 4,500 feet
Maps:
   7.5 minute Winfield
   San Isabel National Forest

Ice Mountain is the central summit and the highest of The Three Apostles in the Collegiate Peaks Wilderness. It is considered the most difficult high summit to climb in the Sawatch Range. Its ascent should only be attempted by experienced climbers. On the other hand, Apostle North is a walk-up and the long hike and climb to it can be accomplished by those with varying abilities.

Drive to Winfield as in hike number 32. Turn south and park shortly after crossing Clear Creek on a bridge.

Walk southwest up the rough road, taking the right fork after three-fourths mile. Another mile and a quarter south a barrier halts all vehicle traffic. Continue to hike south on the

The Three Apostles, with Ice Mountain in the center, from a vantage point near Hamilton.

former road and then trail to the townsite of Hamilton. A quarter mile south of Hamilton, South Fork Clear Creek splits into three main branches. Turn right into this area, cross the creek to the west, and find a well-beaten path leading south along the western side of the central branch of the creek. Follow this path to timberline.

After leaving the timber, bear left and head southeast toward the vast basin on the north side of Ice Mountain. A good route climbs southeast along the edge of the timber left of a cliff band at 12,000 feet. Shortly before reaching the massive cliffs guarding the northwest ridge of Apostle North, turn south and traverse above the cliff band into the center of the basin. Depending on the season, climb the long snowfield in the basin or ascend steeply over endless boulders. Continue east to the 13,460-foot saddle between Ice Mountain and Apostle North.

Apostle North is a direct climb north over talus from the 13,460-foot saddle. Return to the saddle after climbing Apostle North.

Ice Mountain is much more difficult. The ridge from the

Apostle North's summit serves as a good point to inspect the ridge route on Ice Mountain.

13,460-foot saddle presents some cliffy sections that can be difficult to negotiate under certain conditions. The route up the ridge generally follows the ridge crest south and it has some exposure in places. At the 13,800-foot level there is one section where the ridge line becomes too precipitous. This necessitates a short steep climb of a narrow couloir to the right of the ridge. This couloir with its northern exposure can be problematical under certain ice or snow conditions. Once up this steep section, the rest of the rocky climb to the summit is more straightforward.

Extreme care is needed on the descent from Ice Mountain. It is best to follow the ridge back toward Apostle North to the 13,460-foot saddle. Then follow the ascent route back to the trailhead.

35. IOWA PEAK (13,831 feet)
EMERALD PEAK (13,904 feet)

General description:
   **A long trail-hike approach with straightforward but
   tedious off-trail travel to these rounded summits**
Hiking distance: 16 miles
Starting elevation: 9,660 feet
Elevation gain: 5,700 feet
Maps:
   7.5 minute Winfield
   7.5 minute Mount Harvard
   San Isabel National Forest

The Collegiate Peaks Wilderness part of the Sawatch Range is the home of many high peaks in close proximity to the Collegiate Fourteeners. Iowa Peak and Emerald Peak receive little attention since they are surrounded by higher summits. In addition, they are not visible from the commonly traveled lower-level vantage points.

Emerald Peak, center, and less-prominent Iowa Peak to its left as viewed from the south.

Drive west on the Clear Creek road as in hike number 32, this time stopping after eight miles at Vicksburg. A fenced trailhead parking area is south of the road.

Follow a trail south across Clear Creek on a bridge. Stay on the scenic trail as it climbs south, sometimes steeply, up Missouri Gulch. In five and a half miles you reach 13,220-foot Elkhead Pass.

From Elkhead Pass, descend on trail to the west end of the first switchback south of the pass. Leave the trail, continue descending to 12,800 feet, and then contour southwest to an isolated small lake on a grass bench at 12,717 feet. Turn right

47

and climb northwest over gentle slopes to the Missouri Mountain-Iowa Peak saddle at 13,540 feet. Turn left and follow the ridge south to Iowa Peak. Continue south on the broad ridge down to a wide saddle and up to Emerald Peak.

To return, descend northeast from Emerald Peak on easy talus slopes and tundra to the lake at 12,717 feet. Traverse back to the trail south of Elkhead Pass and follow it over the pass and north back to the trailhead.

36. UNNAMED 13,762

General description:
An extremely long hike and a short rocky climb
Hiking distance: 24 miles
Starting elevation: 8,920 feet
Elevation gain: 5,000 feet
Maps:
  7.5 minute Harvard Lakes
  7.5 minute Mount Harvard
  San Isabel National Forest

This peak is one of the most remote high summits in the Sawatch Range. It can be approached from Pine Creek, Texas Creek, Clohesy Lake, or over Elkhead Pass. A long and tiring but more direct approach is up the Pine Creek valley into the Collegiate Peaks Wilderness. Because of the excellent trail that leads to the base of the peak, strong hikers can make this climb in a day; however, some may prefer to backpack to one of the scenic campsites along the Pine Creek trail.

Drive on US 24 thirteen miles north of Buena Vista or twenty-one miles south of Leadville. Turn west on Chaffee County road 388. Take a left fork after a quarter mile and drive another mile and a quarter to an informal camping area where passenger cars should be parked.

Walk up the rough road left of the camping area a mile and a quarter to the beginning of an excellent trail. Follow this trail ten miles as it slowly ascends Pine Creek to remote Silver King Lake. The trail crosses the Main Range Trail after two miles and forks left at a junction with the trail to Elkhead Pass six miles farther.

At sparkling Silver King Lake, find a rocky trail leading southeast to a 13,100-foot pass on the Continental Divide northeast of the 13,762-foot summit. Turn right at the pass and climb the ridge southwest. Climb around some rough spots on the right before walking out onto the broad summit.

Under some road conditions, many passenger cars may not be able to negotiate an eroded road section a half mile from the highway. Also, there may be a locked gate shortly beyond the eroded section that would prevent driving to the informal camping area. This would add two more miles to this already long hike and would make a backpack more enticing.

Sawatch Range—
Southern Area

Mount Ouray

37. UNNAMED 13,631

General description:
A pleasant long hike on forested jeep roads to high inactive mines with a finish on rocky talus slopes
Hiking distance: 10 miles
Starting elevation: 9,900 feet
Elevation gain: 3,800 feet
Maps:
7.5 minute Italian Creek
7.5 minute New York Peak
Gunnison National Forest

This far-off summit in the Collegiate Peaks Wilderness is best approached from the south. Drive to the Taylor Park Reservoir area, either from Buena Vista over Cottonwood Pass or north from US 50. Proceed to the road junction where the Cottonwood Pass road joins the road around the east side of Taylor Park Reservoir. Drive north from the road intersection east of the reservoir past Dinner Station Campground. Continue two miles beyond the Pothole Reservoirs to Tellurium Creek. A hundred yards east of Tellurium Creek at 9,866 feet a jeep track heads north along the east side of the creek. Good campsites are available along the first hundred yards of the road. Park in this area.

Walk north up the jeep track. The road soon crosses a tributary of Tellurium Creek and after a mile and a quarter comes to a fork at 10,540 feet. Take the right fork around the north side of a swampy area and climb to the remains of the Enterprise Mine at 11,700 feet. From the mine take another old abandoned road northwest and contour through a couple of switchbacks to an old mining area at 12,540 feet.

From the end of the road beyond the mines, climb north up the unstable talus slope to a saddle at 13,300 feet. Follow the ridge on more stable footing a quarter mile northwest to the summit.

This peak has a northern approach that is much longer.

From Colorado 82 between Aspen and Independence Pass drive the Lincoln Creek road south to Grizzly Reservoir. This road continues as a jeep road to the ghost town of Ruby. Climb west from Ruby to the ridge well north of the summit to avoid the east-face cliffs. Finish with a walk along the ridge to the summit.

38. UNNAMED 13,626

General description:
   A trail walk and a stiff rocky climb
Hiking distance: 10 miles
Starting elevation: 9,600 feet
Elevation gain: 4,100 feet
Maps:
   7.5 minute Mount Yale
   San Isabel National Forest

This high summit is scarcely noticed as it is a subsidiary summit of Mount Princeton. It is, however, in the more remote area northwest of Mount Princeton and is more difficult to climb than its Fourteener neighbor.

From Buena Vista drive seven miles west on Colorado 306 toward Cottonwood Pass. Take the left fork, Chaffee County 344, and drive three more miles to Cottonwood Lake. Continue around the north side of the lake a quarter mile past Cottonwood Lake Campground. Park near some abandoned buildings.

To start the hike, find a crossing to the left to get south of South Cottonwood Creek. There is no established crossing, so find the best way across on rocks or logs. Pick up a trail that switchbacks up the ridge that is across the creek south of Cottonwood Lake Campground. Follow this trail to mine tailings at 10,500 feet. Turn right and continue on a less-prominent unmaintained trail west and south. The trail rounds a north-facing basin and emerges on a ridge at 11,300 feet.

The route continues directly south and east up this ridge to the remote summit. The terrain becomes increasingly rougher and slower going as the summit is approached. Two minor false summits are crossed a half mile west of the summit.

If South Cottonwood Creek is too high to cross safely, it may be better to retreat to the picnic area southeast of Cottonwood Lake. Follow fishermen trails westward south of Cottonwood Lake and continue on paths to join the trail south of South Cottonwood Creek.

The peak also can be climbed from the south from two miles east of Alpine by hiking the crude trail up Grouse Canyon.

39. MOUNT MAMMA (13,646 feet)

General description:
A long but simple hike primarily on jeep trails
Hiking distance: 13 miles
Starting elevation: 9,420 feet
Elevation gain: 4,300 feet
Maps:
7.5 minute St. Elmo
San Isabel National Forest

Six summits in the southern Sawatch Range—Mount Mamma, Mount White, Grizzly Mountain, Cyclone Mountain, Carbonate Mountain, and the unnamed 13,870-foot summit—can be combined for climbing in various ways. The choice will depend on whether or not you use a four-wheel-drive vehicle, whether or not you want to climb other summits in the area, and whether or not you want to backpack. These descriptions assume day hikes from passenger-car trailheads. This requires more individual hikes than either backpacking or using a four-wheel-drive vehicle.

Mount Mamma is an elongated ridge-top summit east of

Grizzly Gulch and southeast of St. Elmo. It is in an area that has had intense mining activity.

From Nathrop on US 285 drive west on Colorado 162. After thirteen miles, near Alpine, find a jeep road, Chaffee County road 277, turning sharply back left and heading steeply uphill. Park here.

Hike up the steep road. Continue straight ahead at 10,860 feet when the left fork crosses to the east side of Baldwin Creek and heads up Baldwin Gulch. Follow the jeep track up the west side of Baldwin Creek to a junction at 12,000 feet a quarter mile north of Baldwin Lake. Take the right fork through the tundra to the end of the jeep track at an abandoned mine at 12,560 feet. Climb northwest on talus slopes to the summit.

The high point of Mount Mamma is at the south end of a mile-long north-south ridge. While the 1982 St. Elmo 7.5 minute topographic map shows the name "Mount Mamma" near a lower ridge point to the north, the USGS has confirmed that the name applies to the entire massif with 13,646 feet as the high point.

40. UNNAMED 13,870

General description:
An easy ridge walk after ascending a jeep road
Hiking distance: 15 miles
Starting elevation: 9,420 feet
Elevation gain: 5,100 feet
Maps:
7.5 minute St. Elmo
San Isabel National Forest

This unpretentious high summit is dwarfed by Mount Antero to its northeast. It is sometimes referred to as "North Carbonate." Carbonate Mountain is a lower summit two miles south of this peak. The starting point is the same as for Mount Mamma, hike number 39.

Hike up the jeep road, taking the left fork crossing of Baldwin Creek at 10,860 feet. Beyond the creek there is a choice of routes. For a longer but easier walk, stay on the jeep road until it crosses a ridge at 13,089 feet. Leave the road on the right and descend grassy slopes southwest to a saddle at 12,820 feet. The summit is a comfortable ridge walk over broken rocks less than a mile west from the saddle.

A more direct but rougher route leaves the jeep road in Baldwin Gulch at 11,600 feet. Angle south to the center of the drainage. Cross the stream at 11,700 feet, turn west, and ascend the grass slopes to meet the north ridge of the peak at 12,600 feet. Turn left and follow the ridge south to the summit. This route ascends 4,600 feet in a twelve-mile round trip.

If you wish to shorten the climbing day with a backpack up Baldwin Creek, good campsites can be found near the creek crossing at 10,860 feet.

41. MOUNT WHITE (13,667 feet)

General description:
A long scenic trek mostly on little-used trails
Hiking distance: 13 miles
Starting elevation: 8,940 feet
Elevation gain: 4,800 feet
Maps:
7.5 minute Mount Antero
San Isabel National Forest

Mount White is the prominent summit southeast of Mount Antero. Its rugged east ridge is readily visible from the valley between Buena Vista and Salida.

From three and a half miles south of Nathrop on US 285, drive west on Chaffee County road 270. Proceed west on roads

270 and 272 three and a half miles to a junction. Take the left fork and follow road 272 south a mile and a half. Turn right and drive two hundred yards to a trailhead parking area on the north bank of Little Browns Creek.

The new Forest Service trail that climbs up the north side of Little Browns Creek is not shown on the 7.5 minute 1983 Mount Antero map. Hike up this trail as it climbs to the ridge north of Little Browns Creek. After a mile and a half, high up on the ridge north of several beaver ponds, you reach a junction with the Colorado Trail. Turn sharply right and climb steeply on the Colorado Trail as it ascends north on the east side of a ridge. In a half mile, just after the Colorado Trail reaches a high point and begins a long, gradual descent, find a rocky jeep track that crosses the Colorado Trail.

Turn left and hike up the jeep track, which soon becomes a trail. This little-used but easily followed trail contours south into the Little Browns Creek drainage. The trail gradually climbs all the way to the broad saddle at 12,800 feet between Mount Antero and Mount White. After the trail passes tree line, the track becomes faint due to lack of use.

At the saddle the trail joins a jeep track that can be followed through a couple of wide switchbacks to Mount White's west ridge at 13,260 feet. The hike finishes with an easy ridge walk east to the southwest summit. Though very close in height, the southwest summit appears to be higher than the northeast summit.

42. JONES PEAK (13,604 feet) UNNAMED 13,712

General description:
A long trail approach, best done as a backpack, followed by a strenuous climb over talus to the summits

Hiking distance: 18 miles
Starting elevation: 8,940 feet

56

On the trail to the lake between Mount White and Jones Peak.

Elevation gain: 5,300 feet
Maps:
   7.5 minute Mount Antero
   San Isabel National Forest

Jones Peak is the eastern high point of an east-west ridge northeast of Mount Shavano. The higher unnamed summit is at the western end of the ridge and is less visible from the Arkansas River valley.

Drive to the same trailhead used for hike number 41 to

Mount White. Hike up the trail past the junction with the Colorado Trail on the right. This time continue straight ahead. In two hundred yards take the right fork as the Colorado Trail exits on the left. Soon you will cross Little Browns Creek and join the old Browns Creek Trail that enters from the left.

Continue along the trail that stays on the north side of Browns Creek to a lake at 11,286 feet between Mount White and Jones Peak. Due to the length of the approach, hikers may prefer to backpack and camp either at the lake or in the meadows at 9,740 feet.

From a quarter mile beyond the lake, leave the trail on the left and cross Browns Creek. Climb south and southeast up the gully leading to the saddle a quarter mile southwest of the 13,712-foot summit. This is a stiff climb on steep grass slopes followed by a long haul over talus. From the 13,380-foot saddle, head northeast over easy talus slopes to the 13,712-foot summit.

The traverse to the east to Jones Peak is not difficult even though numerous ridge points are encountered along the way. The easiest return route is to retrace your steps west over the 13,712-foot summit.

43. GRIZZLY MOUNTAIN (13,708 feet)

General description:
  An off-trail climb on good footing to a pass and up a ridge
Hiking distance: 6 miles
Starting elevation: 11,480 feet
Elevation gain: 2,800 feet
Maps:
  7.5 minute Garfield
  7.5 minute St. Elmo
  San Isabel National Forest

Of six mountains in Colorado over thirteen thousand feet

with the name "Grizzly," five are named "Grizzly Peak." This is the only Grizzly *Mountain*. It is hidden deep in the southern Sawatch Range surrounded by other summits more visible from the populated areas.

Drive to Maysville on US 50, six miles west of Poncha Springs or eleven and a half miles east of Monarch Pass. Turn north on Chaffee County road 240 and drive eight miles on the North Fork road to a road junction at 11,414 feet. The left fork goes to North Fork Reservoir Campground. Take the right fork another two-tenths of a mile to 11,480 feet, where a jeep track heads northwest toward Billings Lake. Park near the junction. Drivers should be forewarned that the North Fork road can be rough for passenger cars.

Walk up the rough road a half mile. Leave the road on the right shortly beyond tree line and ascend the gentle slope to the north. Climb to an almost flat area east of a 12,831-foot ridge point. Descend the ridge north toward Grizzly Mountain to a 12,540-foot pass. This historic pass, known unofficially as Calico Pass, was once crossed by a well-used trail. From the pass, climb north up the rocky ridge to the summit of Grizzly Mountain.

44. CYCLONE MOUNTAIN (13,596 feet)
CARBONATE MOUNTAIN (13,663 feet)

General description:
  A straightforward hike over two summits on gentle talus slopes
Hiking distance: 7 miles
Starting elevation: 10,744 feet
Elevation gain: 3,300 feet
Maps:
  7.5 minute Garfield
  7.5 minute St. Elmo
  San Isabel National Forest

These two unimposing summits are hidden among a mass of peaks in the southern Sawatch Range. The best approach is from the south.

Drive up the North Fork road as in hike number 43, this time stopping after six miles at the site of Shavano. Park near some abandoned buildings.

Hike north up the east side of the Cyclone Creek drainage on a jeep track that soon becomes a trail. The trail crosses to the west side of the creek after a mile. After another mile it passes a small pond at 11,440 feet. Shortly thereafter, cross to the east side of the creek. Climb northeast into a broad talus-filled gully descending from the Cyclone-Carbonate saddle. Climb up this gully to the saddle at 13,260 feet.

From the saddle climb north along the shale-covered ridge to Cyclone Mountain. Return to the saddle and climb south up the ridge to the summit of Carbonate Mountain.

The most direct descent is the south ridge of Carbonate Mountain to 12,400 feet and then southwest to the trail in Cyclone Creek, a half mile from the starting point.

45. TAYLOR MOUNTAIN (13,651 feet) MOUNT AETNA (13,745 feet)

General description:
A moderate hike with a road and trail to tree line
Hiking distance: 9 miles
Starting elevation: 9,660 feet
Elevation gain: 4,800 feet
Maps:
7.5 minute Garfield
San Isabel National Forest

Taylor Mountain and Mount Aetna are most visible from the highway east of Monarch Pass. The view of Mount Aetna is unique because of the spectacular rockslide gully that extends down the entire south side of the peak.

Drive to Garfield on US 50 between Poncha Springs and Monarch Pass. On the west edge of town a jeep trail leaves the north side of the highway to ascend the Middle Fork South Arkansas River drainage. Park passenger cars in Garfield at the start of this jeep trail.

Hike up the jeep trail a mile and a half to a junction at 10,542 feet. This junction is a quarter mile west of the turnoff on the left to Boss Lake Reservoir. From the junction take a trail that climbs to the remains of a cabin in Hoffman Park. From the cabin, climb the grassy and gravel slopes east to the crest of the southwest ridge of Taylor Mountain. Turn left and ascend the broad ridge north to the summit.

The straightforward traverse to Mount Aetna follows the ridge line west from Taylor Mountain through a 13,020-foot saddle. To descend, return to the Aetna-Taylor saddle. Hike south down gentle slopes to intersect the trail at Hoffman Park for the walk out.

46. MOUNT OURAY (13,971 feet)

General description:
  A short off-trail climb on good footing
Hiking distance: 6 miles
Starting elevation: 10,810 feet
Elevation gain: 3,300 feet
Maps:
  7.5 minute Mount Ouray
  San Isabel National Forest

Mount Ouray stands out as the high point of the portion of the Sawatch Range south of US 50. The climb starts at Marshall Pass. You can drive to Marshall Pass either from US 285 six miles south of Poncha Springs or from Sargents on US 50 west of Monarch Pass.

A good starting place for the climb is at 10,810 feet just east of the Marshall Pass summit, where the eastern approach road turns from west to south. Climb directly north with good footing on varied terrain to a 12,685-foot ridge point on the Continental Divide west of Mount Ouray. Turn right and walk east along the broad ridge to the summit. Some obstructions along the ridge can readily be bypassed.

Elk Mountains

Pyramid Peak

47. CLARK PEAK (13,580 feet)

General description:
  A scenic backpack with a difficult climb over rugged terrain
Hiking distance: 13 miles backpacking; 5 miles climbing
Starting elevation: 9,400 feet
Elevation gain: 3,200 feet backpacking; 2,200 feet climbing
Maps:
  7.5 minute Capitol Peak
  White River National Forest

Clark Peak, a neighbor of Fourteener Capitol Peak, is an imposing summit with sweeping ridges of dazzling white rock. Its remoteness and the rugged climb make its ascent a jewel for experienced mountaineers.

Drive to the town of Snowmass, midway between Aspen and Carbondale on Colorado 82. Turn south and after two miles take the right fork up Capitol Creek. Proceed seven and a half miles to the Capitol Lake trailhead overlooking Capitol Creek.

The trail descends four hundred feet to cross Capitol Creek and then climbs up the scenic creek. After six and a half miles, it reaches crystal-clear Capitol Lake. Maroon Bells-Snowmass Wilderness camping regulations require that you camp in the timbered area below the lake.

Climb east from Capitol Lake up a steep grassy slope. Follow well-beaten paths to the Capitol Peak-Mount Daly saddle at 12,500 feet. Traverse southeast on steep slopes into the broad basin east of the Capitol-Daly ridge. You will lose a hundred feet of elevation in the process. Cross the rocky basin southeast and ascend to a 12,980-foot saddle between two ridge points on the southeast side of the basin. Although not apparent on the topographic map, a small cliff band spans the entire southeast side of the basin. A minor gully of steep broken rock a little right of the 12,980-foot saddle gives access to the top of the ridge.

Turn right at the saddle and climb southwest up the ridge to 13,200 feet. Turn left and traverse southeast to a 13,140-foot saddle west of Clark Peak. From this point climb east over huge boulders of every imaginable shape to the high point at the east end of the Clark Peak ridge. If the rock is wet, great caution is needed. Be careful to maintain footing on the slick lichens that grow on the large boulders.

Clark Peak can be climbed more directly via West Snowmass Creek, but there is a difficult ford.

48. UNNAMED 13,722
UNNAMED 13,932
UNNAMED 13,631

General description:
  A trail approach to difficult climbs on rotten rock, done as two separate day hikes or a two- or three-day backpacking trip
Hiking distance: 11 miles and 12 miles
Starting elevation: 9,580 feet
Elevation gain: 4,900 feet and 4,300 feet
Maps:
  7.5 minute Maroon Bells
  White River National Forest

These three unnamed summits lie south along the ridge that has Pyramid Peak as its highest point. These peaks are made of the same rotten, maroon-colored rock as Pyramid Peak and the Maroon Bells. Due to the difficulties of the climbs, including both the route finding and the nature of the rock, these climbs are only recommended for experienced climbers.

Although the three peaks are on the same ridge, they are described as two separate climbing days due to the difficulties of a ridge traverse. An alternative is a short backpack

The ridge to unnamed 13,932 viewed north from unnamed 13,722.

The final portion of the north ridge of unnamed 13,631.

approach for a two-day or three-day climbing trip.

Drive a half mile west of Aspen on Colorado 82 and turn south and take the right fork to Maroon Lake. During the summer season, you may be required to take a shuttle bus to avoid congestion in the Maroon Lake area.

From the trailhead at the parking area, hike southwest toward Crater Lake. At a trail junction shortly before reaching Crater Lake, take the left fork toward West Maroon Pass. For backpackers, good campsites can be found in a wooded area at 10,680 feet, a mile and a half south of Crater Lake. This is a half mile south of the point where the trail crosses from the west side to the east side of West Maroon Creek. A backpack to this area involves a 1,200-foot climb in the seven-mile round trip.

Begin the ascents of the 13,722- and 13,932-foot summits from the trail at the 10,600-foot level. This is a few hundred yards north of the suggested campsites. Climb east and then southeast on grass and intermittent talus slopes into the broad basin west of the peaks. Cliff bands not shown on the topographic map will be encountered. By traversing on the grassy benches to the left or right, gullies can be found that allow entry into the next higher level.

Once in the basin you will want to take a few moments to examine the imposing face of the peaks to the east. The ascent route to the 13,722-foot summit uses the steep couloir that begins at the 13,420-foot saddle north of the summit. The descent route from the 13,932-foot summit follows the line of the white rock couloir beginning near the top of the peak.

From 11,800 feet in the basin, climb east-southeast into and up the couloir left of the 13,722-foot summit. Stay on the right or south side of the couloir to avoid cliffs. In the steeper sections the route climbs a series of ledges littered with loose debris. After reaching the 13,420-foot saddle, turn right and make the short walk south to the 13,722-foot summit.

To traverse to the 13,932-foot summit, known to climbers as "Thunder Pyramid," return to the saddle. Contour on steep grassy slopes on the east or right side of the ridge at the elevation of the saddle. Pick your way to the first couloir that climbs back to the ridge crest. This talus-filled couloir will bring you back to the ridge crest at 13,840 feet. Turn right and climb up a couple of ridge steps to the sharp summit.

To return to the basin, climb south along the ridge a hundred yards. Descend slowly west toward the steep white-rock couloir. Carefully climb down the couloir. At the 12,000-foot level, turn left above a cliff band and traverse left where easier grassy slopes are available.

The circuit to the two summits is eleven miles with 4,900 feet of climbing from Maroon Lake or four miles with 3,700 feet of elevation gain from the suggested camping area.

To climb the 13,631-foot summit, ascend to the basin from Maroon Lake or from camp as described previously. Continue to the head of the basin. Climb left on long talus slopes to the 13,300-foot saddle just north of the summit. The short climb south up the ridge to the summit is time consuming due to the ridge steps encountered. These steps can be climbed directly or bypassed by traversing on the talus-filled ledges on the east face.

The trip to this summit and back to Maroon Lake is twelve miles with 4,300 feet of climbing. It is five miles and 3,100 feet of elevation gain for the trip from the camping area.

Some experienced climbers may want to undertake the rugged and challenging ridge traverse between the 13,631- and 13,722-foot summits. Others may prefer to attack each of these three summits separately and avoid any ridge traverse.

49. UNNAMED 13,635

General description:
   An easy walk on trail
Hiking distance: 11 miles
Starting elevation: 9,880 feet
Elevation gain: 3,800 feet
Maps:
   7.5 minute Hayden Peak
   White River National Forest

This summit, known unofficially as Electric Pass Peak, is the easiest high summit to climb in the Elk Mountains. A good trail leads almost to the top.

From Colorado 82 just west of Aspen, turn south on the road to Ashcroft, which branches left from the road to Maroon Lake just south of the highway. Drive south twelve miles to a side road on the right a mile beyond Ashcroft. Follow this side road a half mile to a trailhead parking area.

Hike up the popular trail toward Cathedral Lake. Keep right at a series of trail junctions two to three miles from the trailhead where several trails go left to Cathedral Lake. Follow the trail into a large basin and then ascend switchbacks toward a ridge southeast of the 13,635-foot summit. As the trail bears left toward Electric Pass, you can either continue up the ridge to the summit or stay with the trail to Electric Pass and climb north to the summit from there.

50. CATHEDRAL PEAK (13,943 feet)

General description:
   A testy climb with a trail approach and a steep gully ascent to the summit ridge
Hiking distance: 9 miles
Starting elevation: 9,880 feet
Elevation gain: 4,300 feet
Maps:
   7.5 minute Hayden Peak
   White River National Forest

Cathedral Peak is one of the summits in the Elk Mountains composed of the same rotten purple rock that makes the Maroon Bells and Pyramid Peak so visually attractive. Consequently, the ascent of the last thousand vertical feet of Cathedral Peak is more difficult than the map contours indicate. The trailhead and the first part of the hike are the

The rugged north ridge of Cathedral Peak looking from unnamed 13,635.

same as hike number 49.

Hike the popular trail to Cathedral Lake. There are several trails branching left in the final part of the hike to the lake. The most worn path generally is the most direct. Hike to the outlet at the northeast end of the lake. Head northwest to intersect an old but well-preserved miners trail. This trail leads through the rocky basin southeast of Cathedral Peak.

From trail's end at 12,600 feet, head due west to climb a prominent steep gully. This gully intersects the ridge at 13,460 feet at the first saddle south of Cathedral Peak. The gravel-filled gully can be a steep snow climb early in the season. Later, it is a tedious tilted sand box where poor footing and gravity foil your best efforts. Once on the narrow ridge, turn right and climb a quarter mile north to the summit.

Many climbers err in tackling the large face of purple rock to the right of the gully. The map contours do not indicate that this face is particularly steep; however, the nature of the rock leaves climbers wishing they had ascended the gully instead.

51. UNNAMED 13,803

General description:
  A long backpack trail approach and a steep climb up loose fractured rock
Hiking distance: 18 miles backpacking; 4 miles climbing
Starting elevation: 8,760 feet
Elevation gain: 2,600 feet backpacking; 2,800 feet climbing
Maps:
  7.5 minute Hayden Peak
  7.5 minute Maroon Bells
  White River National Forest

This remote peak is on the main ridge crest of the Elk Mountains and is a western neighbor of Castle Peak. Good footing here is a dubious matter because of the highly fractured white rock. For the long approach, most climbers elect to backpack to Conundrum Hot Springs where a warm soak is in the offing.

Drive south on the Ashcroft road as in hike number 49. This time leave the Ashcroft road five miles from Colorado 82. Turn right on a dirt road, number 15B. Descend a few hundred yards to cross Castle Creek on a bridge. The road becomes quite rough but passable as it continues another mile to a trailhead parking area.

Backpack up the fine trail through the picturesque Conundrum Creek valley nine miles to Conundrum Hot

72

Springs at 11,200 feet. Marked campsites can be found both below and beyond the hot springs.

To climb the peak, hike south a quarter mile beyond the hot springs. Leave the trail on the left and hike southeast. After navigating through willows in the drainage, the going becomes easier on grassy slopes beneath the peak's broad west flank.

Climb southeast to the base of the west ridge at 12,000 feet. Turn east and climb steeply up ledges of loose shale. Navigate through minor cliff bands up the peak's west flank. Along the way you will climb up numerous small rock ledges, clamber up loose rock, and ascend steep slopes. The long tedious climb of 1,600 feet brings you to the ridge at 13,600 feet a quarter mile south of the summit. Turn left and hike north on the ridge crest for the more pedestrian finish.

With a rugged jeep trip toward Pearl Pass from the south, a day-hike route northwest up Middle Brush Creek can be followed to this peak.

52. HAGERMAN PEAK (13,841 feet)
SNOWMASS PEAK (13,620 feet)

General description:
   A long trail hike and a difficult climb over rough rocky terrain with some loose rock hazard
Hiking distance: 16 miles
Starting elevation: 9,000 feet
Elevation gain: 5,200 feet
Maps:
   7.5 minute Snowmass Mountain
   White River National Forest

Snowmass Peak should not be confused with Snowmass Mountain, the Fourteener up the ridge northwest of Hagerman Peak. Snowmass Peak, perhaps a harder summit to climb than Snowmass Mountain, is along the ridge east of Hagerman Peak. These peaks are composed of the same highly fractured white rock as Snowmass Mountain and Capitol Peak. They require slow and careful travel across slopes of loose rock.

These two peaks can be climbed either from Snowmass Lake on the north or from Crystal on the south. The southern approach is the one to use for a day hike.

Drive twenty-two miles south of Carbondale on Colorado 133. If coming north on Colorado 133, drive to the northern base of McClure Pass. Turn east for six miles on paved road to Marble. Then drive east five and a half more miles to Crystal. This is on some rough road that generally is passable for passenger cars. Park at a level area a quarter mile east of Crystal just before the road turns left to begin its climb to Schofield Pass.

Hike up the road a third of a mile to a road junction at 9,190 feet. Turn left and walk north on the rough road into Lead King Basin. Continue hiking north into the Maroon Bells-Snowmass Wilderness on a trail that leads north out of a parking area.

Take the left fork at a trail junction at 9,900 feet. Follow a trail that climbs steeply left of the cascading Geneva Lake outlet. Continue along the west side of Geneva Lake. The area west of picturesque Geneva Lake provides good campsites for those not wanting to make the trip from Crystal in a single day.

Follow the trail around the north end of Geneva Lake. Ascend east on trail to a drainage at 11,480 feet. Leave the trail on the left and climb north up the drainage. At 12,000 feet, bear left through tundra and rocks to ascend the broad south-facing slope of Hagerman Peak. Climb up the rough slope over broken rock to the summit.

Descend east along the ridge from Hagerman Peak. Due to the loose rock hazard, the final portion of the descent to the saddle over fractured broken rock must be done carefully. From the saddle at 13,500 feet, make a short but rough ridge climb through large boulders to Snowmass Peak.

The descent from Snowmass Peak must be made with caution. One good route is to follow the ridge east to Trail Rider Pass. Watch for cliffy sections and make your way around them as you weave your way down to the pass. Follow the trail southwest from Trail Rider Pass back to Geneva Lake.

Another route off Snowmass Peak is to return to the 13,500-foot saddle between it and Hagerman Peak. Climb down the steep south-facing gully to intersect the ascent route. Descent of this steep gully, filled with precariously poised loose talus, requires great care.

Sangre de Cristo Range—
Northern Area

South face of Tijeras Peak

53. COTTONWOOD PEAK (13,588 feet)

General description:
A scenic trail hike up a canyon and a comfortable off-trail ridge ascent
Hiking distance: 12 miles
Starting elevation: 8,800 feet
Elevation gain: 5,400 feet
Maps:
7.5 minute Valley View Hot Springs
Rio Grande National Forest

Cottonwood Peak is the highest summit in the northern section of the Sangre de Cristo Range. It is visible from a wider area than its height would indicate. Like many summits in the Sangre de Cristo Range, Cottonwood Peak can be approached either from the east or from the west. We think the western approach is best.

Drive to the junction of US 285 and Colorado 17 in the San Luis Valley. Drive east on Saguache County road GG six and a half miles to a junction. Take the right fork for another half mile. Find a narrow side road on the left turning sharply north up the hill. Most passenger cars can drive this road a half mile. Don't be tempted to drive farther into a brushy area at 9,000 feet or you may suddenly be stopped with no turnaround and find it necessary to back out.

Walk up the trail into Hot Springs Canyon. Although not shown on the topographic map, this little-used trail extends to tree line. Follow the canyon bottom on the sometimes-sketchy trail as it winds east, then north, then northeast, and back north again.

At 11,800 feet, the trail runs out as you leave the scenic canyon. Now you are out of the timber and don't need a trail. Climb the grassy slope directly north. Bear slightly east to reach the crest of the ridge at a minor saddle at 12,300 feet. Turn right for easy hiking east along the broad ridge. There are only minor ridge bumps on the way to the summit.

54. ELECTRIC PEAK (13,598 feet)

General description:
  A long hike on old road, trail, and easy ridge
Hiking distance: 15 miles
Starting elevation: 8,500 feet
Elevation gain: 5,300 feet
Maps:
  7.5 minute Electric Peak
  7.5 minute Valley View Hot Springs
  Rio Grande National Forest

Electric Peak is a hard-to-distinguish summit along the Sangre de Cristo range crest. It can be identified by its long gradual north ridge. It is south of Cottonwood Peak and is just ten feet higher.

From the junction of US 285 and Colorado 17 in the San Luis Valley, drive east on Saguache County GG six and a half miles to a junction. Turn right and drive south one and three-fourths miles to park near a curve midway between points 8,585 and 8,461 on the topographic map.

Walk east on a path on BLM land north of a fence line to skirt private property. Enter the National Forest after a half mile and join an old road that climbs east on the north side of Major Creek. The first mile along Major Creek may be the hardest part of the hike as the creek runs down large gullies washed out in the road bed. Take the left fork at a junction at 10,020 feet. Shortly thereafter the old road ends and a good trail continues, switchbacking to the range crest at 12,460 feet.

From the pass at the range crest, Electric Peak is a mile southeast. The climbing along the crest of the ridge is over easy tundra and rocks, with just one minor false summit to cross.

Electric Peak also can be climbed using the trail to the range crest along Cotton Creek, the next drainage south of Major Creek.

55. RITO ALTO PEAK (13,794 feet)

General description:
  A short off-trail climb after a long hike to a high pass
Hiking distance: 14 miles
Starting elevation: 9,700 feet
Elevation gain: 4,200 feet
Maps:
  7.5 minute Horn Peak (road approach only)
  7.5 minute Rito Alto Peak
  San Isabel National Forest

Making the final approach to the summit of Rito Alto Peak.

Rito Alto Peak is the high point in the middle section of the northern part of the Sangre de Cristo Range. It is easily visible from Westcliffe in the Wet Mountain Valley.

Rito Alto Peak can be approached by four-wheel-drive vehicle on the road that climbs to Hermit Pass from the east. The western approach requires a long trail hike. From a passenger-car trailhead, the eastern approach is also a long hike.

From a quarter mile south of the junction of Colorado 69 and Colorado 96 in Westcliffe, drive west on the Hermit Lake road. After six miles the road turns southwest and begins climbing. Under ideal conditions, passenger cars can drive to the Hermit Lake turnoff at 11,360 feet. More often, passenger cars are stopped after two miles, shortly beyond the Rainbow Trail junction at 9,680 feet. Consider this the trailhead.

Follow the road on up to Hermit Pass, which is at 13,020 feet. After passing Horseshoe Lake, which lies below the road to the left at 11,948 feet, good trails shortcut some of the switchbacks on the road.

From Hermit Pass to Rito Alto Peak the ascent is less than a mile up the ridge to the northwest. The terrain is easy going on tundra and rocks.

56. MOUNT ADAMS (13,931 feet) UNNAMED 13,580 CHALLENGER POINT (14,081)

General description:
 A steep backpack to a lake at timberline and two short, but steep ascents to the neighboring summits
Hiking distance: 12 miles backpacking; 8 miles climbing
Starting elevation: 8,100 feet
Elevation gain: 3,500 feet backpacking; 5,500 feet climbing

Maps:
   7.5 minute Crestone
   7.5 minute Crestone Peak
   7.5 minute Horn Peak
   Rio Grande National Forest

The three summits described here are just north of the Crestone Peaks. Challenger Point, a 14,081-foot summit, located west-northwest on the ridge from Kit Carson Mountain, meets the criteria defining a separate summit. Although this summit is estimated to be 14,100 feet interpolating the contours, the U.S. Geological Survey reports an elevation of 14,081 feet. This gives it a rise of 301 feet above the saddle with Kit Carson. Since few climbers were aware of this summit until it was named in 1987, a route description is provided here.

The three summits are best done in two days of climbing. A backpack from the San Luis Valley up Willow Creek to a lake at timberline is the recommended approach.

From Moffat on Colorado 17, drive east to the picturesque town of Crestone. In the last mile prior to reaching the center of Crestone, the road makes three right-angle turns. At the center of town, two hundred fifty yards north of the last right-angle turn, turn right on a dirt road. Passenger cars can be driven another half mile to 8,100 feet.

Walk a mile and a half up the rough road to the beginning of the trail at 8,860 feet. The trail immediately crosses to the south side of Crestone Creek and climbs rapidly to Willow Creek Park. The steep rocky trail continues up Willow Creek. It reaches the lower of the Willow Creek Lakes at 11,564 feet. Numerous campsites are available near the lake. From this base, Mount Adams lies to the north and Kit Carson Mountain to the south.

To climb Mount Adams, hike due north from the lake outlet into the large grassy cirque southwest of Adams. Ascend directly north to the 12,900-foot saddle west of Mount Adams. Turn right and climb east on solid conglomerate rock. At 13,600 feet a sharp ridge step is bypassed on the right. Turn left and head north for the final pitch to the small summit.

The 13,580-foot unnamed summit is a three-quarter-mile

hike south along the range crest. Climb down the steep rocky slope to the saddle and then hike up the ridge finishing on gentle grassy slopes. To return to camp, descend west into the cirque to rejoin the ascent route. The climb to these two summits entails 2,900 feet of ascent in the four-mile circuit.

To climb Challenger Point, hike east along the trail on the north side of the lake. Midway along the side of the lake, the trail climbs steeply through bushes away from the lake to get on top of a cliff band. Once above the cliffs the trail contours over to the top of a waterfall east of the lake and peters out.

Leave the drainage and continue southeast another quarter mile. At this point you will be able to see on the right a sharp gully leading southwest. This gully begins at the ridge line at 13,860 feet, a quarter mile northwest of the summit. It descends all the way to the valley floor, finishing as a shallow couloir. Turn right and climb the grassy slopes southwest just to the southeast of the couloir.

The route follows a narrow rib as it climbs steeply just to the left of the sharp gully. Although steep, the rib provides solid footing for the climb to the ridge crest. Turn left for the short walk southeast on much gentler terrain to the 14,081-foot summit. This summit requires a 2,600-foot climb in a round-trip distance of four miles from camp.

57. COLONY BALDY (13,705 feet)

General description:
   A trail hike approach finishing with a stiff climb over grass and talus
Hiking distance: 17 miles
Starting elevation: 9,100 feet
Elevation gain: 4,700 feet
Maps:
   7.5 minute Horn Peak
   7.5 minute Crestone Peak
   San Isabel National Forest

This peak rises east of the Sangre de Cristo Range crest and northeast of the Crestone Peaks. Being less spectacular and lower than the Fourteeners, it receives much less attention.

Drive a quarter mile south of the junction of Colorado 69 and Colorado 96 in Westcliffe. Turn west on the Hermit Lake Road. After a mile, turn left and drive south five miles on Macey Lane to Horn Road. Turn right and proceed west and southwest two and a half miles to Horn Creek Ranch. At the ranch entrance, turn right and drive another quarter mile to the forest boundary, the terminus for passenger-car travel.

Walk up the road three-quarters of a mile to the junction with the Rainbow Trail. Turn left and follow the Rainbow Trail as it contours south to Macey Creek. Leave the Rainbow Trail to the right and follow the fine trail west on the north side of Macey Creek. The trail continues southwest to the northernmost Macey Lake at 11,506 feet. Excellent campsites are available here for backpackers.

A sketchy trail continues south around the west side of the lower lake and climbs to another of the Macey Lakes at 11,643 feet. Turn left and cross the lake outlet. Proceed south along the east side of the lake to its south end. Turn left and climb east and northeast on mixed grass and talus to intersect the west ridge of Colony Baldy at 13,100 feet. Hike east up the ridge to the summit.

58. UNNAMED 13,799
UNNAMED 13,980

General description:
    A stiff rocky climb after a long hike or backpack
Hiking distance: 18 miles
Starting elevation: 9,000 feet
Elevation gain: 5,600 feet
Maps:
    7.5 minute Beck Mountain
    7.5 minute Crestone Peak
    San Isabel National Forest

These two summits are high points on the ridge east of Kit Carson Mountain and could be combined with a trip to that mountain. They often are regarded as "just being in the way" on a trip to Kit Carson. For this reason, the 13,799-foot summit has been referred to as "Obstruction Mountain." The 13,980-foot unnamed summit has been recognized as a separate mountain only in recent years. Many climbers go near its summit without climbing it on their way to Kit Carson Mountain.

The two unnamed summits may be approached from the east via South Colony Lakes, the popular starting point for climbing the four Fourteeners in the area. A four-wheel-drive vehicle is needed to drive to near South Colony Lakes. Otherwise, it is a long walk up the road. Since climbing these two summits is a long trek as a day hike from the passenger-car trailhead, a backpack may be well-advised.

Drive four and a half miles south of Westcliffe on Colorado 69 to Colfax Lane. Proceed south five and a half miles to a "T," turn right, and drive west as far as possible. For passenger cars this should be about two miles to 9,000 feet.

Walk up the rough road five miles to 11,040 feet to the beginning of the South Colony Lakes trail. Follow the trail to the lower of the two South Colony Lakes where many well-used campsites can be found. From north of the lower lake, hike on trail to the upper lake and continue west up the wide drainage. Climb out of the west end of the cirque in a steep gully with a well-worn gravel path. This brings you to the far south end of a broad saddle, known as the "Bears Playground," at 13,140 feet on the range crest.

Walk north across the tundra and bear slightly west up the rocks to climb the 13,799-foot unnamed summit. Follow the ridge west to get to the 13,980-foot unnamed summit. This involves a gradual descent to a 13,460-foot saddle and a steep but short climb on grass and knobby slabs.

The 13,980-foot unnamed mountain has two summits of almost equal height about a hundred and fifty yards apart. You probably will want to climb both of them to be sure of climbing the true summit.

59. TIJERAS PEAK (13,604 feet)
PICO ASILADO (13,611 feet)

General description:
   Two difficult peaks for experienced climbers in a remote scenic area best done on a three- or four-day backpacking trip
Hiking distance: 8 miles backpacking; 17 miles climbing
Starting elevation: 9,240 feet
Elevation gain: 3,200 feet backpacking; 9,100 feet climbing
Maps:
   7.5 minute Beck Mountain (approach trail only)
   7.5 minute Crestone Peak
   San Isabel National Forest

These peaks are in a remote area of the Sangre de Cristo Range south of the Crestone Peaks. There are usually more fishermen than climbers on the approach trails. Pico Asilado, in particular, lives up to its name by being well-hidden, as it can be seen only from a few ridges and summits. While the climbs are recommended only for experienced climbers, a trip into this scenic country is well worth the effort.

Drive on Colorado 69 to Colfax Lane, four and a half miles south of Westcliffe. Turn directly south on paved road and drive five and a half miles to a "T." Turn left and go east a quarter mile and then drive south five miles to the Rainbow Trail, which leaves the road on the right. Passenger cars should be parked in the vicinity of this trailhead.

Walk up the steep rough road that continues south and turns west. In two and a half miles there is a barrier halting vehicle traffic. Continue on a trail another mile to Music Pass at 11,380 feet. This gives a view of the valley of Sand Creek. Tijeras Peak is the summit directly west.

Lower Sand Creek Lake is the best staging point for a climb of Tijeras Peak while camping at Upper Sand Creek Lake

Descending the steep rocky ramp through the cliffs on Tijeras Peak.

makes the climb of Pico Asilado shorter. Some climbers may prefer to move camp between the two climbs, while others will want to make the two climbs from one of the two lakes. We will assume you will want to camp first at Lower Sand Creek Lake.

Descend northwest from Music Pass on the trail. In a clearing in the valley, pass a trail junction at 10,980 feet where the trail down Sand Creek cuts back sharply to the left. A third of a mile farther, just as you reach the edge of the clearing and the trail enters the timber, look for a trail crossing Sand Creek to the left. There may be more trails in this area than you need, and they may not agree with the topographic map. The object is to bear left and southwest to ascend the five hundred feet to Lower Sand Creek Lake. Good camping spots can be found along the east side of the lake.

To climb Tijeras Peak, round the lake on its north side and climb and contour generally northwestward. The biggest obstacle is a long cliff band that extends southeast to northwest between the 12,200 and 12,400-foot level. As you get west of the lake and out of the timber you can view this cliff band. There appear to be several breaks in the cliff band, but the best one for climbing is approximately centered between sheer cliffs on the right and on the left. This break is in the form of a rocky ramp leading from the lower right to the upper left.

Climb up the ramp of solid rock, which may be carrying some streams of water at times during the summer. Once up this steep rocky ramp, the going is much easier. Note carefully the location of the top of the ramp so you can find it on the descent. Walk west up the slope to the right of Tijeras Peak to a saddle at 13,260 feet, left of a minor ridge point. Climb southwest up the rocky ridge from the saddle to the summit. This ascent is a three-mile round trip from the lake with 2,200 feet of elevation gain.

The climb of Pico Asilado is both harder and longer. The route goes past the camping area at the east side of Upper Sand Creek Lake, whether or not you move camp to that lake. Hike north in the timber from the east side of Lower Sand Creek Lake. Bear northwest to stay left of the cliffs on the nose of the ridge between the two lakes. Cross the ridge at the 12,000-foot level and descend northwest to the campsites on the east side of Upper Sand Creek Lake.

Cross to the north side of the lake outlet and descend north two hundred vertical feet through the timber. Intersect a crude path at the 11,600-foot level. This point is directly west of another small lake in a swampy area at 11,420 feet. The path climbs north up a wide ramp between cliff bands into a broad basin west of Marble Mountain. The path becomes more sketchy as it ascends the lush basin. Hike on north to a 12,740-foot saddle on the range crest between Marble Mountain and Broken Hand Peak. Turn left and climb south up the ridge toward Milwaukee Peak. Pick up a well-built trail at 13,200 feet that goes along the east side of the ridge. Follow it to a 13,300-foot saddle on the ridge crest just north of Milwaukee Peak.

There are two routes to Pico Asilado from the 13,300-foot saddle. Each takes you over another summit first. The first route is much shorter and much more difficult. The second route described is longer with more elevation gain but is much easier.

The shortest route is over the summit of Milwaukee Peak. The ascent of Milwaukee Peak is only 222 vertical feet in a quarter mile, but the climb is quite difficult. Leave the trail where it crosses the ridge crest and climb south into the notch at the saddle. Climb south out of the notch to immediately reach a ramp that contours south along the east side of the ridge. While the ramp is at least two feet wide at its narrowest point, there is great exposure. Some climbers may prefer the security of a fixed rope. Once to the end of this ramp, bear right on safer terrain to the ridge crest. Continue over large rocks and steep steps to the summit.

Descend the west ridge of Milwaukee Peak to a 13,220-foot low point along the ridge to Pico Asilado. Climb west and southwest up the left-hand side of the ridge toward Pico Asilado. Proceed to a small saddle on the ridge at 13,420 feet just below the summit block. Drop south off the left side of the ridge a hundred vertical feet. Find a series of ledges and narrow gullies that climb very steeply up the southeast side of the summit block. Intersect the ridge just east of the high point and climb to the summit. There are several difficult sections of this ascent that require searching out the best route. This climb from Lower Sand Creek Lake covers nine miles with 3,800 feet of elevation gain for the round trip.

The second route to Pico Asilado is much longer with more

The difficult ridge from Milwaukee Peak to Pico Asilado. The climb uses the ledges and gullies on the left side of the summit block.

elevation gain, but has no technically difficult climbing. Descend east from the 13,300-foot saddle north of Milwaukee Peak. Follow the good trail on long switchbacks down into the basin. Again, this trail does not follow the route of the trail indicated on the topographic map. The fine trail descends well to the north of the center of the drainage. When the trail becomes sketchy in a meadow at 12,300 feet, continue down the north side of the drainage toward the upper reaches of Cottonwood Creek.

After passing a patch of timber at 11,800 feet, turn left and cross the drainage to the south. Contour beneath a band of cliffs on your left to get to a small lake at 11,820 feet.

At the lake, turn left and ascend grassy slopes and unstable talus southeast to a saddle at 12,860 feet. This saddle is between a 12,989-foot ridge point and a 13,020-foot summit northeast of it. From the saddle, walk up the easy ridge northeast to the 13,020-foot summit. Descend northeast to a 12,660-foot saddle. Climb east up the moderate ridge toward the summit.

When the ridge becomes steep at 13,200 feet, climb to the right into a wide couloir just south of the main summit ridge. The couloir rejoins the ridge at the 13,500-foot level for the final brief ridge walk to the summit.

This long hike with many ups and downs climbs 6,900 feet in the 14-mile round trip from Lower Sand Creek Lake to Pico Asilado.

The distances and elevation gains in the heading for this trip are based on a camp at Lower Sand Creek Lake and following the second longer route to Pico Asilado. You could follow one route to Pico Asilado and return by the other. However, we would not recommend returning over Milwaukee Peak if you have not come up that way, because of possible difficulty in finding the best descent route. On the return you can pick up a trail east of Upper Sand Creek Lake that will lead back over Music Pass.

Sangre de Cristo Range—
Southern Area

West Spanish Peak

60. UNNAMED 13,828

General description:
A trail approach to a comfortable cross-country climb
Hiking distance: 11 miles
Starting elevation: 10,140 feet
Elevation gain: 4,400 feet
Maps:
7.5 minute Mosca Pass
7.5 minute Blanca Peak
San Isabel National Forest

This often overlooked high summit is in the Sierra Blanca section of the Sangre de Cristo Range. It is the northernmost high point on a ridge east of the Huerfano River.

Drive on Colorado 69 to a half mile west of Gardner. Turn west and follow road 408 through Red Wing and Sharpsdale to the Singing River Ranch. Passage has been permitted through private property on a road that under good conditions is passable for passenger cars. Drive four miles along the Huerfano River beyond the Singing River Ranch headquarters. The end of the road for passenger cars usually is near the forest boundary at 10,140 feet.

Walk south on the road three quarters of a mile to a junction with the Huerfano Trail. Turn left, cross the Huerfano River, and climb east out of the valley on a series of switchbacks. When the trail reaches the ridge crest at 11,060 feet, it levels out. In the next half mile, it comes to a junction with the Ute Trail. Take the right fork southeast on the Ute Trail. The trail descends into a meadow and disappears. Head southeast a half mile to Dutch Creek.

Leave the trail here at 10,960 feet, turn right, and head south up the Dutch Creek drainage. After leaving the timber, hike southeast over rolling terrain to intersect the broad flat ridge dropping north-northeast from the 13,828-foot summit. The climb becomes steeper and rockier as this ridge ascends to join a more well-defined ridge coming up from the east. Follow this ridge southwest and south to the summit.

An ascent of this peak also can be combined with a climb to Mount Lindsey. Hike farther south up the Huerfano River to climb Mount Lindsey. Then climb over or around Iron Nipple to follow the ridge north to the 13,828-foot unnamed summit.

61. CALIFORNIA PEAK (13,849 feet)

General description:
A pleasant trail hike and walk along a broad ridge
Hiking distance: 10 miles
Starting elevation: 10,140 feet
Elevation gain: 4,000 feet
Maps:
  7.5 minute Mosca Pass
  7.5 minute Blanca Peak
  San Isabel National Forest

California Peak is another of those neglected high summits in an area of Fourteeners. It is on the main ridge north of Blanca Peak and Ellingwood Point. California Peak is an ideal objective for those seeking a nice trail hike and easy ridge walking.

Drive to the same trailhead used for hike number 60. Walk south along the road three quarters of a mile to the point where the Huerfano Trail crosses the road. Turn right and take this scenic trail west to the range crest at 11,860 feet. Portions of the trail are obscured by high meadow grass but some large posts indicate the way.

California Peak is south along the ridge. Turn left and make a long gradual climb on gentle tundra slopes. There are some minor ups and downs prior to reaching the broad summit.

62. TWIN PEAKS (13,580 feet)
UNNAMED 13,660

General description:
  A backpack trip to a remote lake and two short rugged
  peak climbs
Hiking distance: 10 miles backpacking; 5 miles climbing
Starting elevation: 9,000 feet
Elevation gain: 3,100 feet backpacking; 3,700 feet
  climbing
Maps:
  7.5 minute Zapata Ranch (approach to trailhead only)
  7.5 minute Twin Peaks
  7.5 minute Blanca Peak (route to unnamed 13,660
  barely on edge)
  Rio Grande National Forest

These remote peaks lie at the north end of the rugged Blanca
massif. Twin Peaks is particularly difficult to access from the
east since it lies well west of the main range crest. The long
approach makes a backpack more convenient if both peaks are
to be climbed in one trip.

The starting point is near Great Sand Dunes National
Monument. Two access roads, Colorado 150 north from US
160 and Sixmile Lane east from Colorado 17, come together a
few miles south of the entrance to the monument. Drive one
mile south of this junction on Colorado 150 to the Zapata
housing development. Turn left and continue southeast on the
Lake of the Falls Road. The road, heading generally southeast,
passes a small pond and crosses a creek bed shortly before
reaching a road fork 3.9 miles from Colorado 150. Park cars
here.

Hike up the right fork. The track soon becomes quite rough
as the jeep trail winds its way toward the base of Zapata Falls
at 9,400 feet. The jeep trail soon turns right at a pipeline which
you follow to a trailhead west of the falls. From here a well-
constructed but sometimes obscure trail continues up South

Zapata Creek. Avoid the North Fork Trail—the left two miles beyond the falls. The trail continues all the way to remote South Zapata Lake at 11,900 feet. The last half mile of the trail above timberline is indistinct, but a trail is not necessary in the lush tundra. Good isolated campsites are available in the vicinity of the lake.

To climb Twin Peaks, ascend west and southwest from South Zapata Lake on grassy slopes. Head for a minor ridge southwest of the lake. Climb to a flat area on this ridge at 12,660 feet. Bear right and walk up grass and talus slopes west to the 13,460-foot saddle between the two summits of Twin Peaks. The north peak on the right is the higher. This climb from camp is 1,800 feet in two and a half miles for the round trip.

For the 13,660-foot unnamed summit, hike up the valley a quarter mile southeast of South Zapata Lake. Turn left and climb northeast up the loose steep talus slope. Continue the tedious climb to the ridge crest. Aim for an elongated 13,620-foot point on the ridge. This portion of the ridge is midway between the 13,660-foot unnamed summit and a 13,618-foot ridge point north of Ellingwood Point. Turn left and proceed along the narrow ridge to the summit. The round trip from camp gains 1,900 feet in two and a half miles.

The 13,660-foot unnamed summit also can be climbed from the north in combination with California Peak. It is a long up and down hike on the ridge from California Peak, and more difficult than the north ridge to California Peak.

Still another approach to the 13,660-foot summit is from the east. It uses the trail up the Huerfano River to Lily Lake. The rugged east face of the peak requires a climb to the 13,577-foot summit north-northwest of Lily Lake. This brings you to the ridge crest for the ridge traverse west to the summit.

63. HAMILTON PEAK (13,658 feet)

General description:
A long backpack on a jeep road, a trail climb, and a long ridge walk
Hiking distance: 12 miles backpacking; 9 miles climbing
Starting elevation: 8,000 feet
Elevation gain: 4,000 feet backpacking; 3,800 feet climbing
Maps:
7.5 minute Twin Peaks
7.5 minute Blanca Peak
Rio Grande National Forest

Hamilton Peak is a ridge point at the end of the long ridge extending south-southeast from Blanca Peak. It is dwarfed by its neighboring Fourteeners. Hamilton Peak is seldom visited due to access problems.

A direct approach from the south up Blanca Creek is not suggested. Changing ownership of the approach roads has made access too uncertain a matter. Therefore, an approach from the west side via Lake Como is described here. To reach Hamilton Peak, an ascent of the fourth highest Fourteener, Blanca Peak, is required.

From three and one-fourth miles north of US 160 on Colorado 150, drive up an unmarked dirt road northeast. After one and a half miles, at 8,000 feet, the road becomes too rocky for safe passenger-car travel. Park here.

Without a four-wheel-drive vehicle, or without the nerve to drive one up the rough road, it is best to backpack six miles up the road to Lake Como. Though the Lake Como area is privately owned, good campsites can be found along the trail beyond the lake.

From Lake Como, a well-preserved mining trail continues past Blue Lakes and Crater Lake to the 13,700-foot saddle northwest of Blanca Peak. It is a short climb to the right on well-beaten paths up the narrow ridge to the summit of Blanca

Peak. From this highest point in the Sangre de Cristo Range, the ridge to Hamilton Peak extends south-southeast. Don't make the mistake of following the ridge southwest that goes to Little Bear Peak!

After the abrupt descent from Blanca Peak, hike the occasionally narrow ridge south-southeast with minor ups and downs. You reach the summit of Hamilton Peak in a mile and a half. Use the ridge traverse to return over Blanca Peak.

64. WEST SPANISH PEAK (13, 626 feet)

General description:
A comfortable trail and off-trail ridge climb to a prominent summit
Hiking distance: 7 miles
Starting elevation: 11,248 feet
Elevation gain: 2,500 feet
Maps:
7.5 minute Cucharas Pass
7.5 minute Herlick Canyon (corner only)
7.5 minute Spanish Peaks (summit area only)
San Isabel National Forest

The Spanish Peaks are twin summits prominent far beyond what their elevations would indicate. Standing alone well east of the main Colorado mountain ranges, they are visible from as far north as Colorado Springs and from far east on the plains. Though the two peaks are similar in appearance, the west peak is almost a thousand feet higher.

Drive to Cucharas Pass on Colorado 12, either south from US 160 or west from Trinidad. Turn northeast and drive the dirt road 415 to Cordova Pass at 11,248 feet. This pass was named Apishapa Pass until the U.S. Board on Geographic Names adopted the name Cordova Pass in 1978. Cordova Pass also can be reached by a back road west from Interstate 25 at Aguilar.

From Cordova Pass, follow a trail that heads northeast through open meadows and forest a little to the right of the ridge crest. In a little over a mile the Apishapa Trail comes in on the right. Continue on the trail as it climbs along the ridge on switchbacks for another mile to timberline. Hike northeast up the ridge on gravel paths and large talus to the elongated summit area. The unobstructed view in all directions will impress you with the isolation of this summit.

65. RED MOUNTAIN (13,908 feet) VERMEJO PEAK (13,723 feet) PURGATOIRE PEAK (13,676 feet)

General description:
   A backpack to a timberline camp followed by a long strenuous ridge traverse to the three summits
Hiking distance: 8 miles backpacking; 14 miles climbing
Starting elevation: 9,240 feet
Elevation gain: 2,400 feet backpacking; 6,800 feet climbing
Maps:
   7.5 minute Taylor Ranch
   7.5 minute El Valle Creek
   7.5 minute Culebra Peak

These three summits are located in the southern portion of Colorado's Sangre de Cristo Range. They are only a few miles north of the New Mexico state line. These are the only summits covered in the route descriptions that are not shown on a national forest map.

Access to these peaks is available from the west through the privately owned Taylor Ranch. The trailhead is the same as used for the neighboring Fourteener, Culebra Peak. Backpackers and climbers have been welcome to use the Taylor Ranch lands after a guest fee is paid at the caretaker's residence.

From San Luis on Colorado 159, drive southeast on Colorado 152 four and a half miles to Chama. Continue east three and a half miles on the Whiskey Pass road to the bridge over Culebra Creek. Immediately after crossing the bridge, turn south on a dirt road. After a half mile, turn left at a "T". Drive east another mile and turn right at a road fork. Drive south another two miles to the Taylor Ranch buildings. The guest fee should be paid to the caretaker before proceeding farther.

Passenger cars usually can drive another half mile east to a road fork at 9,240 feet. Beyond this point the road becomes quite steep, but may be passable if graded recently.

Assuming the road is not passable beyond 9,240 feet, hike up the right fork of the road. Follow the road east as it climbs steeply through aspen to a broad ridge of open meadows. The road continues along the ridge to a junction, called Four Corners, in a saddle at 11,220 feet. Proceed straight ahead another mile to the road end for all vehicles in a timberline meadow at 11,600 feet. Good camping with a backdrop of the San Luis Valley is available here next to a tumbling stream.

Hike southeast across the tundra aiming to intersect the ridge at a 13,220-foot saddle northwest of Culebra Peak. If you get too high on the left, merely follow the ridge down to the saddle. Continue along the ridge southeast. If you don't want to climb over Culebra Peak, you can readily bypass it on the southwest side by bearing right at the 13,900-foot level. Either from Culebra Peak or from its southwest side, head to the ridge leading south from Culebra to Red Mountain. Follow the ridge south over one minor ridge point. Climb the talus slope southeast to the summit of Red Mountain.

The footing becomes better as you continue south along the ridge to Vermejo Peak. This peak has an elongated summit area with the northeast point being the highest.

The long ridge traverse continues on grassy and gravel slopes west from the lower southeastern summit of Vermejo Peak. First hike west through a 12,909-foot saddle. Bear left and climb south up the ridge to an unnamed 13,466-foot summit.

Descend south from the 13,466-foot summit to a 12,827-foot saddle. Climb steeply south to the summit of Purgatoire Peak. From this southernmost thirteener in the Colorado portion of the Sangre de Cristo Range, the view from the symmetrical summit cone is totally unobstructed.

The return route depends on your preference for ridge walking compared with sidehilling. The entire ridge route could be retraced, although the total elevation gain this would entail would be very exhausting; therefore, a west side return route with a good deal of sidehilling is described here.

From Purgatoire Peak climb back over the 13,466-foot unnamed summit to the 12,909-foot saddle west of Vermejo Peak. Descend north down the scree slope into the broad basin at the head of North Vallejos Creek.

At the 11,500-foot level at a level area in the drainage, begin traversing to the right. Contour into a southwest-facing cirque on the southwest side of Culebra Peak. Bear left and traverse at the 11,600-foot level southwest out of the cirque around the end of a broad ridge. This traverse leads across sandy ground between cliff bands above and below. After crossing two gullies above the lower cliffs, the going becomes easier.

Continue contouring at the 11,600-foot level into the next broad cirque. This cirque begins at the saddle northwest of Culebra Peak. Once in the center of the cirque, climb northwest over a tree-covered ridge at the 12,000-foot level. Note an old roadbed below and northwest of the ridge crest. Descend northwest through intermittent meadows into the next drainage. Intersect the old roadbed at the 11,600-foot level. This road contours northwest through a gap east of an 11,733-foot ridge point and leads back to the camping area.

Access restrictions and use regulations on Taylor Ranch lands have changed frequently over the years and will continue to do so. It is important to check the current status before attempting this hike.

San Juan Mountains— La Garita Wilderness

Unnamed 13,895 from the north

66. STEWART PEAK (13,983 feet)
BALDY ALTO (13,698 feet)

General description:
  A comfortable off-trail hike up a valley and on rolling
  ridges
Hiking distance: 11 miles
Starting elevation: 11,020 feet
Elevation gain: 3,700 feet
Maps:
  7.5 minute Elk Park
  7.5 minute Stewart Peak
  Gunnison National Forest

Stewart Peak, only seventeen feet short of 14,000 feet, was
once classed as a Fourteener. Its demotion to the ranks of the
Thirteeners makes it a summit seldom visited. Baldy Alto's
name reflects the Spanish influence in the derivation of many
of the feature names in this area. The hike to these two summits
in the La Garita Wilderness is pleasant walking in open
country.

The trailhead can be reached in a number of ways, but each is
a long drive from the main highways. One entry is from
Colorado 114 twenty miles south of US 50. From here turn
west and follow Saguache County road NN-14 as it heads
south. After seven miles, turn right on county road 15-GG at
the south end of Upper Dome Reservoir. After four miles, turn
right again on county road 14-DD which becomes Forest
Service road 794. Drive twelve miles winding generally
southwest. After crossing Chavez Creek, go one and a half
miles farther south to the north side of Nutras Creek. Park
here.

Hike southwest on the north side of Nutras Creek on old
jeep tracks, sketchy trails, and assorted cow paths. Continue
until high in the basin at the head of the creek near 13,000 feet.
From here you can climb directly north to Stewart Peak. An
alternate is to take a more gradual route northwest to a saddle
southwest of Stewart Peak. Turn right for a short ridge walk to
the summit of Stewart Peak.

Descend southwest to the 13,540-foot saddle and then descend south, bypassing a 13,795-foot ridge point. Contour southeast to a 13,100-foot saddle. Climb up the ridge southeast to the summit of Baldy Alto.

For the return trip, you may descend directly north from Baldy Alto to the upper part of the Nutras Creek drainage. Turn right and follow the valley east to the trailhead.

67. ORGAN MOUNTAIN (13,799 feet)

General description:
  A long gentle trail approach with an easy off-trail peak climb
Hiking distance: 16 miles
Starting elevation: 10,300 feet
Elevation gain: 3,600 feet
Maps:
  7.5 minute Elk Park
  7.5 minute Halfmoon Pass
  7.5 minute San Luis Peak
  Gunnison National Forest

Organ Mountain is an isolated summit on the long ridge extending east from the Fourteener, San Luis Peak. Make the long drive on unpaved roads described for hike number 66. From the Nutras Creek trailhead for that hike, drive another two and a half miles south. Park north of Stewart Creek in an area overlooking Cochetopa Creek to the east.

Cross Stewart Creek and walk a hundred yards south on the road and another hundred yards southwest on a trail to a gate. Beyond the gate, follow the Skyline Trail, which skirts private property and leads up the west side of Cochetopa Creek. Two miles beyond the Canyon Diablo trail junction, the trail crosses a drainage coming in from the north at 11,280 feet.

Soon after crossing the drainage, leave the trail on the right. Hike north through the timber to tree line. Bear left and hike northwest up the gently-sloping grassy terrain to the summit.

Organ Mountain lives up to its name when viewed from the south.

68. UNNAMED 13,895
LA GARITA PEAK (13,718 feet)

General description:
An easy hike on trail and rolling grassy terrain
Hiking distance: 12 miles
Starting elevation: 9,900 feet
Elevation gain: 4,500 feet
Maps:
7·5 minute San Luis Peak
7.5 minute Halfmoon Pass
Rio Grande National Forest

These summits are along the crest of the main ridge of the La Garita Mountains northeast of Creede, along the boundary of the La Garita Wilderness. The rolling country makes for pleasant hiking.

From Creede, drive north a mile and take a right fork along East Willow Creek. Three and a quarter miles north of the junction, where the main road turns sharply left to the southwest, find a 4WD road continuing north. Park here.

Walk northeast on a rough road that crosses a drainage, climbs over a ridge, and then heads north on the west side of Willow Creek. After a mile, when the road enters a meadow after crossing Whited Creek, leave the road on the right and hike east. Cross East Willow Creek and climb a hundred feet to meet a north-south trail. This shortcuts the trail shown on the 7.5 minute San Luis Peak quadrangle. Turn right and walk south on the trail, which crosses a creek and heads east on the south side of the drainage. Continue east up this trail to timberline. When the trail bends southeast and the drainage curves northeast, leave the trail on the left, cross the creek, and climb a narrow ridge that curves northeast. Go north on gradual slopes to the unnamed 13,895-foot summit.

Follow the wide rolling ridge southeast. Bypass or cross over two ridge points, the highest being 13,770 feet. Continue along the ridge to La Garita Peak. Come off the summit down the slopes west and southwest to pick up the trail back toward the starting point.

These peaks also can be climbed by using the approach up Cochetopa Creek as described for Organ Mountain. This allows access to the long ridge north of the unnamed 13,895-foot summit.

San Juan Mountains— Big Blue Wilderness

Coxcomb Peak

69. REDCLIFF (13,642 feet)

General description:
A trail hike and a comfortable off-trail climb
Hiking distance: 10 miles
Starting elevation: 10,460 feet
Elevation gain: 3,300 feet
Maps:
  7.5 minute Courthouse Mountain (trailhead area only)
  7.5 minute Wetterhorn Peak
  Uncompahgre National Forest

Redcliff with its distinctive rugged north face and its equally conspicuous neighbor, Coxcomb Peak, are obvious landmarks visible from US 550 south of Montrose. Redcliff and Coxcomb Peak both are best approached from the valley of West Fork Cimmaron River. Redcliff is the easiest climb of the peaks surrounding this valley. Coxcomb Peak is the hardest. It is difficult to climb both peaks in a single day, so they are presented as two separate day hikes.

Drive to Owl Creek Pass, either from US 50 via Silver Jack Reservoir or from US 550 between Montrose and Ouray. Turn south at a big switchback a quarter mile east of Owl Creek Pass. Follow this road south along the west side of West Fork Cimmaron River as far as the road is passable. Passenger cars usually can go two miles up the West Fork.

Hike up the rough road through a recently timbered area. Cross to the east side of the drainage near a washed-out bridge. Continue south to the road end at 10,740 feet. Follow a trail that climbs along the east side of the West Fork. After emerging from the timber, leave the trail on the left. Hike southeast up a drainage toward the obvious saddle between Redcliff on the left and Coxcomb Peak directly ahead. Climb to this saddle on grassy benches, tundra, and rocks. Turn left at the saddle and climb north on tundra and rocks to the summit of Redcliff.

70. COXCOMB PEAK (13,656 feet)

General Description:
  A difficult climb, with rope recommended, that should
  be attempted only by experienced climbers
Hiking distance: 12 miles
Starting elevation: 10,460 feet
Elevation gain: 4,000 feet
Maps:
  7.5 minute Courthouse Mountain (trailhead area only)
  7.5 minute Wetterhorn Peak
  Uncompahgre National Forest

Coxcomb Peak's unique appearance when viewed from the
north or south shows that it has a most appropriate name. The
cliff bands that distinguish this landmark also pose problems
for climbers.

The two most difficult parts of the climb to Coxcomb Peak
are climbing to the top of the summit block and getting across a
cleft in the summit ridge to the true summit. While the best
approach to Coxcomb Peak is from the north, the best place to
climb its summit block is from the south.

Drive to the same trailhead as used for hike number 69. Hike
to timberline as in the climb of Redcliff. Continue south on the
trail to a 12,500-foot pass west of Coxcomb Peak.

There is a choice of routes from the pass. It depends on what
you like the most, or perhaps on what you dislike the least. The
objective is to get to the south side of the summit block of
Coxcomb Peak, just west of the summit. You can continue
down from the pass on trail, losing perhaps four hundred feet
of elevation. Then make a rather easy climb north-northwest
up the tundra and rocks. The other choice is to make a tedious
contour around the south side of Coxcomb Peak at
approximately the same elevation as the pass. These two routes
converge at 12,500 feet on the southwest side of the ridge
extending south from the west end of the summit block.

Continue to climb northeast on the steep rocky slope to the

Coxcomb Peak's imposing summit block appears unclimbable when viewed end on.

base of the summit-block cliffs at 13,300 feet. Look for a prominent couloir twenty yards left of a buttress that marks the southernmost extremity of the Coxcomb Peak summit cap.

Ascend a short steep pitch to get into the couloir. Scramble up to the start of a steep chimney. Climb the chimney fifty feet to get on easier ground. At the top of the chimney exit to the right onto more gentle slopes. Many climbers will want the protection of a rope in ascending the steep chimney particularly if the rock is wet. Once out of the chimney, climb north over broken rock to the summit ridge.

Turn right and follow the ridge east toward the summit. The walking is simple until you come to a cleft in the ridge that is vertical on its west side but more gradual on its east side. While the fifteen-foot vertical wall can be down-climbed to get to the base of the cleft, it is best to rappel or belay down. Leave the rope in place while you climb to the summit. From the base of the cleft in the ridge, the rest of the climb to the summit is on good footing along the narrow ridge.

With the fixed rope in place, the return out of the cleft in the ridge can be made safely. It may be advisable to use the rope again on the descent down the chimney from the summit block.

71. MATTERHORN PEAK (13,590 feet)
SILVER MOUNTAIN (13,714 feet)
UNNAMED 13,681

General description:
   One short off-trail climb and one long ridge walk above timberline that can be done separately as day hikes or combined in a backpacking trip
Hiking distance: 7 miles and 19 miles
Starting elevation: 10,380 feet
Elevation gain: 3,400 feet and 6,200 feet
Maps:
   7.5 minute Uncompahgre Peak
   Uncompahgre National Forest

Matterhorn Peak, similar in appearance to its Fourteener neighbor Wetterhorn Peak, gets its name from like European origins. Silver Mountain and its unnamed neighbor are rounded points on the rolling ridge extending north from Uncompahgre Peak. These summits in the Big Blue Wilderness are best approached from the south.

Matterhorn Peak can be climbed in a short day hike. The other two summits are remote enough to take an extremely long day. Some climbers may prefer to combine these three summits in a two- or three-day backpacking trip.

From Lake City drive west on the road up Henson Creek toward Engineer Pass. When the road forks at the Capitol City townsite at 9,715 feet, leave the Engineer Pass road. Turn right and drive two miles to the trailhead at Matterhorn Creek. Park here.

Hike north up the rough road on the east side of Matterhorn Creek. The road soon is closed to vehicles. It is a two-mile hike to a tilted timberline meadow at 11,700 feet, which has good campsites by the creek. The old road turns east at 11,200 feet and you must take a left turn and head north at a "T" at 11,300 feet.

To climb Matterhorn Peak, continue up the old road to 12,200 feet. As the road turns east, leave the road on the left and cross a minor drainage to the north. Climb north up the long south ridge of Matterhorn Peak. Bear northwest to the summit. At first the long ridge is broad and grassy. The climb finishes steeply over broken rock.

To get to Silver Mountain and its neighbor, be prepared for a long day. Hike the old road to a 12,458-foot saddle southeast of Matterhorn Peak. Leave the road a half mile farther east at a large bend to the south at 12,280 feet. Cross a drainage and head northeast cross country toward Uncompahgre Peak. Climb to the 12,800-foot contour where the grade steepens. Angle left and traverse to the north side of Uncompahgre Peak. This traverse crosses the head of several gullies and takes you right of 12,779- and 12,900-foot knolls.

The route descends northeast to a 12,660-foot saddle on the north side of Uncompahgre Peak. Continue north along the largely grassy ridge. The first two ridge points, 13,310 feet and 13,371 feet, are best crossed. Then bear right and bypass some spires on the ridge. A prominent 13,467-foot ridge point as well as a rounded 13,300-foot ridge point to the north can be bypassed on the left by contouring on steep talus and scree at the 13,200-foot level. Climb directly north to the summit of Silver Mountain. The climbers should have a conference to determine the highest point on the large flat summit area.

The unnamed 13,681-foot summit is reached by hiking north along the gentle plateau. Descend to a 13,180-foot saddle and bear left to hike northwest along the ridge to the high point. Retrace your steps along the ridge to return.

* * * * *

The authors found an alternate route from the north to Silver Mountain and unnamed 13,681 that enables you to climb four other Thirteeners. From the Little Cimmaron road, hike south on the Fall Creek trail. Follow a long but easy-walking loop over unnamed 13,016 and 13,051, Silver Mountain, unnamed 13,681 and 13,100, and Sheep Mountain. Return north on the trail along the Little Cimmarron River to the road, where a short car shuttle is welcome after such a long hike.

San Juan Mountains—
Lake City Area

Half Peak

72. HALF PEAK (13,841 feet)
UNNAMED 13,674
UNNAMED 13,660
POLE CREEK MOUNTAIN (13,716 feet)
CARSON PEAK (13,657 feet)
UNNAMED 13,580
UNNAMED 13,581

General description:
A scenic four- or five-day backpack to a remote high lake with three moderate climbs in rolling country
Hiking distance: 10 miles backpacking; 29 miles climbing
Starting elevation: 9,620 feet
Elevation gain: 2,500 feet backpacking;
11,000 feet climbing
Maps:
7.5 minute Redcloud Peak
7.5 minute Pole Creek Mountain
Gunnison National Forest
Rio Grande National Forest

The seven peaks described in this section lie on a high plateau between the upper reaches of Lake Fork Gunnison River and the Rio Grande River. The terrain is generally rolling grassy tundra broken by occasional cliff bands and isolated summits. During the late summer months, the lush tundra ensures that herds of grazing sheep far outnumber climbers. Seven summits can be climbed in three days of hiking from a backpacking base camp at Cataract Lake.

These seven summits, as well as eight more in the following four descriptions, have easy access from the same road southwest of Lake City. Drive two miles south of Lake City on Colorado 149. Take the right fork, the paved Lake Fork road, toward Lake San Cristobal. Beyond the lake, follow the good

115

unpaved road along Lake Fork Gunnison River. At a junction a mile and a half beyond Mill Creek Campground, take the left fork. Drive a little over a mile farther, passing through the ghost town of Sherman. A trailhead area is on the left.

An excellent trail winds south up Cataract Gulch. The first problem is to cross to the south side of Cottonwood Creek. This may require wading unless a new bridge has been provided. The 1964 topographic map shows a trail entirely east of Cataract Gulch, however, the actual trail crosses the gulch several times near beautiful waterfalls. Above the timber, the trail wanders east of the drainage. It crosses back to the west side to complete the five-mile backpack route to Cataract Lake. Good camping may be found in the flat area at the north end of the lake.

Half Peak and its 13,674-foot unnamed neighbor to the north can be climbed together in the same day. Hike northwest from Cataract Lake past two small lakes. Continue northwest beyond the willows over rolling tundra. Climb to a 12,940-foot saddle northeast of Half Peak. Turn left and ascend southwest up the steepening ridge. The last hundred feet of the ridge up to the summit plateau is steep and good route-finding is essential around rock spires and through breaks in the cliffs. The high point of Half Peak is on the northwest end of the tilted summit plateau.

To get to the 13,674-foot summit, return to the 12,940-foot saddle the way you came up. The topographic map might indicate an easy ridge walk from here to the unnamed summit. Unfortunately, there is a series of spires on the ridge just south of the 13,674-foot unnamed summit. This necessitates dropping off the ridge on the east side.

Hike north up the broad grassy ridge from the saddle. After climbing four hundred feet to the 13,340-foot level, contour to the right. Hike over to the edge of the ridge on the gentle southeast-facing slope. Drop more steeply northeast losing four hundred vertical feet. Turn left and traverse over large talus northward at the 12,940-foot level. Reach a point directly east of the 13,674-foot summit. Turn left and climb northwest over grass and talus to the ridge crest north of the summit. A short steep climb left along the ridge on broken rock will bring you to the high point. A traverse right around the 13,620-foot false summit will avoid the steepest ridge section. The summit overlooks the pinnacles to the south that the route took such pains to circumvent.

To return to camp, retrace your route around the pinnacles. This requires descending to 12,940 feet east of the pinnacles. Regain four hundred feet of elevation to return to the broad grassy ridge at the 13,340-foot level. Navigate south and east across the rolling tundra back to Cataract Lake. A lower traverse that avoids climbing back to the ridge is not advised, because of dense willows in the lower section of Cataract Gulch. The circuit of these two summits covers seven miles and ascends 3,500 feet from Cataract Lake.

The second day hike from camp is to the unnamed 13,660-foot summit and Pole Creek Mountain. Walk south around the west side of Cataract Lake. Climb a short slope southeast to a 12,380-foot pass southeast of the lake. Angle south-southwest across the gentle slopes of the upper drainage of Pole Creek. Pick up the north end of the broad grassy ridge that leads south to the 13,660-foot summit. Follow the ridge south over a few minor ridge points to the summit block. The high point is on the south end of a crumbling rotten forty-foot-high rock outcrop. It is best climbed from the northeast side. There is one steep section with some exposure.

Descend east and then southeast over rolling terrain to a broad grassy 12,820-foot saddle. Hike south up the ridge to the flat summit of Pole Creek Mountain. On this ascent bypass a series of ridge spires by staying to the right on the west side of the ridge crest.

To return to camp descend north to the 12,820-foot saddle and contour northwest across the rolling tundra at approximately the 13,000-foot level. Intersect the ascent route well north of the 13,660-foot summit. Duplicate your route back to Cataract Lake. This hike requires 3,500 feet of ascent and covers ten miles.

For the hike to the last three summits return to the 12,380-foot saddle southeast of Cataract Lake. To start toward Carson Peak turn left at the saddle. Contour east into the far reaches of the Pole Creek drainage. Follow the drainage east-northeast to a 12,900-foot pass west of the head of Lost Trail Creek. Turn left and ascend grassy slopes north and northeast to the ridge crest at 13,250 feet. Turn right and descend east on the ridge crest to a 13,100-foot saddle. Continue the comfortable ridge walk by gradually climbing east to the elongated summit.

To head toward the 13,580-foot unnamed summit, return to the 12,900-foot pass west of the head of Lost Trail Creek. Hike south up the broad ridge. Pass well west of a 13,552-foot ridge point. Arrive at a 13,340-foot saddle just north of the summit. A short walk southwest brings you quickly to the 13,580-foot high point.

The ridge between the 13,580-foot unnamed summit and the 13,581-foot objective has numerous obstacles. Therefore, it is necessary to follow a fairly circuitous route to the 13,581-foot unnamed summit. Return northeast to the 13,340-foot saddle. Bear right and ascend the ridge east, staying south of the rock spires and cliffs. Reach grassy slopes and climb over a 13,568-foot ridge point. Descend to a flat grassy area on the ridge crest at 13,300 feet. Here you are a little west of the low point on the ridge.

Unfortunately, the ridge cannot be followed directly to the summit. A series of spires at the low point stands in the way. The shortest detour is to climb down approximately two hundred feet off the north side of the ridge. Turn right and contour east on steep talus and scree at the 13,100-foot level. Once beyond the spires turn right and ascend steeply to the ridge crest at 13,300 feet. From here the short walk to the summit at 13,581 feet is a simple matter. For those who want to avoid this difficult ridge traverse, easier but longer routes to the 13,581-foot summit could be followed from lower down on either Lost Trail Creek or West Lost Trail Creek.

On the return follow the same route back to the 13,340-foot saddle north of the 13,580-foot summit. Descend northwest on gentle slopes to the Pole Creek drainage. Continue back to Cataract Lake. The trip to these three summits covers twelve miles with 4,000 feet of ascent.

The five peaks described here for the second and third days of climbing also can be approached conveniently from the southeast. A backpack can follow the trails up Lost Trail Creek and West Lost Trail Creek. These trails start near Lost Trail Campground west of Rio Grande Reservoir. Camp can be located in the upper reaches of West Lost Trail Creek.

73. UNNAMED 13,795

General description:
A trail hike, a steep rocky climb to a ridge, and a gradual ridge walk
Hiking distance: 8 miles
Starting elevation: 10,420 feet
Elevation gain: 3,600 feet
Maps:
7.5 minute Redcloud Peak
Gunnison National Forest

This summit is the high point on the long lumpy ridge extending east from the Fourteener, Handies Peak. Drive to the road junction a mile and a half past Mill Creek Campground as in hike number 72. Take the rougher right fork four miles to a trailhead area. Here Silver Creek enters the Lake Fork from the right and Grizzly Gulch is on the left.

Hike southwest on trail along the northwest side of Grizzly Gulch. There is a fine bridge for crossing the Lake Fork. It is located behind an abandoned cabin west of the road two hundred yards northwest of the culvert over Silver Creek. Shortly after leaving the last timber two miles from the trailhead, turn left at 11,840 feet. Climb southeast to a small lake at 12,323 feet.

From the lake climb south up the steep slope into a small cirque north of the 13,795-foot summit. Bear right and climb southwest to the ridge crest. Aim a little to the right of a 13,580-

foot saddle just west of the summit. Turn left and proceed southeast for the gradual ridge walk to the summit.

74. UNNAMED 13,832
UNNAMED 13,811

General description:
A pleasant long hike on trail and broad ridges
Hiking distance: 14 miles
Starting elevation: 10,420 feet
Elevation gain: 5,000 feet
Maps:
    7.5 minute Redcloud Peak
    Gunnison National Forest

These two high unnamed summits largely go unnoticed because of their proximity to two Fourteeners, Redcloud Peak and Sunshine Peak. The trailhead area is the same as for hike number 73.

Hike the trail northeast up Silver Creek. The trail stays high above the creek on the northwest side for the first mile and a half. It continues up the drainage, climbing on switchbacks to a pass at 13,020 feet. At the pass, most of the foot tracks go southwest up the ridge to Redcloud Peak. To get to these unnamed summits, hike northeast along the ridge. Contour right, south of a 13,561-foot ridge point. Bear southeast along the south side of the ridge crest to avoid a series of false summits. Climb southeast to the 13,832-foot summit.

Descend east along the ridge and cross or bypass a 13,632-foot false summit. Descend northeast to a 13,260-foot saddle. Climb northeast up the gradual slope to the 13,811-foot summit. To return, retrace your route over the 13,832-foot summit and on to the pass northeast of Redcloud Peak.

A shorter route to these two summits can be followed

directly north from the Lake Fork road in the vicinity of Bent Creek; however, the rugged nature of the area makes the route described here a much better one.

75. UNNAMED 13,691
UNNAMED 13,688

General description:
A nice trail hike and a comfortable long ridge walk
Hiking distance: 11 miles
Starting elevation: 10,651 feet
Elevation gain: 3,800 feet
Maps:
  7.5 minute Redcloud Peak
  Gunnison National Forest

These two summits cannot be seen from any of the well-traveled roads in the area. They guard the head of the fishhook-shaped valley above Cooper Creek.

Drive up the road along Lake Fork Gunnison River as in hike numbers 73 and 74. Continue a mile and a quarter beyond the trailhead area for those two hikes. A trailhead parking area is on the right just before the road crosses Rock Creek.

The trail starts as an old jeep track leading east with little gain in elevation. It soon turns north and climbs along the west side of Cooper Creek. After a stretch on the east side of Cooper Creek, it returns to the west side at a trail junction at 11,560 feet. At the 12,200-foot level, where Cooper Creek bends west toward the outlet from Cooper Lake, stay with the trail north up the ridge. The trail leads to the site of an old mining prospect on top of the ridge at 12,860 feet.

The ridge walk over generally good footing goes east and south around the north end of the Cooper Creek basin. First turn right and either climb or bypass a 13,484-foot ridge point.

Then make a gradual climb east to the unnamed 13,691-foot summit.

Descend southeast along the ridge to a 13,220-foot saddle. Proceed southeast and south over several minor ridge points. Climb south to the unnamed summit at 13,688 feet. A descent from the summit could be made down the steep slope northwest in to the basin, however, it is better to return north along the ridge until the slopes to the west become more gentle. A long talus descent west will bring you into the drainage south of the 13,691-foot summit. Follow the drainage northwest and west. You can pick up the remnants of a trail along the south side of the drainage. The trail leads southwest along the southeast side of Cooper Creek. When you get to a trail junction at 11,560 feet, rejoin the ascent route and return southwest the way you came.

76. WOOD MOUNTAIN (13,660 feet)
UNNAMED 13,688
UNNAMED 13,722

General description:
  A hike on a popular jeep road and a ridge traverse with one difficult section
Hiking distance: 9 miles
Starting elevation: 11,300 feet
Elevation gain: 4,200 feet
Maps:
  7.5 minute Handies Peak
  Gunnison National Forest

The three summits are on or near the ridge crest between Engineer Pass and Cinnamon Pass. The 13,722-foot unnamed summit dominates the skyline as you approach the turn to Cinnamon Pass from the North Fork Animas River road north of Silverton.

Drive west along Lake Fork Gunnison River as in the previous four hikes. This time drive toward Cinnamon Pass as far as possible. Under good conditions, passenger cars can reach an intersection at 11,300 feet. Here the Cinnamon Pass road bears right and makes a big switchback up the hill. The left fork continues south along Lake Fork toward American Basin.

Walk up the road toward Cinnamon Pass. Leave the road at 12,200 feet a quarter mile after crossing minor drainage. Climb northwest up grassy slopes. Intersect the south ridge of Wood Mountain at 12,700 feet, a little north and east of Cinnamon Pass.

The route to Wood Mountain is along the ridge north and northwest. This is generally on good footing with some slow rocky sections.

From the summit of Wood Mountain, descend west along the ridge to a saddle at 13,300 feet. As you descend, examine the ridge extending north to the 13,688-foot unnamed summit. Bypassing the spires and cliffs on the first part of this ridge is the hardest part of this three-peak climb.

The ridge extending north takes off a quarter mile west of Wood Mountain at 13,540 feet. The best route begins farther west at the 13,300-foot saddle. Descend north from the saddle two hundred vertical feet. Turn right and contour on talus along the west side of the ridge. Aim to reach an area a little north of the 13,340-foot low point of the ridge between Wood Mountain and the 13,688-foot summit. Beyond the spires and steep cliffs, turn right and climb steep couloirs of loose rock to the ridge crest. From this part of the ridge, the climb north to the summit is much less demanding.

Return carefully from the 13,688-foot summit to the 13,300-foot saddle west of Wood Mountain. Walk west and either climb or contour left of a 13,708-foot ridge point. Continue south along the narrow rocky ridge, bypassing several minor ridge points. Climb south to the 13,722-foot unnamed summit.

To return, descend the rocky ridge east into the basin

southwest of Wood Mountain. Circle the basin east and south to the jeep trail west of Cinnamon Pass. Hike on the road east over Cinnamon Pass and back to your starting point.

A variation on the return is to take the right fork in the road a half mile east of Cinnamon Pass. Walk east on a parallel old road that is less used by vehicles.

* * * * *

Quite a few additional Thirteeners can be climbed on trips to this area. A Cataract Lake camp described in Chapter 72 makes a good base for climbing unnamed peaks 13,450 and 13,524 and Bent Peak in combination with Carson Peak. Unnamed 13,164 can be climbed with a hike to Half Peak.

The climb to unnamed 13,795 can be extended by following the ridge east to unnamed 13,454. The remote 13,180-foot unnamed summit northeast of unnamed 13,691 and 13,688 can be approached from the ridge extending northeast from between these higher peaks.

When at Cinnamon Pass for the hike to Wood Mountain, it is a short hike to Cinnamon Peak.

San Juan Mountains—
Weminuche Wilderness

Knife Point

77. WHITE DOME (13,627 feet)
PEAK ONE (13,589 feet)

General description:
   A long scenic backpack to a camp at a high lake and a short steep climb to the two summits

Hiking distance: 15 miles backpacking; 4½ miles climbing
Starting elevation: 10,460 feet
Elevation gain: 3,800 feet backpacking;
   1,900 feet climbing
Maps:
   7.5 minute Howardsville
   7.5 minute Storm King Peak
   San Juan National Forest

These two peaks serve as sentries guarding the northern access to the Weminuche Wilderness and the Grenadier Range. They are best approached from the north using a trail that follows the Continental Divide.

Drive east from Silverton on Colorado 110 to Howardsville. Turn south on Forest Service road 589. Drive south four miles along Cunningham Creek. Park near old mine remains where the road turns right and fords Cunningham Creek. This area serves as the trailhead for a high trail along the Continental Divide to the vicinity of Eldorado Lake. The lake's alpine meadows serve as fine campsites for backpackers basing their climbs at the lake.

From your parking place, cross to the west bank of Cunningham Creek amid debris of the abandoned mining area. Hike a quarter mile south along the west bank on a jeep trail. As the road turns west, find the start of a trail crossing to the east side of Cunningham Creek. Wading may be necessary in high water periods. Take the left fork at a trail junction after a half mile. The trail climbs rapidly east and southeast toward the Continental Divide. Beyond timberline, bear right at a creek crossing at 12,060 feet. Follow the trail west and south of a 12,302-foot ridge point to intersect the divide. Follow the well-used trail south, passing east of a 12,905-foot summit.

Continue south along the broad rolling ridge. White Dome's sweeping ridges provide sharp contrast with the gentle terrain near at hand. Follow the trail as it joins old vehicle tracks south on the crest of the Continental Divide. After the trail climbs over the west shoulder of a 12,924-foot ridge point, Eldorado Lake comes into view down to the right. Descend southwest through the meadow to the lake. Fine campsites are located at the east end of Eldorado Lake.

Hike along the south shore line to the west end of Eldorado Lake. Angle southwest past two small ponds around to the northwest side of White Dome. Head directly south up the talus to the 13,180-foot saddle west of White Dome. Turn left and climb east up the rocky ridge to the summit. The climb is over the white quartzite rock from which the peak gets its name.

Return west to the saddle. Hike southwest along the ridge to Peak One. A 13,401-foot ridge point can by bypassed on the right. Two minor ridge points farther along can be avoided on the left. Climb to the summit of Peak One.

From Peak One, return to the saddle west of White Dome. Descend north back to camp at Eldorado Lake.

78. ARROW PEAK (13,803 feet)
VESTAL PEAK (13,864 feet)
TRINITY PEAK WEST (13,765 feet)
TRINITY PEAK (13,805 feet)
TRINITY PEAK EAST (13,745 feet)

General description:
  A backpack partly on steep rough trail and several difficult climbs in a five-day trip
Hiking distance: 10 miles backpacking; 10 miles climbing
Starting elevation: 8,860 feet (at railroad stop)

Elevation gain: 2,700 feet backpacking; 8,600 feet climbing
Maps:
   7.5 minute Snowdon Peak
   7.5 minute Storm King Peak
   San Juan National Forest

These five peaks are in the western part of the Grenadier Range of the San Juan Mountains. They form a line of impressive summits when viewed from the vicinity of Molas Lake. All of them can be climbed on a backpacking trip into the northern part of the Weminuche Wilderness. The best camping destination is the basin in the upper part of the creek that flows from Vestal Lake into Elk Creek.

The shortest backpack starts from the Elk Park stop on the Durango-Silverton narrow-gauge railroad. For those who prefer not to ride the railroad, the hike can begin at Molas Lake, south of Silverton on US 550, a mile and a quarter north of Molas Pass. The parking area is a tenth of a mile from the highway on the south entrance to Molas Lake. From here, a trail leads four miles down to the Animas River north of Elk Park. This trail, not shown on the 1972 Snowdon Peak topographic map, heads south on old roads from the parking area. It bears east on the north side of Molas Creek, and then descends to the Animas River on numerous switchbacks. The trail crosses the river on a bridge at 8,900 feet and then gradually ascends the slope east of the Animas River. It meets a trail coming up from the railroad stop at a junction at 9,200 feet.

Whether reaching this junction from Molas Lake or from the railroad stop, the route continues up the fine trail along Elk Creek. Follow the trail three miles to a flat area at 9,980 feet. This popular area is located on the north side of Elk Creek near two small lakes. Here you leave the excellent trail. Round the east side of the larger lake, climbing over rocks, and continue south to find a crossing of Elk Creek. Once across the creek, bear southwest. Try to pick up one of the indistinct trails on the east side of the drainage originating at Vestal Lake. The several

128

The Trinity Peaks, left, Vestal Peak, center, and Arrow Peak, right of center, are the bastions of the Grenadier Range.

trails in this area are not good, but are better than bushwhacking.

After crossing a minor side drainage coming in from the east at 10,040 feet, the trails along the creek may look attractive, however, a higher trail one hundred feet above the stream is better. Some steep climbing brings you to an area where the gradient becomes more gradual at 10,660 feet. At 11,300 feet, after another steep stretch, good campsites begin to appear. Other campsites may be found alongside meadows in the next half mile. If you want to camp above timberline, you can go all

The Trinity Peaks as viewed from the ascent route on Arrow Peak with Vestal Peak's smooth north ridge in the foreground.

the way to Vestal Lake at 12,220 feet. It is only two miles from Elk Creek to a camp in the meadows at 11,300 feet, and perhaps two and a half miles to Vestal Lake, but the steep rough climb makes it seem a lot longer. An afternoon arrival on the train from Silverton barely allows enough time to make camp in the meadows before dark.

There are several ways these five peaks can be grouped for climbing. All five can be done in one day, but it would be an extremely long one. Arrow Peak and Vestal Peak can be done in a day, or Vestal can be combined with one or more of the Trinity Peaks. Our description assumes that Arrow is climbed one day, Vestal another, and the three Trinitys on a third day.

Arrow Peak has the reputation of being one of the hardest major mountains in Colorado to climb. It doesn't deserve that reputation if you use the route we suggest, although there are other difficult and more dangerous routes to the top. If you are camped in the meadows, start toward Arrow by climbing south up the grassy benches toward the peak. When you reach a more level bench at 11,900 feet, angle left and climb southeast into the broad basin between Arrow Peak and Vestal Peak.

At 12,200 feet, look for a channel, much like a ramp, on the right leading southwest from the basin all the way to the top of Arrow Peak. This route offers 1,600 feet of good but rather steep climbing, much of it on smooth solid rock. Follow up the rocky ledges and steps in this channel. When the ramp becomes steeper near the top, bear left to finish on the northeast ridge.

Two more-difficult routes up Arrow Peak go directly up the north ridge or utilize the south face couloir. If you have come up our recommended route, we suggest going back the same way. Don't be tempted to come down the south side to combine Arrow and Vestal on the same trip. Returning off Arrow Peak by the ascent route will involve another 700 feet of climbing up through the basin to the broad saddle between Arrow and Vestal, however, it is a safer way to combine Arrow and Vestal than descending Arrow Peak by an unknown and difficult route.

For the climb of Vestal Peak, ascend the rocky couloir between Arrow Peak and Vestal to the saddle at 12,860 feet between the two peaks. Work around the south side of Vestal Peak, gaining altitude slowly to remain below the cliffs at 13,200 feet. When you get almost directly south of the summit, find a shallow couloir that you can ascend to the summit. In this south-facing couloir the climbing is steep but not difficult, although there is some loose rock danger.

Don't rely on the USGS 7.5 minute quadrangles for the topography near the summit of Vestal Peak. The Storm King Peak quad dated 1964 shows the elevation of Vestal Peak as 13,664 feet. The 1975 photo-inspected version shows the correct elevation, but with misleading topography near the summit. That map would have you believe that there is an area of gradual climbing between 13,400 and 13,600 feet and then very steep climbing near the top—the gradient is nearly even the entire way, with only slight steepening near the top.

Vestal Peak also is climbed from the north up the Wham Ridge. This has been done unroped, but can be dangerous if wet weather strikes during the ascent, negating good friction on the smooth rock.

For the climb of the Trinity Peaks, the approach is from the pass between Vestal Peak and Trinity Peak West. If you are combining one or more Trinity Peaks with a climb of Vestal Peak, the ridge from Vestal can be used to reach this pass. Otherwise, from a camp in the meadows, follow the trail up the valley to another meadow at 11,740 feet. Turn right, cross the creek, and ascend south going east of Vestal Lake. Cross the boulder field in the basin and finally ascend the steep slopes to the 12,860-foot pass between Vestal Peak and Trinity Peak West. Trinity Peak West is a rocky ridge climb east and northeast from the pass.

The middle Trinity Peak, the highest of the three, is the most difficult to climb. From Trinity Peak West, descend east to the 13,380-foot saddle between the two peaks. Ascend to the east staying below the ridge crest on the south side. There are numerous choices along this portion of the route with cairns marking the unlikely looking but feasible passage. Contour below the crest to a point directly beneath the summit. Turn left and climb more steeply north to the summit of 13,805-foot Trinity Peak.

Trinity Peak East from the middle Trinity is fairly direct, rocky and slow, but with no particular problems. Descend east in a shallow couloir just south of the east ridge of the middle Trinity Peak. From the 13,340-foot saddle, ascend the west ridge of Trinity Peak East. Stay to the south side of the ridge as you near the summit.

The return to camp from Trinity Peak East is best made by descending the northeast ridge. This ridge descent brings you to a pass at 13,060 feet. From this pass, a trail of sorts leads northwest back down to the valley floor. Passing a lake at 12,396 feet, the route continues down the valley to the camping meadow. For Trinity Peak East alone, this is the best ascent route from a camp in the meadows.

The following statistics may be helpful in planning your trip. The pack-in to the 11,300-foot meadow involves 2,700 feet of elevation gain in five miles from Elk Park. It is nine miles from Molas Lake, with 1,800 feet of elevation to be regained on the return. All five peaks in a single day would be 6,000 feet of elevation gain in only seven miles, but it would seem like a lot more. As day hikes from an 11,300-foot base camp in the meadow, Arrow Peak is a 2,600-foot climb in a three-mile round trip, Vestal Peak is a 2,600-foot climb in a four-mile round trip, and the Trinity circuit is a 3,400-foot climb in seven miles.

79. PEAK SEVEN (13,682 feet)
STORM KING PEAK (13,752 feet)
MOUNT SILEX (13,628 feet)
THE GUARDIAN (13,617 feet)

General description:
A week-long backpacking trip to ascend four remote, rugged peaks, requiring a two-day approach and at least two days for the climbs

Hiking distance: 17 miles backpacking; 10 miles climbing
Starting elevation: 8,880 feet
Elevation gain: 5,400 feet backpacking; 5,000 feet climbing
Maps:
7.5 minute Snowdon Peak
7.5 minute Storm King Peak
San Juan National Forest

These four remote peaks are clustered deep in the heart of the Weminuche Wilderness. They are located at the east end of the rugged Grenadier Range. Access from any direction usually takes a minimum of two days' backpacking.

The first day's backpack is the same as used for Arrow Peak and the other summits in the western Grenadier Range. The second day's backpack crosses the range crest to the upper Tenmile Creek drainage. Since the peak climbs require at least two days, generally six days are required for the trip. Because the approach is the same, all nine of the Grenadier Range summits could be combined in an eight- to ten-day wilderness camping trip.

Follow the backpacking route described in hike number 78 to camp in the meadow at 11,300 feet. The route continues through the rugged 12,860-foot pass between Vestal Peak and Trinity Peak West. To reach this pass continue up the trail along the north side of the drainage to a large meadow at 11,740 feet. Cross the creek and hike south up over the grassy benches east of Vestal Lake. The final climb to the pass is somewhat slow since crossing the boulder field prior to the last pitch up to the pass can be tedious with a full pack.

From the 12,860-foot pass east of Vestal Peak, make a descending contour southeast and east over mixed tundra and talus. Aim to intersect in a mile the drainage extending northeast from Balsam Lake. With the proper traverse you will join the drainage in a meadow at 12,020 feet. Here the valley turns from northeast to east. Climb east upstream another quarter mile to the vicinity of two small ponds at 12,180 feet. Good camping is available here. The off-trail backpack from the 11,300-foot meadow requires 1,800 feet of climbing, a tedious descent, and covers three and a half miles.

From a camp near the two small ponds, Storm King Peak and Peak Seven make one good climbing day. Mount Silex and The Guardian take another day. Though not technically difficult, these four rugged summits require route-finding skills and a good deal of care and caution.

For Peak Seven angle southeast over the tundra. Climb to a small lake at the saddle between Peak Eight and Peak Seven. Turn right and climb due west to a minor saddle at 13,020 feet on the north ridge of Peak Seven. Turn left at the saddle and climb south up the ridge to the summit.

To get to Storm King Peak, return to the small lake at the Peak Eight-Peak Seven saddle. Descend north to approximately 12,500 feet. Turn right and contour east beneath Peak Eight's north face. Climb to the 12,820-foot saddle south of Storm King Peak. Turn left and climb north a little left of the ridge crest. At 13,200 feet climb into a narrow southwest-facing couloir filled with loose talus that leads up to the left of the ridge. When the couloir broadens out, again bear left for the final two-hundred-foot climb to the summit.

For the descent return south to the 12,820-foot saddle. Head west down the grassy valley to camp. These two summits require a climb of 2,800 feet in a four-mile round trip from camp.

To get to Mount Silex, climb again to the 12,820-foot saddle south of Storm King Peak. Make a descending contour east beneath the precipitous north face of Peak Nine. A rock shelf at 12,400 feet south of Lake Silex allows you to traverse well above the lake. Once past the lake, climb southeast up the steep rock slope to a saddle at 12,820 feet southwest of Mount Silex. Turn left and climb northeast up the ridge to the summit. There are a few difficult rock ridge steps along the way. Careful route selection should avoid any technical difficulties.

To proceed to The Guardian, return down the southwest ridge of Mount Silex. Descend a hundred vertical feet to the 13,500-foot contour. Leave the ridge on the left and descend south on scree in a broad couloir another three hundred vertical feet. Turn left and make a descending traverse southeast to the 13,060-foot Silex-Guardian saddle. Continue southeast, bypassing a 13,220-foot ridge point southeast of the saddle at the same elevation as the saddle. When the ridge narrows at 13,200 feet, avoid exposure by climbing on ledges right of the ridge crest. Regain the ridge at 13,400 feet for the final rocky walk to the summit. The Guardian gains its name from its imposing presence over the Vallecito Creek drainage extending south toward Vallecito Reservoir.

To return to camp carefully retrace the route to the Silex-Guardian saddle. Contour left across ledges and then scree on Silex's south face to the southwest ridge of Mount Silex. Descend southwest to the saddle for the return to camp the way you came. These two summits involve a hike of six miles from camp and a 3,200-foot elevation gain for the round trip.

A southern approach to the camp used to climb these summits follows the trail up Vallecito Creek. After fording Vallecito Creek, find a trail that goes up the north side of Leviathan Creek to tree line. Climb northwest through the Peak Eight-Peak Seven saddle to reach the camping area at the two ponds. Mount Silex and The Guardian also can be climbed directly from Leviathan Creek using the drainage on the southwest side of the two summits. Such an approach can be made from the excellent campsites near tree line along Leviathan Creek.

80. JAGGED MOUNTAIN (13,824 feet)
PEAK SIX (13,705 feet)

General description:
  **A backpack with one rugged off-trail section, a
  straightforward climb to Peak Six, and a difficult
  climb to Jagged Mountain**
**Hiking distance: 15 miles backpacking;
  9 miles climbing**
Starting elevation: 8,212 feet
**Elevation gain: 3,300 feet backpacking;
  5,700 feet climbing**
Maps:
  7.5 minute Snowdon Park
  7.5 minute Storm King Peak
  San Juan National Forest

Jagged Mountain is one of the most difficult summits to climb in Colorado's highest hundred. Only experienced climbers skilled in route finding should attempt it. The climb can be made without rope although most will prefer to have it

Mount Silex, left, and Storm King Peak, right, from the vicinity of Hunchback Pass.

along. The backpack is mostly on good trail with one short difficult section. Peak Six offers a scenic backpack into a remote area and a moderate climb for those who might not want to attempt Jagged Mountain.

Take the narrow-gauge railroad from Durango or Silverton to Needleton. It is best to go from Durango if you want to reach a high camp the same day and make the minimum four-day trip. Cross the Needleton foot bridge, turn left, and walk north on the east side of the Animas River. A well-beaten path takes you across Pigeon Creek and across an unnamed creek in the first half mile. Then comes the most difficult part of the backpack. Where the ridge between the unnamed creek and Ruby Creek cliffs out at the Animas River, there is no good route to continue north.

Several paths follow high, intermediate, and low routes. We will guarantee that whatever route you select you will wish you had taken another one. The low route, that uses some rocks along the river, may be best if the water is low. One of the paths is so steep that it has had a fixed rope in place, one of the few places you may need rope on a so-called trail.

Once across the ridge, a nice path continues another mile and a quarter to Noname Creek. A good trail starts east on the north side of the creek. Its beginning is near an old telephone pole. Follow the trail east as it stays north of Noname Creek, sometimes climbing high above the creek. After three and a half miles, the trail leaves the trees and enters a long meadow at 10,760 feet. A half mile farther, avoid the trail that turns right and leads south toward Twin Thumbs. Take the left fork trail that continues east along the north side of Noname Creek.

A good camping area to aim for is located another half mile farther at 11,020 where Noname Creek forks. The right fork leads up a valley south toward Sunlight Peak, while the left fork climbs steeply northeast. Good campsites also are available farther down in the big meadow. One is at the site of an old cabin, but these locations make the peak climbs longer.

From the campsite area at 11,020 feet, hike steeply northeast on a trail that climbs well to the west of the creek. This trail leaves the floor of the main valley at the base of an avalanche runout located a hundred yards west of the creek junction. The trail leads out of the timber into a swampy area at 11,820 feet. Bypass to the left of the bog. Hike east along the north side of the drainage past a small lake at 12,180 feet. As you approach a steep rocky ascent to the pass north of Jagged Mountain, favor the right-hand slopes for this climb.

From the narrow pass at 13,020 feet, carefully study Jagged Mountain to the south. Jagged Mountain has several summits. It is not practical to climb from one to another, so it is important to climb the proper summit. The true summit is just right of the first prominent couloir on the left side of the summit block. Prior to August this will be a large snow-filled

Jagged Mountain as viewed across the valley from Leviathan Peak. The ascent route uses the sharp notch to the right of the central summit block.

couloir. Contour south to the base of the prominent couloir. Climb steeply south just to the right of the couloir over technically easy terrain. Head toward the west side of the upper reaches of the couloir.

After gaining as much altitude as possible next to the couloir, you come to the base of a cliff face. This forces you to climb to the right on steep terrain. Gain the saddle at 13,620 feet just to the right or northwest of the highest summit crag of Jagged Mountain. The two hundred feet of climbing to the saddle can be done mainly on sloping sandy ledges. The steep sections between the ledges may be more comfortable with rope if the rock is not dry.

From the 13,620-foot saddle, turn left and contour and climb over the rock ledges. Stay to the right of and well beneath the ridge crest. This brings you to the southwest side of the summit. Look for a steep route leading left toward the summit. There is a choice of several not-too-easy routes involving rock slabs or ledges. Since there is considerable exposure, rope again may be advisable. As you near the summit, the climbing becomes easier. It is a 2,900-foot climb in the four-mile round trip from the camping area to Jagged Mountain.

Don't be tempted to combine Peak Six with Jagged Mountain in a one-day trip from the camp at 11,020 feet, as this may make too long a day. If time and energy are left over after climbing Jagged, Leviathan Peak is available as a short climb northeast after you return to the 13,020-foot pass.

For Peak Six, follow the same route from camp to the small lake at 12,180 feet. Bear left and climb north over ledges through dwarf trees to a large lake at 12,552 feet. Pass west of the lake and walk north up moderate slopes to a 12,900-foot pass between Peak Five and Peak Six. Turn right and follow the rocky ridge east and northeast to the top. Peak Six has two summits with the southeast one appearing higher. The trip to Peak Six from camp and back covers five miles with a 2,800-foot elevation gain.

81. TURRET PEAK (13,835 feet)
PIGEON PEAK (13,972 feet)
PEAK FIFTEEN (13,700 feet)
MONITOR PEAK (13,695 feet)
PEAK THIRTEEN (13,705 feet)
ANIMAS MOUNTAIN (13,786 feet)

General description:
A tough route-finding backpack and climbs ranging from easy to very difficult, requiring five to seven days

Hiking distance: 10 miles backpacking; 14 miles climbing
Starting elevation: 8,212 feet
Elevation gain: 3,800 feet backpacking; 12,400 feet climbing
Maps:
  7.5 minute Snowdon Peak
  7.5 minute Storm King Peak
  7.5 minute Mountain View Crest
    (one climb barely on edge)
  7.5 minute Columbine Pass
    (for alternate approach only)
  San Juan National Forest

Pigeon Peak is a striking landmark on the west edge of the Needle Mountains in the Weminuche Wilderness. The other summits are in a more remote area east of Pigeon Peak. Access to these peaks is difficult and you are unlikely to see as many backpackers and climbers as in other parts of the Weminuche Wilderness.

Each of the various approaches to these peaks requires a long and difficult backpack. The hiking usually begins at Needleton on the Animas River. Most climbers prefer to take the Durango-Silverton narrow-gauge railroad. From Needleton, the objective is to get to the grassy meadow at 11,600 feet on Ruby Creek one mile east of Ruby Lake. This area affords a good base for climbing and provides a beautiful campsite beneath the spectacular Turret Needles.

The shortest approach is to cross the bridge over the Animas River at Needleton and walk upstream on the east bank, cross Pigeon Creek, and go one quarter of a mile farther to a grassy meadow. A rough, but well-defined trail begins at this meadow and contours up to Ruby Creek, reaching an avalanche-cleared area at 10,400 feet on the south side of Ruby Creek.

The initial problem is locating the start of the trail. To find the start of the Ruby Lake trail, leave the river trail and hike to the southeast corner of the meadow and locate the beginning of

Turret Peak and the more diminutive Peak Fifteen to its left from atop Monitor Peak.

the trail. Another approach is to leave the river trail at the abandoned mine machinery one passes shortly before reaching the meadow. Climb the embankment and bushwhack northeast until you intersect the Ruby Lake trail.

The trail crosses to the north side of the unnamed creek at 9,500 feet. At this point two trails leave the creek. Take the right-hand trail which initially climbs very steeply on poor footing. The trail climbs to the crest of the ridge between the unnamed creek and Ruby Creek at 10,340 feet. From the ridge crest, the trail traverses east with some ups and downs until it reaches Ruby Creek at the 10,400-foot avalanche cleared area.

Continue east upstream on the south side of the creek. When the trail becomes less distinct, cross to the north side of the creek.

142

Pick up a trail leading to Ruby Lake and around the north side of the lake. Beyond the east end of Ruby Lake, a rugged trail climbs north away from the creek. Once out of the timber, the trail climbs well to the north of the creek to avoid the worst of the thick willows. The trail returns to the creek at the 11,600-foot meadow.

It is difficult to reach the meadow at 11,600 feet the same day you arrive at Needleton on the train. A morning arrival from Durango is essential, if you are to backpack to the meadow before dark. The afternoon train from Silverton leaves too little time to get to the meadow that same day. If you are unable to reach the 11,600-foot meadow, other suitable camping locations can be found. One is near a tiny pond just west of Ruby Lake. Other campsites are on the south side of the creek east of Ruby Lake, and on the south side of the creek at 11,300 feet. All of these locations make the climbs longer, except for a climb of Pigeon Peak from the basin on its west side.

A second approach to the 11,600-foot meadow on Ruby Creek also starts at Needleton. Hike north on the trail along the east side of the Animas River. Follow the route up Noname Creek as described in hike number 80. From the southeast part of the long clearing at 10,800 feet, follow the trail up the Noname Creek tributary coming in from the south. This takes you in the direction of Twin Thumbs. At 11,000 feet a trail crosses the creek and climbs steeply west toward the imposing east face of Monitor Peak. The trail fades out near tree line at 11,600 feet. Climb southwest over tundra toward the saddle at 12,700 feet south of Monitor Peak. This saddle allows access to the upper reaches of Ruby Creek. A trail of sorts follows down the north side of Ruby Creek to the meadow at 11,600 feet.

A third approach follows the trail up Needle Creek to Chicago Basin. A steep wet trail leaves the Forest Service trail at 11,200 feet at the upper end of Chicago Basin and climbs to two small lakes at 12,500 feet. From these lakes a short climb leads to Twin Thumbs Pass, an unofficially named pass at 13,060 feet between Twin Thumbs and Glacier Point. Descend the north side of the pass about five hundred vertical feet. Traverse west to the 12,820-foot pass north of North Eolus. The descent from Twin Thumbs Pass in early summer requires an ice axe and possibly crampons due to the steep shaded snow on the north side. From this 12,820-foot pass, descend to the upper Ruby Creek lake at 12,580 feet. Traverse to the second approach route at 12,600 feet, one hundred feet below the 12,700-foot pass south of Monitor Peak. Descend to the 11,600-foot meadow as in the second approach.

The first approach route can be done in one long day from Needleton, either after arriving from Durango or after camping along the Animas River. The second and third approaches require two days and would normally be used when making climbs in other areas of the Weminuche Wilderness.

Once at the 11,600-foot base camp, Pigeon Peak and Turret Peak can be climbed in one day. Peak Fifteen requires a second day. Monitor Peak, Peak Thirteen, and Animas Mountain take a third day.

For Turret Peak and Pigeon Peak, cross to the south side of Ruby Creek. Climb the grassy slopes, rocks, and early-season snowfields southwest to the 13,100-foot Pigeon-Turret saddle. Turret Peak is a simple ridge climb east and southeast on sandy rock.

For Pigeon Peak, return to the Pigeon-Turret saddle. Descend and contour west to the 12,780-foot saddle south-southwest of the Pigeon summit. This allows access to the basin on the west side of Pigeon Peak. Descend the basin west-northwest to 12,200 feet. Contour north one-fourth mile to the drainage on the northwest side of Pigeon Peak. Climb the grassy and rocky drainage northeast and east to meet the north ridge of Pigeon Peak at 13,660 feet. Follow the north ridge or the steep slopes just west of the ridge south to the summit. Pigeon Peak has two summits, the west one being the higher, with one large rock as the high point. Unless you are prepared for a long and difficult rappel off the southeast face of Pigeon Peak, return to camp the way you came via the Pigeon-Turret saddle. These two peaks require an ascent of 5,000 feet in a five-mile round trip from camp.

If camped west of Ruby Lake, a better approach to Pigeon Peak alone is to climb southwest to the northwest ridge, contour southeast to the basin west of Pigeon, and then follow

Pigeon Peak, with its precipitous northeast face on the right, as seen from Turret Peak.

the route to the summit previously described.

For Peak Fifteen, follow the route over the 13,100-foot Pigeon-Turret saddle. Descend southwest to the 12,780-foot saddle on the south side of Pigeon Peak. Climb down into New York Basin to the south. Contour east at the twelve-thousand-foot level. Look for a couloir on your left ascending to the notch between Peak Fifteen on the left and Peak Sixteen on the right. Climb up this steep couloir to two hundred feet below the saddle. Here the couloir becomes very narrow and climbing is easier on the rock left of the couloir. Once at the saddle it is a straightforward job to turn right and rock-scramble east and north to the summit of Peak Sixteen, only eighty feet above the saddle. This spot provides an excellent perch to pick out the best route up Peak Fifteen.

Peak Fifteen is tricky to climb due to the smooth sandy nature of the crumbling rock. From the saddle, climb west up the ridge fifty vertical feet. Traverse to the right ten yards on a one-foot-wide ledge to the edge of the north face. Climb fifty vertical feet more to a wider sandy shelf. Traverse west across the south face seventy-five yards to a gully that allows access through the final cliff band to the summit ridge. The high point is fifty yards west on the farthest west point of the ridge.

In the early summer, the couloir to the saddle between Peak Fifteen and Peak Sixteen will be snow-filled even though south facing, requiring the use of an ice axe and possibly crampons. Return to camp the same way. The ascent of Peak Fifteen and Peak Sixteen and the return to camp is 4,400 feet in six miles.

For climbers based in Chicago Basin the upper reaches of New York Basin can be reached by climbing to the Mount Eolus-North Eolus saddle at 13,860 feet and descending to the Peak Fifteen couloir entrance at 12,400 feet. The snow slope on the north side of Eolus is in the shade until late in the day, necessitating use of ice axe and crampons, particularly on a morning descent. The problem with this route is that 1,500 feet of elevation must be regained to return to Chicago Basin. The climb is 5,600 feet for the approach to Peak Fifteen from Chicago Basin.

Monitor Peak, Peak Thirteen, and Animas Mountain combine nicely in the same day. Climbing Monitor first makes for the easiest route finding on the three peaks. From the 11,600-foot meadow, climb northeast into the basin south of Animas Mountain. At 13,000 feet, find a ramp that climbs southeast across the southwest face of Peak Thirteen. The ramp leads to a point directly under the 13,380-foot Peak Thirteen-Monitor saddle. The ledge is probably six feet wide at the narrowest spot and is littered with loose rock and sand. From just west of the saddle, climb the ridge south to Monitor Peak. Spires and cliffs south of the saddle can be bypassed on the west side of the ridge. Thereafter, the ridge can be followed to the summit.

Return to the Peak Thirteen-Monitor saddle. Climb directly north to the base of the cliffs on the south face of Peak Thirteen. Turn right and work east and north along a shelf, with a slight descent on the east side. From the east side of Peak Thirteen, turn left and climb west and north on ledges to the summit.

Descend the north side of Peak Thirteen on ledges a hundred vertical feet. Contour left to the northwest ridge. Descend to the saddle northwest of Peak Thirteen. Contour northwest on the left side of a wide 13,620-foot ridge point between Peak Thirteen and Animas Mountain. From the 13,500-foot saddle just east of Animas Mountain, climb northwest to the base of a cliff band. Traverse to the right into a gully and proceed to the head of the gully. Climb out of the gully up a series of narrow ledges on the right side. Turn left and ascend the last stretch to the summit on the ridge to the right of the gully.

To return to camp, climb down to the 13,500-foot saddle east of Animas Mountain. Descend six hundred feet on the sandy scree slope south of the saddle. Turn right and traverse west across several minor gullies. Enter a broad cliff-bound gully that has a high wall on its west side. Descend this gully to the grassy slopes at 12,600 feet. Turn right for the gentle hike down to the camp in the meadow.

The trip over these three peaks from camp and back has 3,000 feet of elevation gain in just three miles, however, much of the climbing is slow going on difficult terrain.

82. JUPITER MOUNTAIN (13,830 feet)
GRIZZLY PEAK (13,700 feet)
GLACIER POINT (13,704 feet)

General description:
  A backpack into a popular area, one
  easy climb, and one difficult climb
Hiking distance: 14 miles backpacking; 12 miles climbing

Starting elevation: 8,212 feet
Elevation gain: 3,500 feet backpacking; 6,200 feet climbing
Maps:
  7.5 minute Snowdon Peak (trailhead area only)
  7.5 minute Mountain View Crest
  7.5 minute Columbine Pass
  7.5 minute Storm King Peak
  (Glacier Point on map edge)
  San Juan National Forest

These three peaks are in the area around Chicago Basin. Since there are also three Fourteeners surrounding Chicago Basin, most climbers overlook these high Thirteeners on their first trip to this scenic area in the Weminuche Wilderness.

The shortest backpacking route to Chicago Basin is from the narrow-gauge railroad stop at Needleton. Other alternate approaches begin from Purgatory Campground on US 550 or at Vallecito Campground.

From the east end of the Animas River foot bridge at Needleton, follow the trail south. After a level mile, the trail from Purgatory Campground joins on the right. Five miles of steady uphill hiking east along the north side of Needle Creek brings you to a trail junction in a meadow at 11,000 feet. Most foot traffic continues left, toward the upper end of Chicago Basin. The best camping areas for these climbs are along the trail to the right toward Columbine Pass. Cross Needle Creek and ascend another seven hundred feet in a mile to a flat area at the edge of the timber at 11,700 feet. Excellent campsites can be found near the junction with the trail coming up from the upper end of Chicago Basin.

Jupiter Mountain is a direct ascent from the camping area. Hike northeast to the left of a drainage. Climb the slopes on mixed grass and rock between the drainage and the ridge to its left. Reach the west ridge of Jupiter Mountain at 13,400 feet. Make a gradual climb to the summit, with some large rocks to negotiate near the top.

This climber has a lofty perch atop one of the large boulders on the summit of Grizzly Peak.

The approach to Grizzly Peak is from the basin north of Hazel Lake which lies south of Jupiter Mountain. To combine Jupiter and Grizzly in one day from Chicago Basin, it is necessary to descend from Jupiter Mountain into this basin. This descent is the most difficult part of a trip combining these two peaks. Those seeking an easier route to Grizzly Peak might prefer to climb that peak another day by following our suggested return route from Grizzly Peak.

Descend southwest from the summit of Jupiter Mountain if you wish to continue on toward Grizzly Peak. Continue southwest down the ridge to get beyond the steep cliffs on the south face. Work around large boulders toward the south. Climb down steep rocky slopes to the 13,200-foot level on the south face. Turn left and contour east along the base of steep cliffs. Descend slightly and work along the cliff base to a point southwest of the saddle between Jupiter Mountain and Grizzly Peak.

Look for a prominent ramp ascending left to right beginning a hundred feet below the saddle. Walk up this broad ramp on grass and rock as it climbs southeast around the right side of the ridge. This leads to a large couloir that splits the southwest face of Grizzly Peak just north of the summit. Climb up this couloir to the saddle at 13,500 feet just northwest of the summit.

To reach the high point, climb out onto the north face from the saddle. Ascend to the left of the ridge crest over large irregular-shaped boulders. Climb up through these boulders to the top. There are two high points approximately twenty-five yards apart, in the form of two large boulders on the summit ridge.

To return to camp, return to the west end of the ramp beneath the Jupiter-Grizzly saddle. Descend southwest into the basin north of Hazel Lake. Circle the basin to the west side of Hazel Lake. Climb to a 12,780-foot saddle west of Hazel Lake and north of Hope Mountain. Follow a trail west from this saddle that circles west on the north side of the basin above Columbine Lake. This brings you to Columbine Pass at 12,700 feet. A good trail from the pass winds west and north down to the camping area. The round trip to Jupiter Mountain and Grizzly Peak is a six-mile hike from camp with 3,200 feet of elevation gain.

To get to Glacier Point from the camping area, you can

either descend into the upper end of Chicago Basin before climbing north or follow a contour route around the east side of the basin. A good trail descends from the camping area to a junction a hundred yards west of Needle Creek at 11,200 feet.

Turn back sharply to the right and follow the trail as it climbs steeply along the west side of Needle Creek. The contour route follows well-beaten game paths north along the east side of the basin. After contouring around the head of the basin, this route joins the lower route at the trail west of Needle Creek at 11,800 feet.

Hike on north up Needle Creek to a pair of large lakes at 12,500 feet. Turn left and climb west from the northwest end of the northern lake. Continue up on good footing to intersect the ridge that extends south-southeast from Glacier Point at 13,500 feet. The short walk north to the summit is a simple matter. The trip to Glacier Point and back to camp via the low route climbs 3,000 feet in six miles.

83. MOUNT OSO (13,684 feet)

General description:
   A long two-day approach backpack on a trail to a base at a high lake for the moderate off-trail summit climb, making a four- or five-day trip
Hiking distance: 34 miles backpacking; 6 miles climbing
Starting elevation: 7,916 feet
Elevation gain: 5,000 feet backpacking; 2,800 feet climbing
Maps:
   7.5 minute Vallecito Reservoir (trailhead area only)
   7.5 minute Columbine Pass
   7.5 minute Storm King Peak
   7.5 minute Rio Grande Pyramid (trail approach through map corner)
   7.5 minute Emerald Lake
   San Juan National Forest

This remote summit is in the high eastern plateau of the Weminuche Wilderness. It is the high point rising east of Vallecito Creek when viewed from the summits of the Grenadier Range and Needle Mountains.

Drive north from US 160 at Bayfield or east from Durango to Vallecito Reservoir. From the north end of the reservoir drive north another three miles to the road end at Vallecito Campground. The trailhead parking area is in the northeast corner of the campground.

The trail climbs north up Vallecito Creek and Rock Creek to Rock Lake in a total of seventeen miles. Though the trail makes for easy backpacking, the distance covered suggests a two-day approach hike. Follow the trail upstream eight miles to a junction with a trail going left up Johnson Creek to Columbine Pass. Continue north another five miles under the imposing presence of The Guardian to the Rock Creek trail junction.

Turn right on the Rock Creek trail. It climbs southeast up the northeast side of Rock Creek another three and a half miles prior to crossing to the west side of the creek for the final half mile to Rock Lake at 11,841 feet. Fine campsites are found in the vicinity of Rock Lake.

To climb Mount Oso, continue south on the trail to a 12,420-foot pass above Rock Lake. Follow the trail as it continues along the ridge west of the pass. Leave the trail on the right when it turns left and begins to descend to Half Moon Lake. Hike southwest over a gentle 12,620-foot ridge. Drop southwest over the grassy slopes, losing four hundred feet of elevation, into the wide drainage west and northwest of Moon Lake. Once in the center of the basin, turn right and climb west. Aim to ascend to the southeast ridge of Mount Oso at 13,000 feet. Use a shallow grassy and gravel couloir that climbs steeply to the left of the east-face cliffs. Once on the ridge, climb northwest to the broad summit plateau. Cross the rocky plateau and continue northwest for the final pitch to the summit.

152

84. RIO GRANDE PYRAMID (13,821 feet)

General description:
A long scenic hike with a moderate rocky climb
Hiking distance: 20 or 21 miles
Starting elevation: 9,340 feet
Elevation gain: 4,800 feet
Maps:
   7.5 minute Weminuche Pass
   7.5 minute Rio Grande Pyramid
   Rio Grande National Forest

Rio Grande Pyramid is a lofty summit east of the highest summits of the Weminuche Wilderness. Since it is so isolated, its pyramid shape is conspicuous from many distant vantage points.

The long hike and climb of Rio Grande Pyramid can be made in a day, but some climbers may prefer to make a backpack trip. The starting point is near Rio Grande Reservoir west of Creede.

Drive west from Creede or south from Lake City on Colorado 149. Midway between Creede and Spring Creek Pass, a mile south of Spring Creek Reservoir Picnic Ground, turn west on Forest Service road 520. Drive to Thirtymile Campground, near the dam at the east end of Rio Grande Reservoir. The trailhead is in the southwestern part of the campground.

The trail forks just after leaving the trailhead. The left fork goes south along Squaw Creek to Squaw Pass. The route to Rio Grande Pyramid follows the right fork. The trail rounds the south side of Rio Grande Reservoir and proceeds gradually up the northwest side of Weminuche Creek. In five miles, the trail reaches the Continental Divide near Weminuche Pass. It is difficult to determine the high point of Weminuche Pass in the vast flat meadow. As the trail approaches Weminuche Pass from the north, it stays on high ground west of the pass. A timbered area here provides good campsites for backpackers.

There are two good trail routes from Weminuche Pass toward Rio Grande Pyramid. One route from Weminuche Pass is on a trail not shown on the 1975 photo revised Weminuche Pass topographic map. This recently constructed trail goes directly west from the pass. It ascends steeply and stays near the crest of the Continental Divide. After a couple of miles, at 12,000 feet, the trail moves to the south side of the divide. It stays south of a 12,808-foot ridge point. The Window, a prominent rectangular cut in the Continental Divide south of Rio Grande Pyramid, comes into view. Four miles from Weminuche Pass at 12,300 feet, go left of a 13,278-foot summit east of Rio Grande Pyramid.

Look for an obscure trail that climbs on switchbacks toward the 12,645-foot saddle between the 13,278-foot summit and Rio Grande Pyramid. Even without a trail, climbing toward the saddle is not difficult. Angle toward Rio Grande Pyramid from a flatter area at 12,600 feet. Go left on the south side of a 13,185-foot ridge point.

Climb west up the ridge to the summit. This climb is over rocky terrain and is steep in spots. The climb can be aided by finding crude paths in the gravel patches between the rocky sections. After completing this long climb, enjoy the spectacular view from the summit of Rio Grande Pyramid.

The second slightly longer route continues south on the trail from Weminuche Pass. The trail contours along the west side of Raber Lohr Ditch. It then leaves the ditch and turns west along the side of Rincon La Vaca. After crossing an avalanche chute runout at 10,800 feet, the trail begins to climb through timber. Leave the trail just beyond timberline at the northwest end of a broad switchback at 12,000 feet.

Climb left to avoid the willows blocking the route directly ahead. Make a short climb west to a broad grassy ridge. The Window comes into view on the left. Climb northwest up the broad ridge across the higher trail at 12,300 feet. Finish by climbing the east ridge of Rio Grande Pyramid as described in the first route.

San Juan Mountains— Western Area

Mike on Dallas Peak

85. NIAGARA PEAK (13,807 feet)
JONES MOUNTAIN (13,860 feet)
UNNAMED 13,806

General description:
  An approach on an abandoned road, some easy off-trail hiking, and a moderate rocky traverse between the three peaks
Hiking distance: 9 miles
Starting elevation: 10,720 feet
Elevation gain: 4,400 feet
Maps:
  7.5 minute Handies Peak
  San Juan National Forest

These three summits are east of the Animas River northeast of Silverton. They provide a unique opportunity to ascend three "thirteen-eighters" in a single day hike. The best approach to the ridge traverse between the three peaks is from the west. It uses an old road in Burns Gulch.

Drive east from Silverton on Colorado 110 to Howardsville. Continue north three and a half miles to the townsite of Eureka. The road becomes rougher after crossing to the west side of the Animas River. Drive two and a half miles north of Eureka. Park where the road crosses back to the east side of the Animas River.

Hike south on an old roadbed along the east bank of the Animas River. Shortly after crossing the stream draining Grouse Gulch, the road angles up and begins to climb into Burns Gulch. Follow this road through abandoned mining debris in Burns Gulch to near its terminus at 11,900 feet.

Leave the road and climb over the tundra southeast to the 13,220-foot saddle between Niagara Peak and Jones Mountain. Turn right for the short stiff rocky climb southwest to Niagara Peak.

Return northeast to the 13,220-foot saddle. Continue

northeast and north on easier gravelly terrain to the summit of Jones Mountain.

Descend northeast along the ridge to a 13,340-foot saddle. The last part of this ridge traverse involves a rather sharp drop down an abrupt ridge step.

Climb north and east from the saddle. Ascend to the 13,600-foot contour on the south side of the first ridge point northeast of the saddle. There are three intermediate ridge points along the ridge east to the 13,806-foot summit. All can be bypassed on the south side. Traverse east at the 13,600-foot level. The large unstable talus to be crossed makes the half mile to the summit very tedious and slow going. Persevere to a 13,580-foot saddle just west of the 13,806-foot summit. Climb east to the summit.

Return to the 13,340-foot saddle northeast of Jones Mountain. Turn right and descend west on talus into the upper portion of Burns Gulch. Pass a tiny lake at 12,500 feet. Bear left and descend southwest on grassy slopes on the north side of the drainage. Intersect the old mining road just below the point where it crosses the lake outlet.

These three summits also can be climbed from the east side of the range crest. The trip from there is a little longer and steeper. The approach is from Lake City up Lake Fork Gunnison River to American Basin.

86. POTOSI PEAK (13,786 feet) TEAKETTLE MOUNTAIN (13,819 feet)

General description:
   A difficult off-trail climb to two rugged summits
Hiking distance: 6 miles
Starting elevation: 10,780 feet
Elevation gain: 4,500 feet

Maps:
7.5 minute Telluride
7.5 minute Ironton (Potosi Peak only)
7.5 minute Mount Sneffels (Teakettle Mountain only)
Uncompahgre National Forest

These two peaks are on the long ridge of rugged summits extending east from the Mount Sneffels massif. Teakettle Mountain is the distinctive sharp-pointed summit left of Mount Sneffels when viewed from south of Montrose. Potosi Peak's layer-cake appearance dominates the view east from the upper portion of Yankee Boy Basin. Both peaks are well armed with cliffs to test the route-finding skills of the most experienced climbers. The two peaks are best approached from the south via Yankee Boy Basin southwest of Ouray. Strong climbers can combine the two summits in one long day hike.

From a half mile south of Ouray on US 550, turn right on Colorado 361 toward Camp Bird Mine. The unpaved road climbs steeply up Canyon Creek. After five miles, a half mile short of Camp Bird Mine, take the right fork. This road climbs steeply a mile and three-fourths up Sneffels Creek to the townsite of Sneffels. The road is quite spectacular for a short stretch as it traverses a narrow shelf cut out of the cliff face high above the creek. Under good conditions passenger cars can drive a half mile beyond Sneffels to a road fork at 10,780 feet.

Hike up the right fork of the road as it climbs steeply another three-fourths mile. Leave the road on the right where it levels out momentarily at 11,360 feet at the far eastern end of Yankee Boy Basin. Climb north up the tilted slopes of seasonally blooming columbine, aiming for a steep grassy gully. The gully allows access through a minor cliff band to gentler grassy slopes above.

Once above the cliff band, examine the rugged slopes above. A prominent 13,568-foot rock outcrop, referred to as "Coffeepot" by some climbers, is readily visible on the ridge above. The route with the most solid footing is in a shallow couloir that extends southwest from the Coffeepot summit.

From the "Coffeepot" the distinctive summit of Teakettle Mountain is clearly visible.

Climb up toward the base of the rock rib just left of this couloir. At 12,400 feet, begin angling right into the center of the couloir. Continue climbing steeply up the unstable chip-rock for the toilsome haul to the ridge. At 13,400 feet things level out, giving the opportunity to stand upright again. Here you are just south of the Coffeepot summit.

To climb Potosi Peak turn right and descend the ridge southeast to a 12,980-foot saddle. Climb southeast from the saddle up the ridge toward Potosi. At the base of a high cliff band at 13,400 feet, contour right along the west side of the summit block. Continue around a corner into the base of a steep narrow couloir that faces southwest. This difficult couloir with much loose rock may look inviting. While it can be used to get to the summit, it is not recommended. A longer but more pedestrian route is available farther east.

Continue to contour around the next corner. The traverse leads around the south-southwest ridge of the peak and onto the southeast face. Continue your traverse around to the right side of the face and climb an easier, gravel-filled gully. Turn left and climb out onto the surprisingly large, flat summit area.

Return to the base of Coffeepot. If you elect not to continue on to Teakettle Mountain this day, descend left to the valley floor.

To continue to Teakettle, traverse around the left side of Coffeepot. Look for a broad couloir left of the ridge crest. This couloir can be used to get down the southwest side of the ridge crest. Climb down to a point a little below a 13,380-foot saddle. A narrower and steeper couloir can be seen left of the ridge line a little beyond the low point. Use this couloir to start the climb up Teakettle Mountain. Climb up the ridge from the top of the couloir. Keep left of the ridge line. The route negotiates through a series of intermittent cliff bands on wide sloping gravel shelves and sandy gullies.

The high point of Teakettle Mountain is a pinnacle on the far west end of the ridge line. The distinctive handle of the teakettle comes into view left of the high point. Stop long enough to take photos of climbers standing in the handle opening.

The summit pinnacle is best climbed from its east side. Follow a gully on the south side of the ridge that leads to a saddle right of the base of the pinnacle. Climb left over boulders and ledges. Find a ten-foot vertical jam crack on the east side of the pinnacle. Climb this final pitch to the tiny summit area. Some climbers may want a rope belay on this last short, but exposed, rock pitch.

To return retrace the route to the Teakettle-Coffeepot saddle. Turn right and scree southwest down a wide couloir to gentle grassy slopes. Angle left to intersect the ascent route.

Climbers doing Teakettle Mountain singly may be tempted to use the descent couloir as an ascent route. Experience suggests that the appreciably better footing of the recommended ascent route more than compensates for the additional elevation gain required to go over the Coffeepot summit.

For climbers desiring only to scale Potosi Peak, a more direct route is available. From a quarter mile east of the Sneffels townsite, climb steeply north passing above the Torpedo Eclipse Mine. This route joins the route described above at the base of the final cliff bands at the left side of the southeast face.

87. CIRQUE MOUNTAIN (13,686 feet)

General description:
   A simple climb to an impressive summit with fine views
   of the neighboring peaks
Hiking distance: 6 miles
Starting elevation: 10,780 feet
Elevation gain: 3,000 feet
Maps:
   7.5 minute Telluride
   7.5 minute Mount Sneffels
   Uncompahgre National Forest

Cirque Mountain is the easiest to climb of all the peaks surrounding Yankee Boy Basin. Cirque Mountain makes an ideal objective for those who do not want to attempt the more difficult summits in the area. Its summit provides a great vantage point for viewing the surrounding spectacular peaks.

Although Cirque Mountain has an impressive steep north face, its southern flank gives easy access to the summit. The trailhead is the same as for hike number 86.

Take the right-hand road at the trailhead. Hike a mile up the steep road into Yankee Boy Basin. Leave the road on the right at the end of a level stretch at 11,420 feet. Climb northwest into a wide grassy valley. This valley is left of a protruding ridge directly north. Hike up the valley all the way to a 13,060-foot saddle. This saddle, known as Dyke Col, is left and west of Cirque Mountain. Kismet, an unofficially named 13,694-foot summit, is west and on the left of Dyke Col.

Turn right at Dyke Col and follow the chip-rock ridge east to the summit. A 13,500-foot ridge point midway along the ridge can be easily bypassed on the north side.

Cirque Mountain has two well-spaced summit points of almost equal height. The western one is higher.

88. GILPIN PEAK (13,694 feet)
MOUNT EMMA (13,581 feet)

General description:
   A simple approach hike with difficult climbs to each of the summits
Hiking distance: 7 miles
Starting elevation: 10,780 feet
Elevation gain: 3,900 feet
Maps:
   7.5 minute Telluride
   Uncompahgre National Forest

These mountains guard the south side of Yankee Boy Basin. Since they have higher neighbors, these two peaks often go unvisited until a second or third climbing sojourn to Yankee Boy Basin. Both summits are difficult to climb because of loose rotten rock and require good route-finding ability. The trailhead is the same as for hike number 86.

Hike a mile up the steep right fork of the road into Yankee Boy Basin. After a level stretch the road divides at 10,420 feet. Take the left branch a short distance to the edge of a high bank above Sneffels Creek. Cross the creek and hike southwest. Climb up the wide grassy valley right of Stony Mountain. At 12,200 feet, a half mile from the creek, angle right. Hike west toward the low point between Gilpin Peak on the right and Mount Emma on the left. Head for the center of a rock-filled basin at 12,740 feet directly northeast of the low point on the ridge. The spires on the ridge on each side of the low point look forbidding, but are avoided on the peak climbs.

Climb to the right toward Gilpin Peak. Ascend around the right side of a cliff of black rock at 13,000 feet. This will put you at the bottom of a flat buttress that climbs steeply to join the main southeast ridge at 13,420 feet. Climb up this buttress with great care. The buttress is a series of rotten shale ledges that become progressively narrower and steeper. Handholds and footholds should be tested carefully. The steepest part is near the top. Any stance on this lofty perch will seem precarious.

Note the point where you intersect the ridge. You will need to find it on the way back. Turn right for a short climb northwest up the chip-rock ridge to the high point.

To get to Mount Emma from Gilpin Peak, retrace your route to the rock-filled basin beneath the saddle. This time contour southeast along the east side of the ridge. Head for a minor 13,027-foot ridge point on a spur that extends east from the main ridge crest. Turn right at this ridge point and climb west to the main ridge crest. Turn left and climb southwest up the ridge toward the summit towers. Ridge steps in the layered rock can be surmounted by traversing either left or right of the main ridge line.

The main summit block consists of a set of black rock towers well guarded by cliffs. The easiest access is found by contouring right along the northern base of the easternmost towers. This will bring you to a gravel-filled gully. This gully leads up to a saddle in the ridge at the east end of the western towers. Turn right and climb steeply west to the surprisingly level summit area.

The last pitch up the western towers may take a little exploring to find a suitable combination of jam cracks and sandy ledges to provide a safe route. A rope belay may be helpful for some climbers in this final stretch.

For either Gilpin Peak or Mount Emma alone, use the route described above to the basin at 12,740 feet and follow the ascent route for either peak.

163

89. LOOKOUT PEAK (13,661 feet)

General description:
A short steep climb on loose rock
Hiking distance: 3 miles
Starting elevation: 11,700 feet
Elevation gain: 2,000 feet
Maps:
  7.5 minute Ophir
  San Juan National Forest

Lookout Peak is within a mile of Ophir Pass in the area west of Silverton. The road over Ophir Pass is classified as a four-wheel-drive road. While the west side is too steep for passenger cars, passenger cars can drive to the pass from the east side under good conditions.

Drive west on the Ophir Pass road from US 550 between Silverton and Ouray. The unpaved road leaves the highway five miles north of Silverton. It makes a sharp angle northwest and descends to cross Mineral Creek. The road becomes progressively rougher as the pass is approached. If your vehicle will not make it to Ophir Pass, a walk up the final portion of the road can add some distance to this short hike. Park a quarter mile east of Ophir Pass, if you drive that far.

Hike north passing right of a small knoll. Angle northwest on progressively rockier slopes. Climb into a shallow basin on the southeast side of Lookout Peak. At 12,500 feet climb steeply left on loose talus to gain the south ridge of the peak.

Turn right and climb north. There are some steep sections on rotten rock. Continue north along the ridge to the summit.

90. FULLER PEAK (13,761 feet)
VERMILLION PEAK (13, 894 feet)
GOLDEN HORN (13,780 feet)
PILOT KNOB (13,738 feet)
US GRANT PEAK (13,767 feet)

General description:
   A moderate climb to three peaks one day and difficult
   climbs to a peak on each of two subsequent days
Hiking distance: three hikes varying from 9 to 11 miles
Starting elevation: 9,860 feet
**Elevation gain: 5,000 feet on one hike and 4,100 feet each
   on two hikes**
Maps:
   7.5 minute Ophir
   Uncompahgre National Forest

These five summits form an impressive group as they lord
over the confines of Ice Lake Basin. All five can be climbed in
various combinations from South Mineral Campground,
Lower Ice Lake Basin, or Ice Lake. The summits are largely
loose rotten rock with much talus.

Each of these peaks can be climbed on day hikes from South
Mineral Campground. A base camp in Lower Ice Lake Basin
or at windswept Ice Lake may be preferred by some climbers.
This description combines Fuller Peak, Vermillion Peak, and
Golden Horn in a single day. Pilot Knob and US Grant are
each described as separate day hikes. More modest climbs can
be made to any of the first three summits individually as a day
hike. Pilot Knob and US Grant are much more difficult and
should be attempted only by experienced climbers.

From US 550 two miles north of Silverton, drive four and a
half miles west to South Mineral Campground. Park just west
of the campground entrance.

Hike up the trail that leaves the road just east of Clear Creek.
It climbs steeply west and northwest up the hillside. Continue

on the good trail toward Ice Lake Basin. Avoid a trail coming in from the right from the Clear Lake road. Cross flat Lower Ice Lake Basin just above 11,400 feet. Continue on trail to 12,257-foot Ice Lake in a broad upper basin. It is a 2,500-foot climb in three miles from South Mineral Campground to Ice Lake.

Hike south from Ice Lake to climb Fuller Peak, Vermillion Peak, and Golden Horn. Ascend the ridge west of expansive Fuller Lake. Climb up the rocky ridge directly south to the summit of Fuller Peak.

Descend northwest to a 13,500-foot saddle. Vermillion Peak is a direct climb up the ridge northwest from the saddle. Obstructions on the ridge can be bypassed on the left. The summit of Vermillion Peak is the highest in the area.

A descent northeast down the ridge from Vermillion Peak toward Golden Horn may look inviting; however, difficult ridge steps hidden from view make this route inadvisable. Instead, to reach Golden Horn from Vermillion Peak, return back along the ridge to the saddle between Vermillion and Fuller. Contour left across the basin from the Vermillion-Fuller saddle to the 13,380-foot saddle between Vermillion Peak and Golden Horn.

Ascend Golden Horn by climbing the rocky ridge northeast from the saddle. You can weave left and right to avoid obvious obstructions. The gradual ascent route to Golden Horn is quite a contrast to the spectacular vertical drop on its north side.

Descend from Golden Horn by retreating to the saddle between it and Vermillion Peak. Climb east down the loose rock to the ridge west of Fuller Lake for the return. The total elevation gain from Ice Lake is 2,500 feet in the five-mile circuit.

Pilot Knob is one of the most difficult summits to climb in the second hundred highest peaks in Colorado. One reason is the poor quality of the rock. Prior to climbing Pilot Knob, be sure to inspect it carefully from Ice Lake. From this perspective the peak has three summits with the north summit being the highest. The following ascent route places one on the crest a little north of the low point between the central and north summits.

166

Looking toward Pilot Knob from Golden Horn. The right-most ridge point is the summit.

Hike southwest and climb a loose talus slope to reach the ridge a hundred yards to the right (northeast) of the Pilot Knob's summit. Hike the ridge southwest to the base of the Knob and traverse west across the north face to gain access to the west face. Traverse south along the west face two hundred yards to gain a couloir which permits access to the Knob's crest. This couloir is located a short distance south of a permanent snow-field beginning at the base of the west side cliffs.

After a short scramble up this couloir exit left and follow a series of ledges to gain access to the summit crest a little north of the north and central summit saddle. Turn left and scramble along the airy crest. A series of spectacular pinnacles require

167

an exposed down climb and traverse on the west face in order to reach the northernmost high point.

There is a more direct but more difficult route which uses a rotten, yellow couloir on the east face of the crest. This couloir, which is easily visible from Ice Lake, enables one to attain the crest at the same point as the west side route. By either route the climb from Ice Lake is 1,400 feet in a three-mile round trip.

For the difficult climb to US Grant, leave the trail at the east end of Lower Ice Lake Basin. Climb up the grassy slopes north and northwest to Island Lake. If you are camped at Ice Lake, traverse northeast on sheep trails and climb north over the ridge to Island Lake. Climb west-northwest to the 13,220-foot saddle left of US Grant Peak and right of a 13,540-foot summit unofficially named V 4.

Climb north up the south ridge of US Grant until you encounter a major cliff band. Ascend steeply up a twelve-foot step at the center of the ridge by climbing a crack to a four-foot-wide ledge. Traverse right on the exposed ledge twenty yards to a couloir that penetrates the cliff band above the ledge. Climb the broad couloir to easier ground for a stroll to the summit. The elevation gain from Ice Lake is 1,700 feet in the three-mile round trip.

91. ROLLING MOUNTAIN (13,693 feet)

General description:
  A hike up an old road and trail and a moderate off-trail climb
Hiking distance: 12 miles
Starting elevation: 9,860 feet
Elevation gain: 4,100 feet

Maps:
7.5 minute Ophir
San Juan National Forest

Rolling Mountain is a broad-based summit that dominates the head of the valley above South Fork Mineral Creek. Drive to the same starting point as in hike number 90. Cross the culvert over Clear Creek and hike southwest up the rough road. Follow the road along the northwest side of South Fork Mineral Creek two miles to a mine. Take the left fork south at the mine. Descend slightly and cross a creek in a wide meadow. Soon the road ends near an old cabin.

Continue south on a recently reworked trail, called the Rico-Silverton Trail. Leave the timber in a swampy area called South Park at 11,100 feet. Continue on the trail beyond a wide ridge to the next broad drainage at 11,600 feet. Leave the trail on the right where a stream flows in from the west. Hike west along the drainage on generally good footing. Climb to a saddle at the head of the drainage. This saddle at 13,180 feet is on the ridge south of Rolling Mountain.

Turn right at the saddle and follow the rocky ridge north. The route curls east in the final stages to reach the summit.

92. GRIZZLY PEAK (13,738 feet)

General description:
   A long drive on unpaved roads, an off-trail hike, and a
   stiff rocky climb to a remote summit
Hiking distance: 8 miles
Starting elevation: 11,200 feet
Elevation gain: 3,000 feet
Maps:
   7.5 minute Engineer Mountain
   7.5 minute Ophir
   San Juan National Forest

This Grizzly Peak, one of four Colorado summits above 13,700 feet with the name "Grizzly," is in a remote area west of Silverton. The best access is from the south. It requires a long drive on unpaved roads. The hike and climb on varied terrain is well worth the effort; however, some careful route-finding is required. The trip is recommended only for those with a yen for adventure.

Drive on US 550 twenty-eight miles north of Durango or twenty-two miles south of Silverton. Turn west on the road to Purgatory Ski Area. The road turns west a little north and across the highway from Purgatory Campground.

Turn right a half mile from the highway and take the right fork at 3.3 miles. Turn right again at 3.7 miles where the left fork goes to Hermosa Park. Take another right fork at 4.9 miles. You are now headed north on a winding road, Forest Service 579, high above Cascade Creek on its west side. Follow this road to its end, which should measure 15.3 miles from the highway. Most of the road you have followed is not shown on the topographic map. The last ten miles are generally good quality for such a remote road, but there are numerous washes to negotiate that may be difficult for some passenger cars. The road gradually deteriorates and then ends abruptly after several switchbacks. At the road end you are at 11,200 feet, north of Graysill Creek, and directly east of a 12,460-foot point on Sliderock Ridge.

Contour northwest through heavy timber, heading the same direction as the final stretch of road. Cross a minor ridge to a drainage that is a northwest tributary of Cascade Creek. Cross the creek at 11,200 feet and pick up a trail that parallels the creek on its northeast side. Turn right and follow the trail east. Bear north around the nose of a wide ridge north of the creek.

Leave the trail on the left after a mile and a half at 11,300 feet. Ascend west on gradual slopes. Climb west and north to ascend two hundred feet into a large basin at 11,500 feet. There are several lakes and some marshy areas in the basin. Hike around the west side of the largest lake. Continue north on level ground, staying left of the marshes. Turn left and ascend the slopes west. Climb northwest through varied terrain. Stay right of cliffs on the west above the swampy area and left of a

170

projecting ridge to the north.

Head northwest for a wide rocky gully to the left of Grizzly Peak's south-facing cliffs. The gully leads to the crest of the southwest ridge of Grizzly Peak at 13,300 feet. The climbing is slow in the rocky gully, but the grade is not overly steep.

After reaching the ridge, turn right and climb north along its crest. The final ascent is up the broad southwest face of Grizzly Peak. Work your way around the large boulders on the gradual climb to the summit.

93. DALLAS PEAK (13,809 feet)
T 0 (13,735 feet)

General description:
A backpack mostly on trail, a difficult roped climb of Dallas Peak and a moderate rocky climb of T 0
Hiking distance: 6 miles backpacking; 7 miles climbing
Starting elevation: 9,420 feet
Elevation gain: 2,000 feet backpacking; 5,000 feet climbing
Maps:
7.5 minute Telluride
Uncompahgre National Forest

Dallas Peak is the highest of the rugged block-top summits on the long ridge extending south and west from Mount Sneffels. T 0 is on the ridge a mile and half west of Dallas Peak. Only experienced climbers skilled in route finding should attempt Dallas Peak. T 0 is an objective that can be attempted by those of more modest abilities.

Dallas Peak is said by many to be the hardest to climb of Colorado's highest summits. It takes a very long hike with a testy climb of the summit block. The trip makes a better backpack than a day hike, especially if the party expects to spend some time doing roped climbing of the summit pitches.

171

The uninviting north face of Dallas Peak is clearly visible from the ridge between it and T 0.

T 0 can be climbed in a day hike separate from Dallas Peak. If both peaks are on the agenda, a backpack will avoid retracing steps for several miles.

Find the Mill Creek Road, which leads north from Colorado 145 a mile west of Telluride. You are permitted to pass through a gate, which should be closed behind you. Drive about a mile and a half to the Telluride water catchment facility at 9,420 feet. Park here.

Hike up a trail leading north and then west to a thin ridge at 10,620 feet separating Mill Creek and Eider Creek. Follow this ridge northward on a sketchy trail. Hopefully find an unmarked trail leading northeast after just less than a mile.

172

This trail takes you into a drainage coming down from the northwest. The area near the center of the drainage at 11,400 feet is a good place for backpackers to camp.

To climb Dallas Peak from camp, hike generally northeast, working around the broad ridge extending south from Dallas Peak. Once east of this ridge, climb north in a large basin to reach an altitude of 12,800 feet below cliffs on the south side of Dallas Peak. Work right toward the east side of the peak on ledges, gaining as much elevation as possible without getting into difficult steep areas. This will take you across a shelf below the summit cliffs but above the top of a cliff band at 13,000 feet on the southeast side of the peak.

Once on the east side of the peak, but still south of the northeast ridge, climb steeply to an area below the vertical summit cliffs. Traverse right to meet the northeast ridge. Follow the ridge as high as possible to near 13,700 feet. Traverse around to the north side of the peak on ledges with some exposure. The highest traverse you can find is generally the best.

Look for a narrow hundred-foot couloir of solid rock running vertically up to the summit. This couloir is steep at first, then has a more moderate section, and is steep again near the top. Rope is desirable at any time of year, and is essential if there is snow and ice in the couloir. The most difficult move is getting into and starting up the couloir. From the top of the couloir it is just a few steps to the summit. From the 11,400-foot camp the elevation gain to Dallas Peak is 2,600 feet in a three-mile round trip.

To climb T 0 from the 11,400-foot camping area, head northwest up the drainage above camp. At the 12,800-foot level, turn left and climb onto a north-south trending ridge. Since the first part of the steep ridge is quite narrow, the best climbing is in small gullies just to the right of the ridge crest. Continue on the ridge until it joins the main east-west ridge between T 0 and Dallas Peak. Caution is advised while climbing on the lower portions of the north-south ridge where the composition is steep rotten-shale rock.

Once on the east-west ridge, the walk left to the summit is an easy matter. From the high camp, the elevation gain to T 0 is

One of the authors stands triumphant on the summit of Dallas Peak.

2,400 feet in a four-mile round trip. T 0 can be climbed alone as a day hike from the parking area, a much easier trip than a day-hike climb of Dallas Peak.

94. GLADSTONE PEAK (13,913 feet)

General description:
   A hike on an old mine road and trail, followed by a difficult rocky ridge climb
Hiking distance: 10 miles

Starting elevation: 9,960 feet
Elevation gain: 4,400 feet
Maps:
    7.5 minute Gray Head (trailhead area only)
    7.5 minute Little Cone (trailhead area only)
    7.5 minute Dolores Peak (mine road only)
    7.5 minute Mount Wilson
    Uncompahgre National Forest

Gladstone Peak is in the Lizard Head Wilderness of the San Miguel Mountains. It is on the ridge between two Fourteeners, Mount Wilson and Wilson Peak. It is separated from each by rough ridges. The approach is from the north via Silver Pick Basin.

Drive on Colorado 145 west from Telluride or east from the intersection with Colorado 62 near Placerville. At Vanadium, midway between these towns, turn south on the Big Bear Creek road, Forest Service 622. Drive four miles south to a junction. Take the right fork south up the hill. Cross to the east side of Big Bear Creek in a quarter mile. After another mile and a quarter take the right fork at 9,712 feet.

The road continues another two and a quarter miles to the abandoned Silver Pick Mill at 10,960 feet. Passenger cars generally can drive some portion of this distance, depending on the condition of the road and road closures. The heading assumes you can drive a half mile farther to a road fork at 9,960 feet.

Hike up the left fork of the road toward Silver Pick Mill. Continue around a gate that may be locked at 10,500 feet. Take the left fork at a junction at 11,120 feet and make a big switchback. Pass a small pond at 11,380 feet. Soon thereafter, when the main road turns east, continue south up through Silver Pick Basin. Follow old mine roads not shown on the topographic map to the vicinity of the Silver Pick Mine. An old mine road, portions of which are reduced to a trail by rockslides, climbs up the right side of the basin. Follow this road as it angles left to a 13,020-foot saddle on the range crest. You look south from the saddle into Navajo Basin, with Mount Wilson and El Diente on the ridge beyond.

Follow a trail left as it contours and climbs east. Intersect the ridge at the east end of Navajo Basin at 13,260 feet. Leave the trail on the right and follow the ridge south. Gladstone Peak is only a mile south along the ridge but the climbing is slow because of the large boulders.

A major ridge point of 13,341 feet can be crossed or bypassed on the east side. After a descent to 13,160 feet, the ridge gets steeper. On this last portion of the climb care is needed in climbing over the loose rocks on the narrow ridge crest. Continue on the ridge crest to the summit of Gladstone Peak.

95. SAN MIGUEL PEAK (13,752 feet)

General description:
A pleasant trail hike and a stiff rocky climb
Hiking distance: 8 miles
Starting elevation: 10,300 feet
Elevation gain: 3,600 feet
Maps:
   7.5 minute Ophir
   Uncompahgre National Forest

San Miguel Peak is a high undistinguished summit southwest of its more prominent neighbors in the Ice Lake Basin area. It is best approached from the west. The route follows a good hiking trail to scenic Lake Hope.

Drive to a point midway between the Ophir Loop and Lizard Head Pass on Colorado 145. Turn east on a road that goes northeast of Trout Lake. Follow the road, Forest Service 626, past Trout Lake along the north side of Lake Fork. Two miles from the highway make a sharp left turn on a side road that starts northwest and then loops back southeast. Continue two more miles to a trailhead parking area at 10,300 feet.

Hike southeast on a good trail that climbs steadily. Leave

the trail a quarter mile beyond the timber, at 11,700 feet. Turn right and walk southeast over grassy open country. This will bring you to the north end of Lake Hope near its outlet. If you miss this turn and follow the trail all the way to the east end of the lake at 11,860 feet, turn right and walk northwest over a small knoll to get to the lake outlet.

Cross the dam at the lake outlet and climb west. Ascend a rounded spur ridge off the main northeast ridge of San Miguel Peak. This ridge feeds into the rocky northeast ridge that you then follow southwest to the summit. The last quarter mile of the ridge route climbs over and through many large, irregular-shaped boulders.

San Miguel Peak has two boulder-strewn summits. The east one is higher.

Casco Peak from French Mountain.

Appendices

Three tabular listings showing all of the Colorado summits thirteen thousand feet and above follow. The first listing shows the summits in descending order of elevation. The second lists the summits grouped by USGS topographic map quadrangles, with the quadrangles listed alphabetically. The third lists summit names alphabetically.

The 636 summits that meet the criterion of rising at least three hundred feet above saddles to higher summits are ranked in order of elevation. The rank of each summit is shown in the first column of each listing. The ranked summits include 417 named and 219 unnamed summits. Unnamed summits are indicated by an "UN," followed by the elevation.

The 104 named high points that do not meet the 300-foot criterion for a separate summit are included in the tabular listings but are not ranked. Named high points are the ones thirteen thousand feet and above with names shown on the latest USGS topographic maps, plus those with names subsequently approved by the United States Board on Geographic Names. There are a total of 740 summits in each tabular listing.

In each tabular listing, the columns showing rank, height in feet, and name, are followed by a column headed "Neighbor." This column shows the name of the nearest higher summit that can be reached along ridges with the least elevation loss from the named summit. The "Neighbor" is useful in locating a particular summit on the topographic map.

The column headed "Drop" shows the number of feet a summit rises above the highest low point on any ridge between it and a higher summit. In effect, the "Drop" represents the minimum descent needed to follow ridges from the named summit to any higher summit. If the figure in this column is three hundred feet or more, the listed mountain is deemed to be a separate summit and is given a rank. The named mountains that are not ranked have a "Drop" of less than three hundred feet.

The column headed "Mi" shows the straight-line distance in miles from the listed summit to the summit in the "Neighbor" column. Distances between summits are measured from the summit point when it is shown precisely on the topographic map or from the center of the highest closed contour. If there is more than one closed contour and no indication of which is highest, the distance is measured from the center of the contour containing the most area. Note that the distance to the nearest neighbor is a straight-line distance. The nearest neighbor may not be the nearest one to reach if you were following the ridge, since some ridges curve so that a summit farther away by ridge distance may be closer by straight-line distance.

If there is no entry in the columns headed "Neighbor," "Drop," and "Mi," it means that the drop between the listed summit and all higher summits is one thousand feet or more. Ordinarily those mountains that have a drop of one thousand feet or more either stand alone or are the highest summit in a group.

The final column labeled "Quad" shows the 7.5 minute USGS topographic map quadrangle on which the summit is located. There are now 7.5 minute maps covering all Colorado areas so it is no longer necessary to use the older, less detailed 15 minute maps.

The elevations of summits and of the low points on ridges used in computing drops are from the latest USGS topographic maps. In cases where no exact elevation is shown, it is necessary to interpolate an elevation from the contour lines. For example, Clark Peak on the 7.5 minute Capitol Peak topographic map quadrangle shows no exact elevation. It has a closed 13,560-foot contour line at the summit but no 13,600-foot contour. Thus, Clark Peak could be any height from 13,560 feet to 13,599 feet. Its elevation is interpolated by assuming the elevation is the midpoint between the contour lines. Consequently, the elevation of Clark Peak is listed as 13,580 feet. Obviously, such a procedure implies spurious accuracy of the elevations of summits for which no exact elevation is recorded; however, it provides a consistent basis for preparing a listing of summits by elevation and gives a fair relationship between peaks.

In the case of mountains with multiple summits, a directional indication (north, east, south, or west) is shown following the official name. When such directional indications are not part of the official name of a summit, an "M" is shown in the tabular listings under the column headed "FN."

Many unnamed summits were identified by letter and numeral designations by the San Juan Mountaineers many years ago to aid in cataloging summits in areas of numerous unnamed peaks. For clarity, these identifiers are shown as the name of separate summits that do not have official names. They are identified by a "Z" under the column headed "FN."

In cases in which more than one summit has exactly the same name, the highest is designated "A," the second highest "B," etc. Unnamed summits of the same elevation also are distinguished by letter designations. Thus, each summit has a unique designation. Note that the numbered peaks of the San Juan Mountains, such as Peak Seven, are written as words while the numbered summits of the Tenmile Range are written as numerals.

Officially named ridges are considered to be summits when they have a high point that is distinct from adjacent higher mountains. In such cases there is at least one closed contour along the ridge.

Benchmarks are considered to be named summits when the benchmark name is the only name for the summit. When summits have both an official name and a benchmark name, the official name is used.

It is difficult to tell where the high point is located on some summits. When a name is spread over an entire ridge, the high point on the ridge is considered to be the summit. Examples are San Joaquin Ridge, Sunshine Mountain, and Yellow Mountain. In other cases, the decision is more difficult. We have followed the general rule that a high point near a named summit on the map is the true summit, unless the summit name seems to apply to a distinctive feature that is lower than the high point. An example is Epaulet Mountain. The summit area consists of two rounded high points, one 13,523 feet and another 13,530 feet. The map name is nearer the lower 13,523-foot point. We consider the 13,530-foot point to be the summit of Epaulet Mountain.

On the other hand, consider some examples of summit names that appear to apply to distinctive features lower than the high point. We consider the 13,248-foot high point on the ridge south of Notch Mountain to be a separate unnamed summit. Thus, Notch Mountain is listed at 13,237 feet, the elevation of the high point near the distinctive feature. Likewise, we consider Jones Peak to be the 13,604-foot ridge point overlooking the Arkansas River valley, while the higher 13,712-foot point on the ridge west of Jones Peak is considered to be an unnamed summit.

It can readily be seen that some decisions on the location of a named summit are arbitrary and leave room for argument; however, we intend our decisions to follow the intentions of those who named the mountains. The United States Geological Survey confirmed the validity of our approach by indicating in correspondence that summit names on maps are not always precisely located at the high point.

Another problem is determining an exact elevation for some summits. Many writers and users of topographic maps regard the elevation of a mountain to be the figure printed on the topographic map quadrangle if there is a number printed near the summit. In many cases, however, a measured elevation printed on the map is not at the high point. For example, at the top of West Needle Mountain there are three closed contours of 13,340 feet. The southwest one has a listed elevation of 13,045. We found, however, that the northeast high point is higher. In such cases we estimate the elevation to be midway between the printed elevation and the next higher contour, thus making 13,062 feet the elevation of West Needle Mountain.

Another example is the unnamed summit between Blanca Peak and Iron Nipple. There are two closed contours of 13,080 feet. The southwest one has a listed elevation of 13,081 feet. We found that the northeast one is higher. Its interpolated elevation is 13,100 feet and that is listed as the elevation of this summit. Our general rule is: If an interpolated elevation of a closed contour is higher than the elevation listed on the map for another closed contour, the interpolated elevation is used unless we have first-hand knowledge from climbing the peak that the listed elevation is the high point. Other examples of summits higher than the printed elevation are Gold Dust Peak and Mount Flora.

These abreviations are used in the tabular listings: "MT" means Mount, "MTN" means Mountain, and "BM" means benchmark.

Special mention should be made of Challenger Point that ranks number 34 on the tabular listings. This summit west of Kit Carson Mountain is not considered a Fourteener, although from the map contours it rises 320 feet above the saddle between it and Kit Carson Mountain. The contours indicate an interpolated elevation of 14,100 feet for the summit. An actual elevation of 14,081 feet for the summit was reported to us by the United States Geological Survey. Using the 14,081-foot elevation, there is a drop of 301 feet from the summit to the saddle between it and Kit Carson Mountain. Thus, the summit qualifies for listing as a separate summit under our standards.

With the increased interest in climbing the highest Colorado summits below the Fourteeners, climbers have been seeking an accepted listing of Thirteeners. Several published lists of Colorado's hundred highest summits have had errors and omissions. As a result, some climbers have been climbing more than a hundred summits to be sure of climbing the right ones. We hope the accompanying lists will prove to be accurate and acceptable so that the proper summits can be climbed to reach any desired goal.

We would sugggest that to climb the hundred highest summits in Colorado, you should climb the Fourteeners plus the ranked summits down through number 100 on the tabular listing. This would give you all the ranked Thirteeners 13,809 feet and above. To climb the 150 highest summits, the ranked Thirteeners down through number 150 should be climbed. This would require climbing the ranked Thirteeners 13,693 feet and above. To climb the two hundred highest Colorado summits, the ranked Thirteeners down through the five summits tied for rankings 198 through 202 should be climbed.

To fill out a high peak climbing schedule more completely,

you may want to climb the named unranked summits on the list. The named but unranked high Thirteeners are climbing objectives similar to the unrecognized Fourteeners such as Conundrum Peak and North Eolus. Once you have climbed the Fourteeners plus the Thirteeners that have route descriptions in this book, you can extend your goal to include other mountains on the list. There are enough peaks to keep the most avid climbers busy for many years. That is what makes Colorado mountain climbing so fascinating.

One final note. Though the mountains may never seem to change in our perception, our knowledge of them is constantly evolving. New topographic maps can change elevations, creating new summits and causing others to disappear. Man can alter the mountains after they are mapped. Ironically, the top portion of Bartlett Mountain, which is shown as 13,555 feet on the topographic map, has been mined and processed for molybdenum. As a result, Bartlett Mountain has been omitted from these lists.

Note: The tables in previous editions listed 637 ranked summits and a total of 741 ranked summits plus named high points. Besides eliminating Bartlett Mountain, an apparent 13,400-foot summit on the Creede 15 minute topographic map was eliminated when the newer 7.5 minute San Luis Peak map indicated it was not a summit. The 13,020-foot summit near Montezuma Peak, omitted from the previous tables, was added. These changes account for the reduction in ranked summits from 637 to 636. In addition, the tables in this edition reflect 7.5 minute maps in all areas, newly named peaks, and minor modifications in some elevations.

Colorado Summits 13,000 Feet and Above

1. Listed by Elevation
2. Listed by Topographic Map
3. Listed Alphabetically

Colorado Summits 13,000 Feet and Above — Listed by Elevation

RANK	HT	NAME	FN	NEIGHBOR	DROP	MI	QUAD
1	14433	ELBERT, MT					MT ELBERT
2	14421	MASSIVE, MT					MT MASSIVE
3	14420	HARVARD, MT					MT HARVARD
4	14345	BLANCA PK					BLANCA PK
5	14336	LA PLATA PK					MT ELBERT
6	14309	UNCOMPAHGRE PK					UNCOMPAHGRE PK
7	14294	CRESTONE PK					CRESTONE PK
8	14286	LINCOLN, MT					ALMA
9	14270	GRAYS PK					GRAYS PK
10	14269	ANTERO, MT					MT ANTERO
11	14267	TORREYS PK		GRAYS PK	560	0.6	GRAYS PK
12	14265	CASTLE PK					HAYDEN PK
13	14265	QUANDARY PK					BRECKENRIDGE
14	14264	EVANS A, MT					MT EVANS
15	14255	LONGS PK					LONGS PK
16	14246	WILSON, MT					MT WILSON
	14238	CAMERON, MT		LINCOLN, MT	138	0.5	ALMA
17	14229	SHAVANO, MT					MAYSVILLE
18	14197	BELFORD, MT					MT HARVARD
19	14197	CRESTONE NEEDLE		CRESTONE PK	457	0.5	CRESTONE PK
20	14197	PRINCETON, MT					MT ANTERO
21	14196	YALE, MT					MT YALE
22	14172	BROSS, MT		CAMERON, MT	312	1.0	ALMA
23	14165	KIT CARSON MTN					CRESTONE PK
	14159	EL DIENTE		WILSON, MT	259	0.8	DOLORES PK
24	14156	MAROON PK					MAROON BELLS
25	14155	TABEGUACHE PK		SHAVANO, MT	455	0.7	SAINT ELMO
26	14153	OXFORD, MT		BELFORD, MT	653	1.2	MT HARVARD
27	14150	SNEFFELS, MT					MT SNEFFELS
28	14148	DEMOCRAT, MT		CAMERON, MT	768	1.3	CLIMAX
29	14130	CAPITOL PK					CAPITOL PK
30	14109	PIKES PK					PIKES PK
31	14092	SNOWMASS MTN					SNOWMASS MTN
32	14083	EOLUS, MT					COLUMBINE PASS
33	14082	WINDOM PK					COLUMBINE PASS
34	14081	CHALLENGER POINT		KIT CARSON MTN	301	0.2	CRESTONE PK
35	14073	COLUMBIA, MT		HARVARD, MT	893	1.9	MT HARVARD
36	14067	MISSOURI MTN		BELFORD, MT	847	1.3	WINFIELD
37	14064	HUMBOLDT PK					CRESTONE PK
38	14060	BIERSTADT, MT		EVANS A, MT	720	1.4	MT EVANS
	14060	CONUNDRUM PK		CASTLE PK	240	0.4	HAYDEN PK
39	14059	SUNLIGHT PK		WINDOM PK	399	0.5	STORM KING PK
40	14048	HANDIES PK					HANDIES PK
41	14047	CULEBRA PK					CULEBRA PK
42	14042	ELLINGWOOD PT		BLANCA PK	342	0.5	BLANCA PK
43	14042	LINDSEY, MT					BLANCA PK

186

Listed by Elevation (continued)

RANK	HT	NAME	FN	NEIGHBOR	DROP	MI	QUAD
	14039	NORTH EOLUS		EOLUS, MT	179	0.2	STORM KING PK
44	14037	LITTLE BEAR PK		BLANCA PK	377	1.0	BLANCA PK
45	14036	SHERMAN, MT					MT SHERMAN
46	14034	REDCLOUD PK					REDCLOUD PK
47	14018	PYRAMID PK					MAROON BELLS
48	14017	WILSON PK		WILSON, MT	877	1.5	MT WILSON
49	14015	WETTERHORN PK					WETTERHORN PK
	14014	NORTH MAROON PK		MAROON PK	234	0.4	MAROON BELLS
50	14014	SAN LUIS PK					SAN LUIS PK
51	14005	HOLY CROSS, MT OF THE					MT OF THE HOLY CROSS
52	14003	HURON PK					WINFIELD
53	14001	SUNSHINE PK		REDCLOUD PK	501	1.3	REDCLOUD PK
54	13988	GRIZZLY PK A					INDEPENDENCE PASS
55	13983	STEWART PK		SAN LUIS PK	883	2.5	STEWART PK
56	13980	UN 13980		KIT CARSON MTN	360	0.2	CRESTONE PK
57	13972	PIGEON PK					SNOWDON PK
58	13971	OURAY, MT					MT OURAY
59	13951	FLETCHER MTN		QUANDARY PK	611	1.2	COPPER MTN
	13951	GEMINI PK		SHERMAN, MT	171	0.7	MT SHERMAN
60	13951	ICE MTN					WINFIELD
61	13950	PACIFIC PK		FLETCHER MTN	570	1.4	BRECKENRIDGE
62	13943	CATHEDRAL PK		CONUNDRUM PK	523	1.4	HAYDEN PK
63	13940	FRENCH MTN					MT MASSIVE
64	13933	HOPE, MT		LA PLATA PK	873	2.9	MT ELBERT
65	13932	UN 13932		PYRAMID PK	312	0.6	MAROON BELLS
66	13931	ADAMS, MT		KIT CARSON MTN	871	1.9	HORN PK
67	13913	GLADSTONE PK		WILSON, MT	733	0.6	MT WILSON
68	13911	MEEKER, MT		LONGS PK	451	0.7	ALLENS PARK
69	13908	CASCO PK		FRENCH MTN	648	1.2	MT ELBERT
70	13908	RED MTN A		CULEBRA PK	448	0.7	CULEBRA PK
71	13904	EMERALD PK		MISSOURI MTN	564	1.3	WINFIELD
72	13898	HORSESHOE MTN		SHERMAN, MT	758	2.8	MT SHERMAN
73	13895	UN 13895					HALFMOON PASS
74	13894	VERMILLION PK					OPHIR
	13876	FRASCO BM		FRENCH MTN	256	0.5	MT MASSIVE
75	13870	UN 13870					SAINT ELMO
76	13865	BUCKSKIN, MT		DEMOCRAT, MT	725	1.5	CLIMAX
77	13864	VESTAL PK					STORM KING PK
78	13860	APOSTLE NORTH	M	ICE MTN	400	0.4	WINFIELD
79	13860	JONES MTN A		HANDIES PK	520	1.7	HANDIES PK
80	13857	CLINTON PK		FLETCHER MTN	517	2.7	CLIMAX
81	13855	DYER MTN		GEMINI PK	475	0.9	MT SHERMAN
82	13852	CRYSTAL PK		PACIFIC PK	632	0.9	BRECKENRIDGE
	13852	TRAVER PK		CLINTON PK	232	0.7	CLIMAX
83	13850	EDWARDS, MT		GRAYS PK	470	1.3	GRAYS PK
84	13849	CALIFORNIA PK		ELLINGWOOD PT	629	2.2	BLANCA PK

Listed by Elevation (continued)

RANK	HT	NAME	FN	NEIGHBOR	DROP	MI	QUAD
85	13845	OKLAHOMA, MT		MASSIVE, MT	745	1.8	MT CHAMPION
	13842	SPAULDING, MT		EVANS A, MT	262	1.1	MT EVANS
86	13841	HAGERMAN PK		SNOWMASS MTN	341	0.6	SNOWMASS MTN
87	13841	HALF PK					POLE CREEK MTN
88	13841	UN 13841		FLETCHER MTN	421	0.7	COPPER MTN
89	13835	TURRET PK		PIGEON PK	735	0.5	SNOWDON PK
90	13832	UN 13832		REDCLOUD PK	812	1.4	REDCLOUD PK
91	13831	HOLY CROSS RIDGE		HOLY CROSS, MT OF THE	331	0.6	MT OF THE HOLY CROSS
	13831	IOWA PK		MISSOURI MTN	291	0.6	WINFIELD
92	13830	JUPITER MTN		WINDOM PK	370	0.6	COLUMBINE PASS
93	13828	UN 13828		LINDSEY, MT	688	1.2	BLANCA PK
94	13824	JAGGED MTN		SUNLIGHT PK	964	1.4	STORM KING PK
95	13823	UN 13823		CASCO PK	883	1.8	INDEPENDENCE PASS
96	13822	SILVERHEELS, MT					ALMA
97	13821	RIO GRANDE PYRAMID					RIO GRANDE PYRAMID
98	13819	TEAKETTLE MTN		SNEFFELS, MT	759	1.7	MT SNEFFELS
99	13811	UN 13811		UN 13832	551	1.2	REDCLOUD PK
100	13809	DALLAS PK		SNEFFELS, MT	869	2.0	TELLURIDE
101	13807	NIAGARA PK		JONES MTN A	587	0.6	HANDIES PK
102	13806	UN 13806		JONES MTN A	466	0.8	HANDIES PK
103	13805	TRINITY PK		VESTAL PK	945	1.2	STORM KING PK
104	13803	ARROW PK		VESTAL PK	943	0.5	STORM KING PK
105	13803	UN 13803		CASTLE PK	423	0.9	MAROON BELLS
106	13801	ORGAN MTN A		SAN LUIS PK	694	2.0	SAN LUIS PK
107	13799	UN 13799		UN 13980	339	0.5	CRESTONE PK
108	13795	ARKANSAS, MT		BUCKSKIN, MT	575	1.9	CLIMAX
109	13795	UN 13795		HANDIES PK	495	1.3	REDCLOUD PK
110	13794	RITO ALTO PK					RITO ALTO PK
111	13794	SQUARE TOP MTN		EDWARDS, MT	814	3.4	MONTEZUMA
112	13786	ANIMAS MTN					SNOWDON PK
113	13786	POTOSI PK		TEAKETTLE MTN	806	1.0	IRONTON
114	13783	RINKER PK		LA PLATA PK	923	1.8	MT ELBERT
115	13781	MOSQUITO PK		BUCKSKIN, MT	561	2.3	CLIMAX
116	13780	GARFIELD PK		GRIZZLY PK A .	360	0.8	INDEPENDENCE PASS
117	13780	GOLDEN HORN		VERMILLION PK	400	0.4	OPHIR
	13780	MCNAMEE PK		CLINTON PK	80	0.5	CLIMAX
118	13768	UN 13768		HOLY CROSS RIDGE	388	0.8	MT OF THE HOLY CROSS
119	13767	US GRANT PK		GOLDEN HORN	747	1.7	OPHIR
120	13765	TRINITY PK WEST	M	TRINITY PK	385	0.4	STORM KING PK
121	13762	UN 13762		HARVARD, MT	822	2.8	MT HARVARD
122	13761	BULL HILL		ELBERT, MT	421	1.6	MT ELBERT
123	13761	DEER MTN		OKLAHOMA, MT	941	1.7	MT CHAMPION
	13761	FULLER PK		VERMILLION PK	261	0.5	OPHIR
124	13752	SAN MIGUEL PK					OPHIR
125	13752	STORM KING PK		TRINITY PK	612	1.3	STORM KING PK
126	13748	SHERIDAN, MT		SHERMAN, MT	608	1.3	MT SHERMAN

Listed by Elevation (continued)

RANK	HT	NAME	FN	NEIGHBOR	DROP	MI	QUAD
127	13745	AETNA, MT					GARFIELD
128	13745	TRINITY PK EAST	M	TRINITY PK	405	0.2	STORM KING PK
	13739	PTARMIGAN PK		HORSESHOE MTN	279	2.5	MT SHERMAN
129	13738	ARGENTINE PK		EDWARDS, MT	638	1.9	MONTEZUMA
130	13738	GRIZZLY PK B		SAN MIGUEL PK	758	1.6	OPHIR
131	13738	PILOT KNOB		GOLDEN HORN	398	0.5	OPHIR
132	13738	SAYRES BM		LA PLATA PK	958	1.9	MT ELBERT
133	13736	UN 13736		DEER MTN	676	1.2	MT CHAMPION
134	13735	T 0	Z	DALLAS PK	395	1.4	TELLURIDE
135	13723	VERMEJO PK		RED MTN A	761	1.3	CULEBRA PK
136	13722	UN 13722 A		UN 13932	302	0.4	MAROON BELLS
137	13722	UN 13722 B					HANDIES PK
138	13716	POLE CREEK MTN					POLE CREEK MTN
139	13714	SILVER MTN A					UNCOMPAHGRE PK
140	13712	UN 13712		SHAVANO, MT	332	0.9	MT ANTERO
141	13711	TWINING PK					MT CHAMPION
	13710	LA GARITA PK		UN 13895	232	1.9	HALFMOON PASS
142	13708	GRIZZLY MTN		UN 13870	568	1.7	SAINT ELMO
143	13705	COLONY BALDY		HUMBOLDT PK	925	1.4	CRESTONE PK
144	13705	SIX, PK		JAGGED MTN	685	1.0	STORM KING PK
	13705	THIRTEEN, PK		ANIMAS MTN	245	0.3	STORM KING PK
	13704	GLACIER PT		NORTH EOLUS	284	0.4	STORM KING PK
	13701	TREASUREVAULT MTN		MOSQUITO PK	281	0.4	CLIMAX
145	13700	FIFTEEN, PK		TURRET PK	320	0.2	SNOWDON PK
146	13700	GRIZZLY PK C		JUPITER MTN	440	0.7	COLUMBINE PASS
147	13698	BALDY ALTO		SAN LUIS PK	518	1.4	STEWART PK
148	13695	MONITOR PK		THIRTEEN, PK	315	0.2	STORM KING PK
149	13694	GILPIN PK		DALLAS PK	720	1.7	TELLURIDE
150	13693	ROLLING MTN		SAN MIGUEL PK	913	2.3	OPHIR
	13692	LOVELAND MTN		BUCKSKIN, MT	192	0.8	CLIMAX
151	13691	UN 13691		UN 13832	471	2.7	REDCLOUD PK
152	13690	WHEELER MTN		FLETCHER MTN	310	1.6	COPPER MTN
153	13688	UN 13688 A		UN 13832	428	1.6	REDCLOUD PK
154	13688	UN 13688 B		UN 13722 B	388	1.1	HANDIES PK
155	13686	CIRQUE MTN		TEAKETTLE MTN	546	0.6	MT SNEFFELS
156	13684	BALD MTN					BOREAS PASS
157	13684	OSO, MT					EMERALD LAKE
	13684	WHITE RIDGE		SHERMAN, MT	184	1.2	MT SHERMAN
158	13682	SEVEN, PK		SIX, PK	422	0.8	STORM KING PK
159	13681	UN 13681		SILVER MTN A	501	1.0	UNCOMPAHGRE PK
160	13676	PURGATOIRE PK		VERMEJO PK	849	1.8	CULEBRA PK
161	13674	UN 13674		HALF PK	734	1.3	REDCLOUD PK
162	13672	TWETO, MT		BUCKSKIN, MT	412	1.2	CLIMAX
163	13670	JACKSON, MT					MT JACKSON
164	13667	WHITE, MT		ANTERO, MT	847	1.3	MT ANTERO
165	13663	CARBONATE MTN		UN 13870	434	2.0	SAINT ELMO

Listed by Elevation (continued)

RANK	HT	NAME	FN	NEIGHBOR	DROP	MI	QUAD
166	13661	LOOKOUT PK		GILPIN PK	841	8.6	OPHIR
167	13660	UN 13660 A		CALIFORNIA PK	400	1.1	TWIN PKS
168	13660	UN 13660 B		POLE CREEK MTN	840	1.5	POLE CREEK MTN
169	13660	WOOD MTN		UN 13688 B	320	0.5	HANDIES PK
	13658	HAMILTON PK		BLANCA PK	278	1.5	BLANCA PK
170	13657	CARSON PK					POLE CREEK MTN
171	13656	COXCOMB PK		WETTERHORN PK	796	1.8	WETTERHORN PK
172	13651	TAYLOR MTN		AETNA, MT	631	1.2	GARFIELD
173	13646	CHAMPION, MT		UN 13736	306	0.6	MT CHAMPION
174	13646	MAMMA, MT		GRIZZLY MTN	546	1.7	SAINT ELMO
175	13642	REDCLIFF		COXCOMB PK	502	0.5	WETTERHORN PK
176	13641	BARD PK					GRAYS PK
177	13635	UN 13635		CATHEDRAL PK	335	0.9	HAYDEN PK
178	13633	PEAK 10		CRYSTAL PK	373	0.9	BRECKENRIDGE
179	13631	UN 13631 A		GARFIELD PK	971	2.2	NEW YORK PK
180	13631	UN 13631 B		UN 13722 A	331	0.7	MAROON BELLS
181	13628	SILEX, MT		STORM KING PK	808	0.8	STORM KING PK
182	13627	WHITE DOME		TRINITY PK EAST	967	2.2	STORM KING PK
183	13626	UN 13626		PRINCETON, MT	486	1.4	MT YALE
184	13626	WEST SPANISH PK					SPANISH PKS
	13620	SNOWMASS PK		HAGERMAN PK	120	0.2	SNOWMASS MTN
185	13617	GUARDIAN, THE		SILEX, MT	557	0.6	STORM KING PK
186	13616	UN 13616		LA PLATA PK	436	1.6	MT ELBERT
	13615	FATHER DYER PK		CRYSTAL PK	115	0.6	BRECKENRIDGE
187	13614	NORTH STAR MTN		WHEELER MTN	434	0.9	BRECKENRIDGE
188	13611	PICO ASILADO		CRESTONE NEEDLE	831	1.7	CRESTONE PK
	13604	JONES PK		UN 13712	144	0.7	MT ANTERO
189	13604	TIJERAS PK		PICO ASILADO	744	1.7	CRESTONE PK
190	13602	GRAY WOLF MTN		SPAULDING, MT	582	1.2	MT EVANS
191	13598	ELECTRIC PK A		RITO ALTO PK	938	6.1	ELECTRIC PK
192	13596	CYCLONE MTN		CARBONATE MTN	336	0.5	SAINT ELMO
193	13590	MATTERHORN PK		WETTERHORN PK	570	0.9	UNCOMPAHGRE PK
194	13589	ONE, PK		WHITE DOME	409	0.8	STORM KING PK
195	13588	COTTONWOOD PK					VALLEY VIEW HOT SPRG
	13587	MCCLELLAN MTN		EDWARDS, MT	167	0.8	GRAYS PK
196	13581	EMMA, MT		GILPIN PK	561	0.8	TELLURIDE
197	13581	UN 13581		CARSON PK	681	1.5	POLE CREEK MTN
198	13580	CLARK PK		CAPITOL PK	440	1.2	CAPITOL PK
199	13580	POWELL, MT					MT POWELL
200	13580	TWIN PKS A		ELLINGWOOD PT	640	1.6	TWIN PKS
201	13580	UN 13580 A		UN 13581	360	1.2	POLE CREEK MTN
202	13580	UN 13580 B		ADAMS, MT	440	0.5	HORN PK
203	13579	CHIEFS HEAD PK		LONGS PK	719	1.4	ISOLATION PK
204	13577	EVANS B, MT		DYER MTN	317	1.2	CLIMAX
	13577	GRAVEL MTN		UN 13688 B	157	0.4	HANDIES PK
205	13577	UN 13577		UN 13660 A	317	0.5	BLANCA PK

190

Listed by Elevation (continued)

RANK	HT	NAME	FN	NEIGHBOR	DROP	MI	QUAD
206	13575	GREYLOCK MTN		WINDOM PK	555	1.2	COLUMBINE PASS
207	13575	ROSALIE PK		EVANS A, MT	675	3.0	HARRIS PARK
208	13574	PARNASSUS, MT		BARD PK	537	1.0	GRAYS PK
209	13573	BROKEN HAND PK		CRESTONE NEEDLE	673	0.8	CRESTONE PK
	13572	WESTON PK		PTARMIGAN PK	272	1.1	MT SHERMAN
	13569	CROWN MTN		NIAGARA PK	229	0.6	HANDIES PK
210	13568	APOSTLE WEST	M	ICE MTN	508	0.6	WINFIELD
211	13566	UN 13566		UN 13691	746	1.9	REDCLOUD PK
212	13565	UN 13565		CULEBRA PK	545	1.4	EL VALLE CREEK
	13561	HAYDEN PK		UN 13635	181	0.8	HAYDEN PK
213	13560	HAGUES PK					TRAIL RIDGE
214	13555	WASATCH MTN		LOOKOUT PK	495	2.1	TELLURIDE
215	13554	FLUTED PK		ADAMS, MT	734	1.2	HORN PK
216	13554	MCCAULEY PK		GRIZZLY PK C	454	0.7	COLUMBINE PASS
217	13553	GIBBS PK		RITO ALTO PK	693	4.2	ELECTRIC PK
218	13553	PETTINGELL PK					LOVELAND PASS
219	13552	TOWER MTN					HOWARDSVILLE
220	13550	UN 13550		UN 13803	530	0.9	GOTHIC
221	13546	UN 13546		ADAMS, MT	646	0.8	HORN PK
222	13542	WHITECROSS MTN		HANDIES PK	562	1.4	REDCLOUD PK
223	13541	UN 13541		UN 13580 B	361	0.8	CRESTONE PK
224	13540	ELEVEN, PK		SUNLIGHT PK	400	0.6	STORM KING PK
225	13540	UN 13540 A		WILSON PK	520	1.0	DOLORES PK
226	13540	UN 13540 B		WOOD MTN	520	2.6	REDCLOUD PK
227	13540	V 4	Z	US GRANT PK	320	0.4	OPHIR
228	13540	WHITE ROCK MTN		UN 13550	800	2.8	GOTHIC
229	13538	EMMA BURR MTN					CUMBERLAND PASS
230	13537	UN 13537		WHITE ROCK MTN	757	2.5	MAROON BELLS
231	13535	UN 13535 A		DEER MTN	555	1.2	MT CHAMPION
232	13535	UN 13535 B		JONES MTN A	515	1.5	HANDIES PK
233	13531	UN 13531		HOPE, MT	431	1.5	MT ELBERT
234	13530	EPAULET MTN		EVANS A, MT	350	1.9	HARRIS PARK
235	13528	BOULDER MTN		MAMMA, MT	588	1.6	SAINT ELMO
236	13528	LEVIATHAN PK		JAGGED MTN	588	0.7	STORM KING PK
237	13528	TREASURE MTN					SNOWMASS MTN
238	13528	V 3	Z	US GRANT PK	388	0.4	OPHIR
239	13524	UN 13524 A		CARSON PK	464	1.4	POLE CREEK MTN
240	13524	UN 13524 B		GIBBS PK	624	3.3	RITO ALTO PK
	13523	BROWNS PK		HURON PK	183	0.7	WINFIELD
241	13522	MILWAUKEE PK		PICO ASILADO	302	0.5	CRESTONE PK
242	13521	STAR PK		CASTLE PK	816	4.1	PEARL PASS
243	13517	TRINCHERA PK					TRINCHERA PK
244	13517	UN 13517		HURON PK	457	1.5	WINFIELD
245	13516	KEEFE PK		UN 13537	496	1.3	MAROON BELLS
246	13514	YPSILON MTN					TRAIL RIDGE
247	13513	UN 13513		GIBBS PK	453	2.4	ELECTRIC PK

Listed by Elevation (continued)

RANK	HT	NAME	FN	NEIGHBOR	DROP	MI	QUAD
248	13510	T 11	Z	LOOKOUT PK	452	1.3	TELLURIDE
249	13510	UN 13510 A					BALDY CINCO
250	13510	UN 13510 B		EMMA, MT	610	5.0	IRONTON
	13509	TELLURIDE PK		UN 13510 B	289	0.5	IRONTON
251	13507	EUREKA MTN		RITO ALTO PK	807	2.0	RITO ALTO PK
252	13505	UN 13505		UN 13631 A	525	1.3	NEW YORK PK
253	13502	FAIRCHILD MTN		YPSILON MTN	922	1.2	TRAIL RIDGE
254	13502	NORTH ARAPAHO PK					MONARCH LAKE
	13500	IRON NIPPLE		UN 13828	200	0.6	BLANCA PK
	13500	NEEDLE RIDGE		SUNLIGHT PK	200	0.4	STORM KING PK
	13500	RED MTN B		GARFIELD PK	120	0.4	INDEPENDENCE PASS
	13500	SIXTEEN, PK		FIFTEEN, PK	80	0.1	SNOWDON PK
255	13500	UN 13500		TWINING PK	360	0.7	INDEPENDENCE PASS
256	13498	UN 13498		UN 13540 A	358	0.6	DOLORES PK
257	13497	HUNTER PK		KEEFE PK	477	1.4	MAROON BELLS
258	13497	PAGODA MTN		LONGS PK	397	0.7	ISOLATION PK
259	13496	MEARS PK		T 0	556	1.3	MT SNEFFELS
260	13492	WHITEHOUSE MTN		TEAKETTLE MTN	592	1.9	OURAY
261	13490	MARCY, MT		UN 13513	430	1.2	ELECTRIC PK
262	13490	UN 13490		UN 13513	990	1.0	RITO ALTO PK
263	13489	GRAYSTONE PK		ARROW PK	509	0.6	STORM KING PK
264	13487	CUATRO PK		TRINCHERA PK	707	2.2	TRINCHERA PK
265	13487	STORM PK A		TOWER MTN	627	1.4	SILVERTON
266	13481	THREE NEEDLES		T 11	421	1.0	TELLURIDE
267	13478	CANBY MTN		CROWN MTN	938	5.6	HOWARDSVILLE
268	13478	THREE, PK		TRINITY PK EAST	498	0.9	STORM KING PK
269	13477	T 10	Z	THREE NEEDLES	537	0.6	IRONTON
270	13475	TWO, PK		THREE, PK	535	0.8	STORM KING PK
271	13475	V 10	Z	GRIZZLY PK B	375	0.7	OPHIR
272	13472	LA JUNTA PK		WASATCH MTN	612	0.7	TELLURIDE
273	13472	UN 13472					MT OURAY
274	13470	SILVER MTN B		WASATCH MTN	410	2.2	TELLURIDE
	13468	MIRANDA PK		UN 13565	288	0.9	EL VALLE CREEK
275	13468	RIDGWAY, MT		TEAKETTLE MTN	448	1.0	MT SNEFFELS
276	13466	UN 13466		VERMEJO PK	557	1.2	CULEBRA PK
277	13463	UN 13463		RED MTN B	563	1.3	INDEPENDENCE PASS
278	13462	TREASURY MTN		TREASURE MTN	522	1.4	SNOWMASS MTN
279	13462	UN 13462 A		BROWNS PK	322	0.6	WINFIELD
280	13462	UN 13462 B		UN 13517	562	1.6	WINFIELD
281	13461	QUAIL MTN		HOPE, MT	921	1.4	MT ELBERT
282	13460	SAN JOAQUIN RIDGE		SILVER MTN B	360	1.3	TELLURIDE
283	13460	SLEEPING SEXTON		NORTH MAROON PK	440	0.6	MAROON BELLS
284	13460	UN 13460		SAYRES BM	440	1.4	INDEPENDENCE PASS
285	13455	UTE RIDGE		WHITE DOME	962	4.9	RIO GRANDE PYRAMID
286	13454	HANSON PK		TOWER MTN	914	3.6	HANDIES PK
287	13454	UN 13454		UN 13795	394	1.0	REDCLOUD PK

192

Listed by Elevation (continued)

RANK	HT	NAME	FN	NEIGHBOR	DROP	MI	QUAD
288	13451	KENDALL PK					HOWARDSVILLE
289	13450	HORN PK		FLUTED PK	710	1.3	HORN PK
290	13450	UN 13450		CARSON PK	350	1.2	POLE CREEK MTN
	13447	HURRICANE PK		HANSON PK	267	0.8	HANDIES PK
291	13441	APACHE PK					MONARCH LAKE
292	13441	S 6	Z	T 0	381	1.0	MT SNEFFELS
293	13436	T 5	Z	TELLURIDE PK	416	2.8	TELLURIDE
294	13435	TAYLOR PK A		STAR PK	815	1.3	PEARL PASS
295	13435	UN 13435		YALE, MT	375	0.8	MT YALE
296	13434	UN 13434		KENDALL PK	534	1.2	HOWARDSVILLE
297	13433	UN 13433		JACKSON, MT	413	0.6	MT JACKSON
298	13432	JENKINS MTN		SAYRES BM	692	4.0	PIEPLANT
299	13432	TWIN SISTER EAST	M				OPHIR
300	13432	UN 13432		SUNSHINE PK	332	0.9	REDCLOUD PK
	13430	GRAY NEEDLE		JAGGED MTN	130	0.3	STORM KING PK
301	13428	VALLECITO MTN		LEVIATHAN PK	568	0.5	STORM KING PK
302	13427	GRIZZLY PK D		TORREYS PK	847	1.5	GRAYS PK
303	13427	UN 13427		WOOD MTN	407	1.4	HANDIES PK
304	13425	MUMMY MTN		HAGUES PK	485	1.4	ESTES PARK
305	13423	SPREAD EAGLE PK		UN 13524 B	443	0.9	ELECTRIC PK
306	13420	EAGLES NEST		POWELL, MT	640	1.2	MT POWELL
	13420	INDEX, THE		ANIMAS MTN	240	0.2	SNOWDON PK
	13420	ROWE PK		HAGUES PK	200	0.4	TRAIL RIDGE
	13420	TEN, PK		JAGGED MTN	280	0.3	STORM KING PK
	13420	TWIN THUMBS		ELEVEN, PK	120	0.2	STORM KING PK
307	13420	UN 13420		SNOWMASS MTN	760	1.2	SNOWMASS MTN
308	13417	UN 13417		OSO, MT	677	0.8	EMERALD LAKE
309	13416	LITTLE GIANT PK		KENDALL PK	556	1.3	HOWARDSVILLE
310	13414	CLEVELAND PK		TIJERAS PK	434	1.4	CRESTONE PK
311	13411	UN 13411		WETTERHORN PK	471	1.2	WETTERHORN PK
312	13410	FOUR, PK		SIX, PK	510	1.2	STORM KING PK
	13409	FINNBACK KNOB		HORSESHOE MTN	149	0.6	MT SHERMAN
313	13409	HILLIARD PK		KEEFE PK	309	0.6	MAROON BELLS
314	13409	NAVAJO PK		APACHE PK	309	0.4	MONARCH LAKE
315	13408	WILCOX, MT		ARGENTINE PK	548	1.1	MONTEZUMA
316	13405	MARIQUITA PK		CUATRO PK	385	1.4	EL VALLE CREEK
317	13402	NINE, PK		STORM KING PK	582	0.5	STORM KING PK
318	13402	RHODA, MT		UN 13434	302	0.4	HOWARDSVILLE
319	13402	UN 13402		UN 13895	422	1.7	HALFMOON PASS
	13401	BALDY CHATO		STEWART PK	181	1.5	STEWART PK
320	13401	UN 13401		TIJERAS PK	301	0.9	CRESTONE PK
321	13401	WHITE BM		WHITE ROCK MTN	381	0.5	GOTHIC
	13397	SOUTH ARAPAHO PK		NORTH ARAPAHO PK	97	0.5	MONARCH LAKE
322	13393	BENT PK		CARSON PK	373	1.2	POLE CREEK MTN
323	13391	PARRY PK					EMPIRE
324	13391	ROGERS PK		EVANS A, MT	515	2.4	HARRIS PARK

193

Listed by Elevation (continued)

RANK	HT	NAME	FN	NEIGHBOR	DROP	MI	QUAD
325	13385	CHICAGO PK		TELLURIDE PK	365	1.3	IRONTON
326	13384	PRIZE BM		UN 13631 A	604	1.6	PIEPLANT
327	13384	UN 13384		CLEVELAND PK	364	0.9	CRESTONE PK
328	13383	BALDY CINCO		UN 13510 A	843	1.9	BALDY CINCO
329	13382	GOLD DUST PK		JACKSON, MT	922	3.1	MT JACKSON
330	13382	WILLIAMS MTN					MT CHAMPION
331	13380	GEISSLER MTN EAST	M	TWINING PK	560	1.1	MT CHAMPION
332	13380	MUSIC MTN		MILWAUKEE PK	400	0.9	CRESTONE PK
333	13380	PRECARIOUS PK		UN 13631 B	640	2.1	MAROON BELLS
334	13380	SOUTH LOOKOUT PK		US GRANT PK	520	1.2	OPHIR
335	13380	UN 13380		WHITE ROCK MTN	480	1.3	GOTHIC
336	13378	ITALIAN MTN					PEARL PASS
337	13377	UN 13377		UN 13411	357	0.5	WETTERHORN PK
338	13375	LAKES PK		COTTONWOOD PK	675	2.1	ELECTRIC PK
339	13374	TWIN SISTER WEST	M	TWIN SISTER EAST	394	0.4	OPHIR
340	13374	UN 13374		HARVARD, MT	394	1.9	MT HARVARD
341	13370	BUCKSKIN BM		SLEEPING SEXTON	908	2.0	MAROON BELLS
342	13370	DOME MTN		TOWER MTN	670	1.3	HOWARDSVILLE
343	13370	GUYOT, MT					BOREAS PASS
344	13369	MONUMENTAL PK					GARFIELD
345	13368	SULTAN MTN					SILVERTON
346	13362	DE ANZA PK A		GIBBS PK	622	1.1	ELECTRIC PK
347	13362	ENGELMANN PK		BARD PK	542	1.8	GRAYS PK
348	13362	PEARL MTN		CASTLE PK	582	2.5	PEARL PASS
349	13359	T 7	Z	TELLURIDE PK	499	1.0	IRONTON
350	13357	WILLOW BM					WILLOW LAKES
351	13352	HOOSIER RIDGE		SILVERHEELS, MT	932	3.3	BRECKENRIDGE
352	13350	HERMIT PK		RITO ALTO PK	330	0.9	RITO ALTO PK
353	13348	MALEMUTE PK		CONUNDRUM PK	368	1.1	HAYDEN PK
	13348	PEERLESS MTN		HORSESHOE MTN	168	0.9	MT SHERMAN
354	13346	UN 13346		GOLD DUST PK	806	1.3	MT JACKSON
355	13345	UN 13345		EMMA BURR MTN	445	1.1	CUMBERLAND PASS
356	13342	BEATTIE PK		FULLER PK	322	0.4	OPHIR
357	13342	UN 13342		UTE RIDGE	726	1.4	RIO GRANDE PYRAMID
358	13340	HERARD, MT					MEDANO PASS
359	13340	OWEN A, MT		UN 13490	600	2.0	ELECTRIC PK
360	13340	UN 13340 A		UN 13417	440	1.2	EMERALD LAKE
361	13340	UN 13340 B		UN 13411	745	1.7	UNCOMPAHGRE PK
362	13339	BROWN MTN		HURRICANE PK	639	1.0	IRONTON
363	13338	KENDALL MTN		KENDALL PK	318	0.7	SILVERTON
364	13336	UN 13336		BUCKSKIN BM	636	1.1	MAROON BELLS
	13335	MAXWELL, MT		M ARIQUITA PK	275	0.8	EL VALLE CREEK
365	13334	CONEY BM		BENT PK	994	1.9	FINGER MESA
366	13334	VENABLE PK		FLUTED PK	634	2.7	RITO ALTO PK
367	13333	DE ANZA PK B		MARIQUITA PK	473	1.0	EL VALLE CREEK
	13333	TWIN PKS B		RINKER PK	233	0.9	MT ELBERT

Listed by Elevation (continued)

RANK	HT	NAME	FN	NEIGHBOR	DROP	MI	QUAD
368	13330	UN 13330		HANSON PK	550	1.9	HANDIES PK
369	13328	CINNAMON MTN		UN 13535 B	308	1.1	HANDIES PK
370	13327	MCHENRYS PK		CHIEFS HEAD PK	907	1.2	MCHENRYS PK
	13326	STORM PK B		LONGS PK	186	0.8	LONGS PK
371	13326	WEST BUFFALO PK					MARMOT PK
372	13325	UN 13325		STORM PK A	465	0.5	SILVERTON
	13322	LEAHY PK		UN 13635	142	0.9	HAYDEN PK
373	13322	UN 13322		JENKINS MTN	902	2.4	PIEPLANT
374	13321	SUNSHINE MTN					HANDIES PK
375	13321	TRICO PK		UN 13510 B	461	0.9	IRONTON
	13319	PALMYRA PK		SILVER MTN B	179	0.5	TELLURIDE
376	13317	UN 13317		UN 13626	737	2.3	SAINT ELMO
377	13315	T 8	Z	T 7	495	0.7	IRONTON
378	13313	UN 13313		BALDY CINCO	413	0.7	BALDY CINCO
379	13312	UN 13312 A		UN 13566	452	0.8	REDCLOUD PK
380	13312	UN 13312 B		PEARL MTN	412	0.6	PEARL PASS
381	13312	UN 13312 C		UN 13463	452	1.0	PIEPLANT
382	13312	WILLIAMS MTN SOUTH A	M	WILLIAMS MTN	572	1.5	THIMBLE ROCK
383	13310	ALICE, MT		CHIEFS HEAD PK	850	1.4	ISOLATION PK
384	13310	AZTEC MTN		JUPITER MTN	610	1.9	COLUMBINE PASS
	13310	EMERY PK		UN 13330	130	0.4	HANDIES PK
385	13310	UN 13310		UN 13340 A	330	0.6	EMERALD LAKE
	13309	ECHO MTN		MCCAULEY PK	209	0.5	COLUMBINE PASS
386	13309	V 2	Z	US GRANT PK	409	0.8	OPHIR
387	13308	UN 13308		UN 13342	606	0.8	RIO GRANDE PYRAMID
388	13307	WARREN, MT		ROGERS PK	367	1.1	MT EVANS
389	13302	UN 13302		OSO, MT	722	1.7	STORM KING PK
390	13301	GEISSLER MTN WEST	M	GEISSLER MTN EAST	481	0.6	MT CHAMPION
391	13300	DALY, MT		CLARK PK	800	1.4	CAPITOL PK
392	13300	EAST BUFFALO PK		WEST BUFFALO PK	480	0.9	MARMOT PK
393	13300	GALENA MTN		CANBY MTN	360	2.1	HOWARDSVILLE
394	13300	MIDDLE PK					DOLORES PK
395	13300	SUMMIT PK					SUMMIT PK
396	13300	UN 13300 A		UN 13505	520	1.4	NEW YORK PK
397	13300	UN 13300 B		TWINING PK	600	2.7	MT CHAMPION
398	13300	UN 13300 C		WETTERHORN PK	440	0.7	WETTERHORN PK
399	13300	UN 13300 D		UN 13302	560	0.6	COLUMBINE PASS
400	13300	UN 13300 E		BEATTIE PK	320	0.6	OPHIR
401	13300	UN 13300 F		UN 13340 B	320	0.6	UNCOMPAHGRE PK
402	13295	UN 13295		SAYRES BM	435	2.7	PIEPLANT
403	13294	JAMES PK		PARRY PK	714	1.5	EMPIRE
404	13294	UN 13294		PETTINGELL PK	314	1.0	LOVELAND PASS
405	13292	ELECTRIC PK B		ARROW PK	832	0.6	STORM KING PK
406	13292	SHEEP MTN A		CANBY MTN	632	1.9	HOWARDSVILLE
	13292	WAVERLY MTN		OXFORD, MT	152	1.1	MT HARVARD
407	13290	DOLORES PK		MIDDLE PK	710	1.1	DOLORES PK

195

Listed by Elevation (continued)

RANK	HT	NAME	FN	NEIGHBOR	DROP	MI	QUAD
408	13286	BONITA PK		EMERY PK	506	0.6	HANDIES PK
409	13285	UN 13285		SAN LUIS PK	665	2.5	SAN LUIS PK
410	13284	UN 13284		UN 13300 B	424	2.7	MT CHAMPION
411	13283	FIVE, PK		FOUR, PK	303	0.6	STORM KING PK
412	13282	TRURO PK		UN 13300 A	822	1.3	NEW YORK PK
413	13282	UN 13282		UN 13300 A	822	1.1	NEW YORK PK
414	13281	GRIZZLY PK E		JENKINS MTN	581	1.9	PIEPLANT
415	13281	LADY WASHINGTON, MT		LONGS PK	301	0.7	LONGS PK
416	13278	UN 13278		RIO GRANDE PYRAMID	633	1.1	WEMINUCHE PASS
417	13277	COMANCHE PK		FLUTED PK	497	1.5	HORN PK
418	13277	RUBY MTN		GRAYS PK	439	1.2	MONTEZUMA
419	13277	KIOWA PK		NAVAJO PK	736	1.3	WARD
	13275	MENDOTA PK		T 5	175	0.8	TELLURIDE
420	13274	SEIGAL MTN		UN 13722 B	374	1.0	HANDIES PK
421	13271	WHITNEY PK		UN 13768	691	1.4	MT OF THE HOLY CROSS
	13270	PECKS PK		BELFORD, MT	50	1.0	MT HARVARD
422	13270	UN 13270		BROKEN HAND PK	490	0.5	CRESTONE PK
423	13269	ANTORA PK					BONANZA
424	13266	GENEVA PK		ARGENTINE PK	926	4.7	MONTEZUMA
425	13266	MARBLE MTN		MILWAUKEE PK	526	1.1	CRESTONE PK
426	13266	WILDHORSE PK		SEIGAL MTN	966	4.0	WETTERHORN PK
427	13265	KNIFE PT		SUNLIGHT PK	325	0.8	STORM KING PK
428	13262	HEISSPITZ, THE		FOUR, PK	362	0.9	STORM KING PK
429	13261	UN 13261		UN 13278	321	0.7	WEMINUCHE PASS
430	13260	UN 13260 A		SEIGAL MTN	520	2.2	HANDIES PK
431	13260	UN 13260 B		PRECARIOUS PK	440	0.8	MAROON BELLS
432	13260	UN 13260 C					VAIL EAST
433	13260	UN 13260 D		CONEY BM	400	1.2	FINGER MESA
434	13260	V 9	Z	ROLLING MTN	397	1.0	OPHIR
	13259	WHITEHEAD PK		RHODA, MT	119	0.4	HOWARDSVILLE
435	13256	BROKEN HILL		MATTERHORN PK	798	2.0	UNCOMPAHGRE PK
436	13255	UN 13255		GRIZZLY PK E	555	1.6	WINFIELD
437	13254	HENRY MTN					FAIRVIEW PK
438	13253	UN 13253		UN 13255	433	2.0	WINFIELD
439	13252	S 8	Z	MEARS PK	552	1.6	SAMS
	13250	BANCROFT, MT		PARRY PK	253	0.7	EMPIRE
440	13248	UN 13248		HOLY CROSS RIDGE	308	1.3	MT OF THE HOLY CROSS
441	13245	UN 13245		UN 13260 C	785	4.0	WILLOW LAKES
442	13244	SPRING MTN		VENABLE PK	464	0.7	HORN PK
443	13244	UN 13244		UN 13336	424	1.1	HIGHLAND PK
444	13242	S 4	Z	S 6	302	0.8	MT SNEFFELS
445	13241	U 3	Z	REDCLIFF	461	0.7	WETTERHORN PK
	13238	LANDSLIDE PK		GENEVA PK	138	0.4	MONTEZUMA
	13237	NOTCH MTN		UN 13248	217	0.9	MT OF THE HOLY CROSS
446	13235	UN 13235		UN 13253	375	0.9	PIEPLANT
447	13234	SNIKTAU, MT		GRIZZLY PK D	520	2.4	GRAYS PK

196

Listed by Elevation (continued)

RANK	HT	NAME	FN	NEIGHBOR	DROP	MI	QUAD
448	13233	BELLEVIEW MTN		MAROON PK	693	1.9	MAROON BELLS
449	13233	TURNER PK					TINCUP
450	13232	HESPERUS MTN					LA PLATA
451	13232	UN 13232 A		SAYRES BM	332	1.7	PIEPLANT
452	13232	UN 13232 B		UN 13260 B	412	0.4	MAROON BELLS
453	13230	UN 13230 A		UN 13308	770	1.9	RIO GRANDE PYRAMID
454	13230	UN 13230 B		UN 13260 C	730	2.0	VAIL EAST
455	13229	RED MTN C		HOOSIER RIDGE	369	0.7	BRECKENRIDGE
456	13229	UN 13229		UN 13565	329	0.6	EL VALLE CREEK
	13228	EIGHT, PK		NINE, PK	288	0.4	STORM KING PK
457	13223	AUDUBON, MT		APACHE PK	843	3.4	WARD
	13222	MACOMBER PK		TOWER MTN	122	0.7	HOWARDSVILLE
458	13222	UN 13222 A		UN 13340 B	322	0.6	UNCOMPAHGRE PK
459	13222	UN 13222 B		UN 13300 D	402	0.8	EMERALD LAKE
	13220	CALIFORNIA MTN		HANSON PK	280	0.6	HANDIES PK
	13220	ELLINGWOOD RIDGE		LA PLATA PK	280	1.5	MT ELBERT
460	13220	GREENHALGH MTN		SHEEP MTN A	400	0.8	HOWARDSVILLE
461	13220	HAGAR MTN		UN 13294	320	0.5	LOVELAND PASS
	13220	KING SOLOMON MTN		LITTLE GIANT PK	280	0.5	HOWARDSVILLE
	13220	LITTLE FINGER		SIXTEEN, PK	120	0.1	SNOWDON PK
462	13220	S 7	Z	MEARS PK	400	1.0	SAMS
463	13220	UN 13220 A		UN 13417	800	1.8	EMERALD LAKE
464	13220	UN 13220 B		UN 13260 C	520	1.6	VAIL EAST
465	13218	ENGINEER MTN		UN 13260 A	438	0.9	HANDIES PK
466	13218	IRVING PK		OSO, MT	638	1.2	COLUMBINE PASS
467	13218	JONES MTN B		EMMA BURR MTN	638	3.0	TINCUP
468	13216	UN 13216		UN 13380	316	0.7	MAROON BELLS
	13215	RED PK A		HOOSIER RIDGE	115	0.7	BRECKENRIDGE
469	13215	UN 13215		PETTINGELL PK	395	1.5	LOVELAND PASS
470	13214	FAIRVIEW PK					FAIRVIEW PK
	13213	CAMPBELL PK		T 0	233	0.5	TELLURIDE
	13213	THIRSTY PK		LAKES PK	233	0.8	ELECTRIC PK
471	13213	UN 13213		UN 13230 B	753	1.5	VAIL EAST
472	13212	UN 13212		UN 13284	312	0.7	MT CHAMPION
473	13209	GLADSTONE RIDGE		JONES MTN B	949	2.6	MT YALE
474	13209	HOMESTAKE PK					HOMESTAKE RESERVIOR
475	13208	POWELL PK		MCHENRYS PK	388	0.4	MCHENRYS PK
476	13208	TEOCALLI MTN		UN 13550	788	2.4	GOTHIC
477	13206	HAYDEN MTN SOUTH	M	T 8	549	1.1	IRONTON
478	13206	UN 13206		UN 13377	306	0.6	WETTERHORN PK
479	13205	EAGLE PK A		THIRSTY PK	545	1.6	ELECTRIC PK
480	13205	JACQUE PK					COPPER MTN
481	13205	NEBO, MT		UN 13230 A	505	0.6	STORM KING PK
482	13204	LENAWEE MTN		GRIZZLY PK D	344	1.0	GRAYS PK
483	13203	BENNETT PK					JASPER
484	13203	TUTTLE MTN		CALIFORNIA MTN	503	1.3	HANDIES PK

197

Listed by Elevation (continued)

RANK	HT	NAME	FN	NEIGHBOR	DROP	MI	QUAD
485	13203	UN 13203		CUATRO PK	303	1.1	TRINCHERA PK
486	13203	WILLIAMS MTN SOUTH B	M	WILLIAMS MTN	423	0.5	MT CHAMPION
487	13202	UN 13202		TWINING PK	422	2.0	MT CHAMPION
488	13201	UN 13201		UN 13300 C	661	1.3	WETTERHORN PK
489	13198	UN 13198		GRIZZLY PK A	658	2.8	INDEPENDENCE PASS
490	13195	PEAK 9		PEAK 10	415	0.6	BRECKENRIDGE
491	13194	LONDON MTN		MOSQUITO PK	534	1.7	CLIMAX
492	13192	MOSS, MT		HESPERUS MTN	372	0.7	LA PLATA
493	13192	UN 13192		UN 13768	372	2.2	MT JACKSON
494	13189	RED PK B		WILLOW BM	929	1.6	WILLOW LAKES
	13188	SHEEP MTN B		SAN MIGUEL PK	128	1.3	MT WILSON
495	13185	VALOIS, MT		AZTEC MTN	325	2.1	COLUMBINE PASS
496	13184	BEAUBIEN PK		MIRANDA PK	604	3.1	EL VALLE CREEK
	13184	ROWE MTN		ROWE PK	44	0.5	TRAIL RIDGE
	13182	BULLION MTN		AZTEC MTN	202	0.8	COLUMBINE PASS
497	13180	GRAND TURK		SULTAN MTN	404	0.6	SILVERTON
	13180	LAVENDER PK		MOSS, MT	280	0.2	LA PLATA
	13180	POINT PUN		GRAYSTONE PK	200	0.6	SNOWDON PK
498	13180	SANTA FE PK		GENEVA PK	480	1.3	MONTEZUMA
499	13180	UN 13180 A		UN 13631 B	320	0.5	MAROON BELLS
500	13180	UN 13180 B		UN 13691	524	2.1	REDCLOUD PK
501	13180	UN 13180 C		WILLOW BM	760	1.6	WILLOW LAKES
	13177	YELLOW MTN		PILOT KNOB	197	0.6	OPHIR
502	13176	COPELAND MTN					ISOLATION PK
503	13172	CONEJOS PK					PLATORO
504	13169	UN 13169		UN 13230 A	989	1.2	RIO GRANDE PYRAMID
505	13168	SHEEP MTN C		UN 13681	592	2.7	SHEEP MTN
506	13165	AMHERST MTN					COLUMBINE PASS
507	13165	UN 13165		CANBY MTN	577	0.7	HOWARDSVILLE
	13164	HELEN, MT		FATHER DYER PK	264	1.0	BRECKENRIDGE
508	13164	KELSO MTN		TORREYS PK	784	1.6	GRAYS PK
509	13164	UN 13164	.	HALF PK	384	1.3	POLE CREEK MTN
510	13162	UN 13162 A		BALDY CINCO	493	1.3	BALDY CINCO
511	13162	UN 13162 B		UN 13550	382	0.9	GOTHIC
512	13159	UN 13159		LOOKOUT PK	379	1.3	OPHIR
513	13158	TWILIGHT PK					SNOWDON PK
514	13158	UN 13158		UNCOMPAHGRE PK	378	1.8	UNCOMPAHGRE PK
515	13157	UN 13157		RIO GRANDE PYRAMID	300	0.9	RIO GRANDE PYRAMID
516	13156	V 5	Z	SOUTH LOOKOUT PK	616	1.3	OPHIR
	13155	BALDY MTN		UN 13244	175	0.6	HIGHLAND PK
517	13155	UN 13155		UN 13285	415	1.7	SAN LUIS PK
518	13153	TAYLOR PK B		POWELL PK	413	1.0	MCHENRYS PK
519	13153	UN 13153 A		HERARD, MT	653	0.9	MEDANO PASS
520	13153	UN 13153 B		ADAMS, MT	373	0.7	HORN PK
521	13151	POMEROY MTN		GRIZZLY MTN	611	2.1	SAINT ELMO
522	13150	ARIKAREE PK		KIOWA PK	570	0.8	MONARCH LAKE

198

Listed by Elevation (continued)

RANK	HT	NAME	FN	NEIGHBOR	DROP	MI	QUAD
523	13150	MONTEZUMA PK		SUMMIT PK	690	1.6	SUMMIT PK
524	13149	BABCOCK PK		MOSS, MT	529	0.7	LA PLATA
525	13148	SOUTH RIVER PK					SOUTH RIVER PK
526	13147	UN 13147		AETNA, MT	527	1.6	GARFIELD
527	13146	FLORA, MT		PARRY PK	686	2.4	EMPIRE
528	13145	UN 13145		LA JUNTA PK	325	0.6	TELLURIDE
529	13144	PRECIPICE PK		U 3	484	1.5	WETTERHORN PK
530	13143	LITTLE HORN PK		FLUTED PK	323	0.9	HORN PK
531	13142	WILLOUGHBY MTN		UN 13336	442	1.8	HIGHLAND PK
	13140	EMERSON MTN		AMHERST MTN	280	0.5	COLUMBINE PASS
	13140	GUYSELMAN MTN		UN 13213	240	0.6	MT POWELL
	13140	ROBESON PK		BARD PK	200	0.9	GRAYS PK
532	13140	TWELVE, PK	Z	NORTH EOLUS	320	0.5	STORM KING PK
533	13140	UN 13140 A		UN 13255	320	0.6	WINFIELD
534	13140	UN 13140 B		JENKINS MTN	320	1.1	PIEPLANT
535	13140	UN 13140 C		TRURO PK	320	0.4	NEW YORK PK
536	13139	HAYDEN MTN NORTH	M	HAYDEN MTN SOUTH	519	1.2	IRONTON
537	13139	SAVAGE PK					MT JACKSON
538	13138	OGALALLA PK		COPELAND MTN	718	1.4	ISOLATION PK
539	13136	HUNCHBACK MTN		WHITE DOME	356	0.8	STORM KING PK
540	13135	FRANCISCO PK		BEAUBIEN PK	435	1.0	EL VALLE CREEK
541	13134	S 9	Z	S 8	354	0.7	SAMS
	13134	SULLIVAN MTN		SANTA FE PK	274	0.6	MONTEZUMA
	13132	SEWANEE PK		UN 13147	232	0.6	GARFIELD
542	13132	UN 13132		UN 13260 A	512	0.9	HANDIES PK
543	13130	EVA, MT		PARRY PK	430	0.8	EMPIRE
544	13130	UN 13130		UN 13180 A	350	0.8	MAROON BELLS
	13129	BLACK BM		UN 13260 C	29	0.2	VAIL EAST
545	13128	LOMO LISO MTN		FRANCISCO PK	308	0.8	EL VALLE CREEK
546	13126	PIKA PK		GOLD DUST PK	506	0.7	MT JACKSON
	13125	KENNEDY, MT		AZTEC MTN	265	0.6	MTN VIEW CREST
	13123	SPILLER PK		BABCOCK PK	183	0.5	LA PLATA
547	13123	UN 13123 A		UN 13498	463	1.1	DOLORES PK
548	13123	UN 13123 B		COTTONWOOD PK	303	0.8	ELECTRIC PK
549	13122	PETERS PK		UN 13222 B	342	0.4	EMERALD LAKE
550	13122	UN 13122		UN 13490	302	1.2	RITO ALTO PK
551	13121	UN 13121 A		GREYLOCK MTN	341	0.5	COLUMBINE PASS
552	13121	UN 13121 B		GUYSELMAN MTN	421	0.6	MT POWELL
553	13118	ISOLATION PK		COPELAND MTN	938	2.2	ISOLATION PK
554	13117	UN 13117		GRIZZLY PK D	377	1.0	GRAYS PK
555	13113	LIZARD HEAD					MT WILSON
556	13112	FITZPATRICK PK		UN 13345	958	2.1	CUMBERLAND PASS
557	13111	COW BM		UN 13132	531	2.3	WETTERHORN PK
558	13111	UN 13111		UN 13510 A	811	4.6	SAN LUIS PK
559	13110	UN 13110		UN 13308	450	1.2	STORM KING PK
560	13109	UN 13109		WHITEHEAD PK	329	0.6	HOWARDSVILLE

Listed by Elevation (continued)

RANK	HT	NAME	FN	NEIGHBOR	DROP	MI	QUAD
	13108	THUNDER MTN		GREYLOCK MTN	248	1.0	COLUMBINE PASS
561	13108	WILLIAMS MTN NORTH	M	WILLIAMS MTN	408	0.8	MT CHAMPION
562	13106	UN 13106		UNCOMPAHGRE PK	726	2.2	UNCOMPAHGRE PK
563	13105	BUSHNELL PK					BUSHNELL PK
564	13105	UN 13105		EMERSON MTN	325	0.4	COLUMBINE PASS
565	13102	UN 13102		MONUMENTAL PK	482	1.7	GARFIELD
566	13100	MIDDLE MTN A		UN 13463	520	1.1	INDEPENDENCE PASS
	13100	SOUTH TWILIGHT PK		TWILIGHT PK	200	0.3	SNOWDON PK
567	13100	UN 13100 A		UN 13681	480	1.8	SHEEP MTN
568	13100	UN 13100 B		PIKA PK	600	2.1	MT JACKSON
569	13100	UN 13100 C		WHITEHOUSE MTN	320	0.5	OURAY
570	13100	UN 13100 D		BLANCA PK	520	1.3	BLANCA PK
571	13100	UN 13100 E		UN 13111	400	1.9	BALDY CINCO
572	13095	KREUTZER, MT		EMMA BURR MTN	355	1.6	TINCUP
573	13095	UN 13095		CHICAGO PK	315	0.5	TELLURIDE
574	13093	UN 13093		SUNSHINE MTN	353	1.4	HANDIES PK
575	13091	UN 13091		UN 13106 A	591	1.8	UNCOMPAHGRE PK
576	13090	UN 13090 A		UN 13140 C	350	1.1	NEW YORK PK
577	13090	UN 13090 B		UN 13245	710	2.0	VAIL EAST
578	13088	PAIUTE PK		AUDUBON, MT	468	0.9	MONARCH LAKE
579	13088	VIRGINIA PK		UN 13140 A	428	0.8	WINFIELD
580	13085	KELLER MTN		UN 13180 C	745	2.1	WILLOW LAKES
581	13085	UN 13085 A		UN 13100 B	625	1.0	MT JACKSON
582	13085	UN 13085 B		UN 13245	465	0.8	VAIL EAST
583	13082	BOREAS MTN		BALD MTN	923	2.9	BOREAS PASS
584	13079	UN 13079		UN 13180 C	659	1.3	WILLOW LAKES
585	13078	UN 13078		UN 13317	738	1.4	SAINT ELMO
586	13078	WHALE PK		LANDSLIDE PK	982	4.8	JEFFERSON
587	13077	SNOWDON PK					SNOWDON PK
	13077	WINFIELD PK		VIRGINIA PK	177	0.7	WINFIELD
	13076	FLORIDA MTN		VALOIS, MT	176	0.8	COLUMBINE PASS
588	13075	NORTH TWILIGHT PK		TWILIGHT PK	335	0.4	SNOWDON PK
589	13075	UN 13075		HANSON PK	415	1.0	HANDIES PK
590	13074	GARFIELD, MT		POINT PUN	374	0.6	SNOWDON PK
591	13074	UN 13074		UN 13300 A	454	1.0	NEW YORK PK
592	13073	BLACKWALL MTN		WILDHORSE PK	453	1.3	WETTERHORN PK
593	13071	HUNTS PK		BUSHNELL PK	891	4.3	WELLSVILLE
594	13070	SHEEP MTN D		UN 13105	370	0.4	COLUMBINE PASS
595	13070	UN 13070		POMEROY MTN	330	0.6	SAINT ELMO
	13069	CHIQUITA, MT		YPSILON MTN	283	1.0	TRAIL RIDGE
596	13069	UN 13069		CROWN MTN	329	3.4	HOWARDSVILLE
	13066	KENDALL BM		KENDALL MTN	286	0.7	SILVERTON
	13062	CENTENNIA L PK		LAVENDER PK	282	0.5	LA PLATA
597	13062	UN 13062 A		SNOWMASS PK	642	1.8	SNOWMASS MTN
598	13062	UN 13062 B		HERMIT PK	842	1.9	RITO ALTO PK
599	13062	WEST NEEDLE MTN		SOUTH TWILIGHT PK	562	0.7	SNOWDON PK

200

Listed by Elevation (continued)

RANK	HT	NAME	FN	NEIGHBOR	DROP	MI	QUAD
	13060	MIDDLE MTN B		UN 13462 A	120	0.6	WINFIELD
	13060	SAINT SOPHIA RIDGE		EMMA, MT	160	0.5	TELLURIDE
600	13060	UN 13060 A		CLARK PK	320	0.5	CAPITOL PK
601	13060	UN 13060 B		UN 13062 B	360	0.4	RITO ALTO PK
602	13058	OWEN B, MT					OH BE JOYFUL
603	13057	UN 13057		UN 13085 B	557	1.0	VAIL EAST
604	13055	UN 13055		KREUTZER, MT	315	1.6	TINCUP
605	13054	UN 13054		EUREKA MTN	594	1.6	RITO ALTO PK
606	13052	HOUGHTON MTN		TUTTLE MTN	472	1.5	HANDIES PK
	13051	LAMBERTSON PK		ITALIAN MTN	231	1.1	PEARL PASS
607	13051	UN 13051		SILVER MTN A	351	1.1	UNCOMPAHGRE PK
608	13050	UN 13050 A		UN 13384	390	0.8	CRESTONE PK
609	13050	UN 13050 B		UN 13345	550	1.5	CUMBERLAND PASS
	13049	GREEN MTN		UN 13165	69	0.6	HOWARDSVILLE
	13047	WEST DYER MTN		DYER MTN	267	0.7	MT SHERMAN
610	13046	UN 13046		SNOWDON PK	386	0.6	SNOWDON PK
	13043	EAGLE PK B		UN 13100 B	223	0.4	MT JACKSON
611	13042	UN 13042		TWIN SISTER EAST	942	2.1	SILVERTON
612	13041	UN 13041 A		UN 13057	581	0.9	VAIL EAST
613	13041	UN 13041 B		UN 13070	301	0.7	WILLOW LAKES
	13041	WOLCOTT MTN		S 6	181	0.6	MT SNEFFELS
614	13039	UN 13039		SLEEPING SEXTON	419	0.9	MAROON BELLS
615	13038	UN 13038		SOUTH ARAPAHO PK	338	0.7	MONARCH LAKE
	13036	UNITED STATES MTN		CHICAGO PK	176	1.0	IRONTON
616	13035	WEST ELK PK					WEST ELK PK
617	13034	UN 13034		UN 13111	654	2.0	BALDY CINCO
618	13033	WILLIAMS MTN SOUTH C	M	WILLIAMS MTN SOUTH A	493	1.4	THIMBLE ROCK
619	13032	ORGAN MTN B		AMHERST MTN	452	0.4	COLUMBINE PASS
620	13028	UN 13028		UN 13060 B	328	0.7	RITO ALTO PK
621	13026	UN 13026		UN 13202	326	1.7	MT CHAMPION
622	13024	UN 13024		UN 13180 C	484	0.8	WILLOW LAKES
	13024	VAN WIRT MTN		UN 13102	284	0.7	GARFIELD
	13023	NIWOT RIDGE		NAVAJO PK	163	0.6	MONARCH LAKE
623	13020	S 10	Z	S 9	360	0.8	SAMS
624	13020	UN 13020 A		UN 13336	320	0.5	MAROON BELLS
625	13020	UN 13020 B		PICO ASILADO	360	0.7	CRESTONE PK
626	13020	UN 13020 C		MONTEZUMA PK	440	0.6	SUMMIT PK
	13019	CUBA BM		CROWN MTN	119	2.7	HOWARDSVILLE
627	13017	UN 13017		UN 13157	400	1.0	RIO GRANDE PYRAMID
628	13016	UN 13016		UN 13051	676	1.5	UNCOMPAHGRE PK
629	13015	UN 13015		UN 13402	315	1.2	HALFMOON PASS
630	13014	CHIEF MTN					LITTLE SQUAW CREEK
	13012	HOPE MTN		JUPITER MTN	232	0.9	COLUMBINE PASS
631	13012	TWIN SISTERS		BUSHNELL PK	552	1.0	BUSHNELL PK
632	13010	UN 13010 A		HAGAR MTN	350	1.2	LOVELAND PASS
633	13010	UN 13010 B					CIMARRONA PK

Listed by Elevation (continued)

RANK	HT	NAME	FN	NEIGHBOR	DROP	MI	QUAD
634	13006	PENNSYLVANIA MTN		EVANS B, MT	699	2.2	CLIMAX
	13003	RUFFNER MTN		S 7	23	0.4	SAMS
635	13003	UN 13003		UN 13026	503	1.9	MT CHAMPION
636	13001	UN 13001		UN 13202	501	0.9	MT CHAMPION

Colorado Summits 13,000 Feet and Above — Listed by Topographic Map

RANK	HT	NAME	FN	NEIGHBOR	DROP	MI	QUAD
68	13911	MEEKER, MT		LONGS PK	451	0.7	ALLENS PARK
8	14286	LINCOLN, MT					ALMA
	14238	CAMERON, MT		LINCOLN, MT	138	0.5	ALMA
22	14172	BROSS, MT		CAMERON, MT	312	1.0	ALMA
96	13822	SILVERHEELS, MT					ALMA
249	13510	UN 13510 A					BALDY CINCO
328	13383	BALDY CINCO		UN 13510 A	843	1.9	BALDY CINCO
378	13313	UN 13313		BALDY CINCO	413	0.7	BALDY CINCO
510	13162	UN 13162 A		BALDY CINCO	493	1.3	BALDY CINCO
571	13100	UN 13100 E		UN 13111	400	1.9	BALDY CINCO
617	13034	UN 13034		UN 13111	654	2.0	BALDY CINCO
4	14345	BLANCA PK					BLANCA PK
42	14042	ELLINGWOOD PT		BLANCA PK	342	0.5	BLANCA PK
43	14042	LINDSEY, MT					BLANCA PK
44	14037	LITTLE BEAR PK		BLANCA PK	377	1.0	BLANCA PK
84	13849	CALIFORNIA PK		ELLINGWOOD PT	629	2.2	BLANCA PK
93	13828	UN 13828		LINDSEY, MT	688	1.2	BLANCA PK
	13658	HAMILTON PK		BLANCA PK	278	1.5	BLANCA PK
205	13577	UN 13577		UN 13660 A	317	0.5	BLANCA PK
	13500	IRON NIPPLE		UN 13828	200	0.6	BLANCA PK
570	13100	UN 13100 D		BLANCA PK	520	1.3	BLANCA PK
423	13269	ANTORA PK					BONANZA
156	13684	BALD MTN					BOREAS PASS
343	13370	GUYOT, MT					BOREAS PASS
583	13082	BOREAS MTN		BALD MTN	923	2.9	BOREAS PASS
13	14265	QUANDARY PK					BRECKENRIDGE
61	13950	PACIFIC PK		FLETCHER MTN	570	1.4	BRECKENRIDGE
82	13852	CRYSTAL PK		PACIFIC PK	632	0.9	BRECKENRIDGE
178	13633	PEAK 10		CRYSTAL PK	373	0.9	BRECKENRIDGE
	13615	FATHER DYER PK		CRYSTAL PK	115	0.6	BRECKENRIDGE
187	13614	NORTH STAR MTN		WHEELER MTN	434	0.9	BRECKENRIDGE
351	13352	HOOSIER RIDGE		SILVERHEELS, MT	932	3.3	BRECKENRIDGE
455	13229	RED MTN C		HOOSIER RIDGE	369	0.7	BRECKENRIDGE
	13215	RED PK A		HOOSIER RIDGE	115	0.7	BRECKENRIDGE
490	13195	PEAK 9		PEAK 10	415	0.6	BRECKENRIDGE
	13164	HELEN, MT		FATHER DYER PK	264	1.0	BRECKENRIDGE
563	13105	BUSHNELL PK					BUSHNELL PK
631	13012	TWIN SISTERS		BUSHNELL PK	552	1.0	BUSHNELL PK
29	14130	CAPITOL PK					CAPITOL PK
198	13580	CLARK PK		CAPITOL PK	440	1.2	CAPITOL PK
391	13300	DALY, MT		CLARK PK	800	1.4	CAPITOL PK
600	13060	UN 13060 A		CLARK PK	320	0.5	CAPITOL PK
633	13010	UN 13010 B					CIMARRONA PK
28	14148	DEMOCRAT, MT		CAMERON, MT	768	1.3	CLIMAX
76	13865	BUCKSKIN, MT		DEMOCRAT, MT	725	1.5	CLIMAX
80	13857	CLINTON PK		FLETCHER MTN	517	2.7	CLIMAX

203

Listed by Topographic Map (continued)

RANK	HT	NAME	FN	NEIGHBOR	DROP	MI	QUAD
	13852	TRAVER PK		CLINTON PK	232	0.7	CLIMAX
108	13795	ARKANSAS, MT		BUCKSKIN, MT	575	1.9	CLIMAX
115	13781	MOSQUITO PK		BUCKSKIN, MT	561	2.3	CLIMAX
	13780	MCNAMEE PK		CLINTON PK	80	0.5	CLIMAX
	13701	TREASUREVAULT MTN		MOSQUITO PK	281	0.4	CLIMAX
	13692	LOVELAND MTN		BUCKSKIN, MT	192	0.8	CLIMAX
162	13672	TWETO, MT		BUCKSKIN, MT	412	1.2	CLIMAX
204	13577	EVANS B, MT		DYER MTN	317	1.2	CLIMAX
491	13194	LONDON MTN		MOSQUITO PK	534	1.7	CLIMAX
634	13006	PENNSYLVANIA MTN		EVANS B, MT	699	2.2	CLIMAX
32	14083	EOLUS, MT					COLUMBINE PASS
33	14082	WINDOM PK					COLUMBINE PASS
92	13830	JUPITER MTN		WINDOM PK	370	0.6	COLUMBINE PASS
146	13700	GRIZZLY PK C		JUPITER MTN	440	0.7	COLUMBINE PASS
206	13575	GREYLOCK MTN		WINDOM PK	555	1.2	COLUMBINE PASS
216	13554	MCCAULEY PK		GRIZZLY PK C	454	0.7	COLUMBINE PASS
384	13310	AZTEC MTN		JUPITER MTN	610	1.9	COLUMBINE PASS
	13309	ECHO MTN		MCCAULEY PK	209	0.5	COLUMBINE PASS
399	13300	UN 13300 D		UN 13302	560	0.6	COLUMBINE PASS
466	13218	IRVING PK		OSO, MT	638	1.2	COLUMBINE PASS
495	13185	VALOIS, MT		AZTEC MTN	325	2.1	COLUMBINE PASS
	13182	BULLION MTN		AZTEC MTN	202	0.8	COLUMBINE PASS
506	13165	AMHERST MTN					COLUMBINE PASS
	13140	EMERSON MTN		AMHERST MTN	280	0.5	COLUMBINE PASS
551	13121	UN 13121 A		GREYLOCK MTN	341	0.5	COLUMBINE PASS
	13108	THUNDER MTN		GREYLOCK MTN	248	1.0	COLUMBINE PASS
564	13105	UN 13105		EMERSON MTN	325	0.4	COLUMBINE PASS
	13076	FLORIDA MTN		VALOIS, MT	176	0.8	COLUMBINE PASS
594	13070	SHEEP MTN D		UN 13105	370	0.4	COLUMBINE PASS
619	13032	ORGAN MTN B		AMHERST MTN	452	0.4	COLUMBINE PASS
	13012	HOPE MTN		JUPITER MTN	232	0.9	COLUMBINE PASS
59	13951	FLETCHER MTN		QUANDARY PK	611	1.2	COPPER MTN
88	13841	UN 13841		FLETCHER MTN	421	0.7	COPPER MTN
152	13690	WHEELER MTN		FLETCHER MTN	310	1.6	COPPER MTN
480	13205	JACQUE PK					COPPER MTN
7	14294	CRESTONE PK					CRESTONE PK
19	14197	CRESTONE NEEDLE		CRESTONE PK	457	0.5	CRESTONE PK
23	14165	KIT CARSON MTN					CRESTONE PK
34	14081	CHALLENGER POINT		KIT CARSON MTN	301	0.2	CRESTONE PK
37	14064	HUMBOLDT PK					CRESTONE PK
56	13980	UN 13980		KIT CARSON MTN	360	0.2	CRESTONE PK
107	13799	UN 13799		UN 13980	339	0.5	CRESTONE PK
143	13705	COLONY BALDY		HUMBOLDT PK	925	1.4	CRESTONE PK
188	13611	PICO ASILADO		CRESTONE NEEDLE	831	1.7	CRESTONE PK
189	13604	TIJERAS PK		PICO ASILADO	744	1.7	CRESTONE PK
209	13573	BROKEN HAND PK		CRESTONE NEEDLE	673	0.8	CRESTONE PK

Listed by Topographic Map (continued)

RANK	HT	NAME	FN	NEIGHBOR	DROP	MI	QUAD
223	13541	UN 13541		UN 13580 B	361	0.8	CRESTONE PK
241	13522	MILWAUKEE PK		PICO ASILADO	302	0.5	CRESTONE PK
310	13414	CLEVELAND PK		TIJERAS PK	434	1.4	CRESTONE PK
320	13401	UN 13401		TIJERAS PK	301	0.9	CRESTONE PK
327	13384	UN 13384		CLEVELAND PK	364	0.9	CRESTONE PK
332	13380	MUSIC MTN		MILWAUKEE PK	400	0.9	CRESTONE PK
422	13270	UN 13270		BROKEN HAND PK	490	0.5	CRESTONE PK
425	13266	MARBLE MTN		MILWAUKEE PK	526	1.1	CRESTONE PK
608	13050	UN 13050 A		UN 13384	390	0.8	CRESTONE PK
625	13020	UN 13020 B		PICO ASILADO	360	0.7	CRESTONE PK
41	14047	CULEBRA PK					CULEBRA PK
70	13908	RED MTN A		CULEBRA PK	448	0.7	CULEBRA PK
135	13723	VERMEJO PK		RED MTN A	761	1.3	CULEBRA PK
160	13676	PURGATOIRE PK		VERMEJO PK	849	1.8	CULEBRA PK
276	13466	UN 13466		VERMEJO PK	557	1.2	CULEBRA PK
229	13538	EMMA BURR MTN					CUMBERLAND PASS
355	13345	UN 13345		EMMA BURR MTN	445	1.1	CUMBERLAND PASS
556	13112	FITZPATRICK PK		UN 13345	958	2.1	CUMBERLAND PASS
609	13050	UN 13050 B		UN 13345	550	1.5	CUMBERLAND PASS
	14159	EL DIENTE		WILSON, MT	260	0.8	DOLORES PK
225	13540	UN 13540 A		WILSON PK	520	1.0	DOLORES PK
256	13498	UN 13498		UN 13540 A	358	0.6	DOLORES PK
394	13300	MIDDLE PK					DOLORES PK
407	13290	DOLORES PK		MIDDLE PK	710	1.1	DOLORES PK
547	13123	UN 13123 A		UN 13498	463	1.1	DOLORES PK
212	13565	UN 13565		CULEBRA PK	545	1.4	EL VALLE CREEK
	13468	MIRANDA PK		UN 13565	288	0.9	EL VALLE CREEK
316	13405	MARIQUITA PK		CUATRO PK	385	1.4	EL VALLE CREEK
	13335	MAXWELL, MT		MARIQUITA PK	275	0.8	EL VALLE CREEK
367	13333	DE ANZA PK B		MARIQUITA PK	473	1.0	EL VALLE CREEK
456	13229	UN 13229		UN 13565	329	0.6	EL VALLE CREEK
496	13184	BEAUBIEN PK		MIRANDA PK	604	3.1	EL VALLE CREEK
540	13135	FRANCISCO PK		BEAUBIEN PK	435	1.0	EL VALLE CREEK
545	13128	LOMO LISO MTN		FRANCISCO PK	308	0.8	EL VALLE CREEK
191	13598	ELECTRIC PK A		RITO ALTO PK	938	6.1	ELECTRIC PK
217	13553	GIBBS PK		RITO ALTO PK	693	4.2	ELECTRIC PK
247	13513	UN 13513		GIBBS PK	453	2.4	ELECTRIC PK
261	13490	MARCY, MT		UN 13513	430	1.2	ELECTRIC PK
305	13423	SPREAD EAGLE PK		UN 13524 B	443	0.9	ELECTRIC PK
338	13375	LAKES PK		COTTONWOOD PK	675	2.1	ELECTRIC PK
346	13362	DE ANZA PK A		GIBBS PK	622	1.1	ELECTRIC PK
359	13340	OWEN A, MT		UN 13490	600	2.0	ELECTRIC PK
	13213	THIRSTY PK		LAKES PK	233	0.8	ELECTRIC PK
479	13205	EAGLE PK A		THIRSTY PK	545	1.6	ELECTRIC PK
548	13123	UN 13123 B		COTTONWOOD PK	303	0.8	ELECTRIC PK
157	13684	OSO, MT					EMERALD LAKE

Listed by Topographic Map (continued)

RANK	HT	NAME	FN	NEIGHBOR	DROP	MI	QUAD
308	13417	UN 13417		OSO, MT	677	0.8	EMERALD LAKE
360	13340	UN 13340 A		UN 13417	440	1.2	EMERALD LAKE
385	13310	UN 13310		UN 13340 A	330	0.6	EMERALD LAKE
459	13222	UN 13222 B		UN 13300 D	402	0.8	EMERALD LAKE
463	13220	UN 13220 A		UN 13417	800	1.8	EMERALD LAKE
549	13122	PETERS PK		UN 13222 B	342	0.4	EMERALD LAKE
323	13391	PARRY PK					EMPIRE
403	13294	JAMES PK		PARRY PK	714	1.5	EMPIRE
	13250	BANCROFT, MT		PARRY PK	253	0.7	EMPIRE
527	13146	FLORA, MT		PARRY PK	686	2.4	EMPIRE
543	13130	EVA, MT		PARRY PK	430	0.8	EMPIRE
304	13425	MUMMY MTN		HAGUES PK	485	1.4	ESTES PARK
437	13254	HENRY MTN					FAIRVIEW PK
470	13214	FAIRVIEW PK					FAIRVIEW PK
365	13334	CONEY BM		BENT PK	994	1.9	FINGER MESA
433	13260	UN 13260 D		CONEY BM	400	1.2	FINGER MESA
127	13745	AETNA, MT					GARFIELD
172	13651	TAYLOR MTN		AETNA, MT	631	1.2	GARFIELD
344	13369	MONUMENTAL PK					GARFIELD
526	13147	UN 13147		AETNA, MT	527	1.6	GARFIELD
	13132	SEWANEE PK		UN 13147	232	0.6	GARFIELD
565	13102	UN 13102		MONUMENTAL PK	482	1.7	GARFIELD
	13024	VAN WIRT MTN		UN 13102	284	0.7	GARFIELD
220	13550	UN 13550		UN 13803	530	0.9	GOTHIC
228	13540	WHITE ROCK MTN		UN 13550	800	2.8	GOTHIC
321	13401	WHITE BM		WHITE ROCK MTN	381	0.5	GOTHIC
335	13380	UN 13380		WHITE ROCK MTN	480	1.3	GOTHIC
476	13208	TEOCALLI MTN		UN 13550	788	2.4	GOTHIC
511	13162	UN 13162 B		UN 13550	382	0.9	GOTHIC
9	14270	GRAYS PK					GRAYS PK
11	14267	TORREYS PK		GRAYS PK	560	0.6	GRAYS PK
83	13850	EDWARDS, MT		GRAYS PK	470	1.3	GRAYS PK
176	13641	BARD PK					GRAYS PK
	13587	MCCLELLAN MTN		EDWARDS, MT	167	0.8	GRAYS PK
208	13574	PARNASSUS, MT		BARD PK	537	1.0	GRAYS PK
302	13427	GRIZZLY PK D		TORREYS PK	847	1.5	GRAYS PK
347	13362	ENGELMANN PK		BARD PK	542	1.8	GRAYS PK
447	13234	SNIKTAU, MT		GRIZZLY PK D	520	2.4	GRAYS PK
482	13204	LENAWEE MTN		GRIZZLY PK D	344	1.0	GRAYS PK
508	13164	KELSO MTN		TORREYS PK	784	1.6	GRAYS PK
	13140	ROBESON PK		BARD PK	200	0.9	GRAYS PK
554	13117	UN 13117		GRIZZLY PK D	377	1.0	GRAYS PK
73	13895	UN 13895					HALFMOON PASS
	13710	LA GARITA PK		UN 13895	232	1.9	HALFMOON PASS
319	13402	UN 13402		UN 13895	422	1.7	HALFMOON PASS
629	13015	UN 13015		UN 13402	315	1.2	HALFMOON PASS

206

Listed by Topographic Map (continued)

RANK	HT	NAME	FN	NEIGHBOR	DROP	MI	QUAD
40	14048	HANDIES PK					HANDIES PK
79	13860	JONES MTN A		HANDIES PK	520	1.7	HANDIES PK
101	13807	NIAGARA PK		JONES MTN A	587	0.6	HANDIES PK
102	13806	UN 13806		JONES MTN A	466	0.8	HANDIES PK
137	13722	UN 13722 B					HANDIES PK
154	13688	UN 13688 B		UN 13722 B	388	1.1	HANDIES PK
169	13660	WOOD MTN		UN 13688 B	320	0.5	HANDIES PK
	13577	GRAVEL MTN		UN 13688 B	157	0.4	HANDIES PK
	13569	CROWN MTN		NIAGARA PK	229	0.6	HANDIES PK
232	13535	UN 13535 B		JONES MTN A	515	1.5	HANDIES PK
286	13454	HANSON PK		TOWER MTN	914	3.6	HANDIES PK
	13447	HURRICANE PK		HANSON PK	267	0.8	HANDIES PK
303	13427	UN 13427		WOOD MTN	407	1.4	HANDIES PK
368	13330	UN 13330		HANSON PK	550	1.9	HANDIES PK
369	13328	CINNAMON MTN		UN 13535 B	308	1.1	HANDIES PK
374	13321	SUNSHINE MTN					HANDIES PK
	13310	EMERY PK		UN 13330	130	0.4	HANDIES PK
408	13286	BONITA PK		EMERY PK	506	0.6	HANDIES PK
420	13274	SEIGAL MTN		UN 13722 B	374	1.0	HANDIES PK
430	13260	UN 13260 A		SEIGAL MTN	520	2.2	HANDIES PK
	13220	CALIFORNIA MTN		HANSON PK	280	0.6	HANDIES PK
465	13218	ENGINEER MTN		UN 13260 A	438	0.9	HANDIES PK
484	13203	TUTTLE MTN		CALIFORNIA MTN	503	1.3	HANDIES PK
542	13132	UN 13132		UN 13260 A	512	0.9	HANDIES PK
574	13093	UN 13093		SUNSHINE MTN	353	1.4	HANDIES PK
589	13075	UN 13075		HANSON PK	415	1.0	HANDIES PK
606	13052	HOUGHTON MTN		TUTTLE MTN	472	1.5	HANDIES PK
207	13575	ROSALIE PK		EVANS A, MT	675	3.0	HARRIS PARK
234	13530	EPAULET MTN		EVANS A, MT	350	1.9	HARRIS PARK
324	13391	ROGERS PK		EVANS A, MT	515	2.4	HARRIS PARK
12	14265	CASTLE PK					HAYDEN PK
	14060	CONUNDRUM PK		CASTLE PK	240	0.4	HAYDEN PK
62	13943	CATHEDRAL PK		CONUNDRUM PK	523	1.4	HAYDEN PK
177	13635	UN 13635		CATHEDRAL PK	335	0.9	HAYDEN PK
	13561	HAYDEN PK		UN 13635	181	0.8	HAYDEN PK
353	13348	MALEMUTE PK		CONUNDRUM PK	368	1.1	HAYDEN PK
	13322	LEAHY PK		UN 13635	142	0.9	HAYDEN PK
443	13244	UN 13244		UN 13336	424	1.1	HIGHLAND PK
	13155	BALDY MTN		UN 13244	175	0.6	HIGHLAND PK
531	13142	WILLOUGHBY MTN		UN 13336	442	1.8	HIGHLAND PK
474	13209	HOMESTAKE PK					HOMESTAKE RESERVIOR
66	13931	ADAMS, MT		KIT CARSON MTN	871	1.9	HORN PK
202	13580	UN 13580 B		ADAMS, MT	440	0.5	HORN PK
215	13554	FLUTED PK		ADAMS, MT	734	1.2	HORN PK
221	13546	UN 13546		ADAMS, MT	646	0.8	HORN PK
289	13450	HORN PK		FLUTED PK	710	1.3	HORN PK

Listed by Topographic Map (continued)

RANK	HT	NAME	FN	NEIGHBOR	DROP	MI	QUAD
417	13277	COMANCHE PK		FLUTED PK	497	1.5	HORN PK
442	13244	SPRING MTN		VENABLE PK	464	0.7	HORN PK
520	13153	UN 13153 B		ADAMS, MT	373	0.7	HORN PK
530	13143	LITTLE HORN PK		FLUTED PK	323	0.9	HORN PK
219	13552	TOWER MTN					HOWARDSVILLE
267	13478	CANBY MTN		CROWN MTN	938	5.6	HOWARDSVILLE
288	13451	KENDALL PK					HOWARDSVILLE
296	13434	UN 13434		KENDALL PK	534	1.2	HOWARDSVILLE
309	13416	LITTLE GIANT PK		KENDALL PK	556	1.3	HOWARDSVILLE
318	13402	RHODA, MT		UN 13434	302	0.4	HOWARDSVILLE
342	13370	DOME MTN		TOWER MTN	670	1.3	HOWARDSVILLE
393	13300	GALENA MTN		CANBY MTN	360	2.1	HOWARDSVILLE
406	13292	SHEEP MTN A		CANBY MTN	632	1.9	HOWARDSVILLE
	13259	WHITEHEAD PK		RHODA, MT	119	0.4	HOWARDSVILLE
	13222	MACOMBER PK		TOWER MTN	122	0.7	HOWARDSVILLE
460	13220	GREENHALGH MTN		SHEEP MTN A	400	0.8	HOWARDSVILLE
	13220	KING SOLOMON MTN		LITTLE GIANT PK	280	0.5	HOWARDSVILLE
507	13165	UN 13165		CANBY MTN	577	0.7	HOWARDSVILLE
560	13109	UN 13109		WHITEHEAD PK	329	0.6	HOWARDSVILLE
596	13069	UN 13069		CROWN MTN	329	3.4	HOWARDSVILLE
	13049	GREEN MTN		UN 13165	69	0.6	HOWARDSVILLE
	13019	CUBA BM		CROWN MTN	119	2.7	HOWARDSVILLE
54	13988	GRIZZLY PK A					INDEPENDENCE PASS
95	13823	UN 13823		CASCO PK	883	1.8	INDEPENDENCE PASS
116	13780	GARFIELD PK		GRIZZLY PK A	360	0.8	INDEPENDENCE PASS
	13500	RED MTN B		GARFIELD PK	120	0.4	INDEPENDENCE PASS
255	13500	UN 13500		TWINING PK	360	0.7	INDEPENDENCE PASS
277	13463	UN 13463		RED MTN B	563	1.3	INDEPENDENCE PASS
284	13460	UN 13460		SAYRES BM	440	1.4	INDEPENDENCE PASS
489	13198	UN 13198		GRIZZLY PK A	658	2.8	INDEPENDENCE PASS
566	13100	MIDDLE MTN A		UN 13463	520	1.1	INDEPENDENCE PASS
113	13786	POTOSI PK		TEAKETTLE MTN	806	1.0	IRONTON
250	13510	UN 13510 B		EMMA, MT	610	5.0	IRONTON
	13509	TELLURIDE PK		UN 13510 B	289	0.5	IRONTON
269	13477	T 10	Z	THREE NEEDLES	537	0.6	IRONTON
325	13385	CHICAGO PK		TELLURIDE PK	365	1.3	IRONTON
349	13359	T 7	Z	TELLURIDE PK	499	1.0	IRONTON
362	13339	BROWN MTN		HURRICANE PK	639	1.0	IRONTON
375	13321	TRICO PK		UN 13510 B	461	0.9	IRONTON
377	13315	T 8	Z	T 7	495	0.7	IRONTON
477	13206	HAYDEN MTN SOUTH	M	T 8	549	1.1	IRONTON
536	13139	HAYDEN MTN NORTH	M	HAYDEN MTN SOUTH	519	1.2	IRONTON
	13036	UNITED STATES MTN		CHICAGO PK	176	1.0	IRONTON
203	13579	CHIEFS HEAD PK		LONGS PK	719	1.4	ISOLATION PK
258	13497	PAGODA MTN		LONGS PK	397	0.7	ISOLATION PK
383	13310	ALICE, MT		CHIEFS HEAD PK	850	1.4	ISOLATION PK

208

Listed by Topographic Map (continued)

RANK	HT	NAME	FN	NEIGHBOR	DROP	MI	QUAD
502	13176	COPELAND MTN					ISOLATION PK
538	13138	OGALALLA PK		COPELAND MTN	718	1.4	ISOLATION PK
553	13118	ISOLATION PK		COPELAND MTN	938	2.2	ISOLATION PK
483	13203	BENNETT PK					JASPER
586	13078	WHALE PK		LANDSLIDE PK	982	4.8	JEFFERSON
450	13232	HESPERUS MTN					LA PLATA
492	13192	MOSS, MT		HESPERUS MTN	372	0.7	LA PLATA
	13180	LAVENDER PK		MOSS, MT	280	0.2	LA PLATA
524	13149	BABCOCK PK		MOSS, MT	529	0.7	LA PLATA
	13123	SPILLER PK		BABCOCK PK	183	0.5	LA PLATA
	13062	CENTENNIAL PK		LAVENDER PK	282	0.5	LA PLATA
630	13014	CHIEF MTN					LITTLE SQUAW CREEK
15	14255	LONGS PK					LONGS PK
	13326	STORM PK B		LONGS PK	186	0.8	LONGS PK
415	13281	LADY WASHINGTON, MT		LONGS PK	301	0.7	LONGS PK
218	13553	PETTINGELL PK					LOVELAND PASS
404	13294	UN 13294		PETTINGELL PK	314	1.0	LOVELAND PASS
461	13220	HAGAR MTN		UN 13294	320	0.5	LOVELAND PASS
469	13215	UN 13215		PETTINGELL PK	395	1.5	LOVELAND PASS
632	13010	UN 13010 A		HAGAR MTN	360	1.2	LOVELAND PASS
371	13326	WEST BUFFALO PK					MARMOT PK
392	13300	EAST BUFFALO PK		WEST BUFFALO PK	480	0.9	MARMOT PK
24	14156	MAROON PK					MAROON BELLS
47	14018	PYRAMID PK					MAROON BELLS
	14014	NORTH MAROON PK		MAROON PK	234	0.4	MAROON BELLS
65	13932	UN 13932		PYRAMID PK	312	0.6	MAROON BELLS
105	13803	UN 13803		CASTLE PK	423	0.9	MAROON BELLS
136	13722	UN 13722 A		UN 13932	302	0.4	MAROON BELLS
180	13631	UN 13631 B		UN 13722 A	331	0.7	MAROON BELLS
230	13537	UN 13537		WHITE ROCK MTN	757	2.5	MAROON BELLS
245	13516	KEEFE PK		UN 13537	496	1.3	MAROON BELLS
257	13497	HUNTER PK		KEEFE PK	477	1.4	MAROON BELLS
283	13460	SLEEPING SEXTON		NORTH MAROON PK	440	0.6	MAROON BELLS
313	13409	HILLIARD PK		KEEFE PK	309	0.6	MAROON BELLS
333	13380	PRECARIOUS PK		UN 13631 B	640	2.1	MAROON BELLS
341	13370	BUCKSKIN BM		SLEEPING SEXTON	908	2.0	MAROON BELLS
364	13336	UN 13336		BUCKSKIN BM	636	1.1	MAROON BELLS
431	13260	UN 13260 B		PRECARIOUS PK	440	0.8	MAROON BELLS
448	13233	BELLEVIEW MTN		MAROON PK	693	1.9	MAROON BELLS
452	13232	UN 13232 B		UN 13260 B	412	0.4	MAROON BELLS
468	13216	UN 13216		UN 13380	316	0.7	MAROON BELLS
499	13180	UN 13180 A		UN 13631 B	320	0.5	MAROON BELLS
544	13130	UN 13130		UN 13180 A	350	0.8	MAROON BELLS
614	13039	UN 13039		SLEEPING SEXTON	419	0.9	MAROON BELLS
624	13020	UN 13020 A		UN 13336	320	0.5	MAROON BELLS
17	14229	SHAVANO, MT					MAYSVILLE

Listed by Topographic Map (continued)

RANK	HT	NAME	FN	NEIGHBOR	DROP	MI	QUAD
370	13327	MCHENRYS PK		CHIEFS HEAD PK	907	1.2	MCHENRYS PK
475	13208	POWELL PK		MCHENRYS PK	388	0.4	MCHENRYS PK
518	13153	TAYLOR PK B		POWELL PK	413	1.0	MCHENRYS PK
358	13340	HERARD, MT					MEDANO PASS
519	13153	UN 13153 A		HERARD, MT	653	0.9	MEDANO PASS
254	13502	NORTH ARAPAHO PK					MONARCH LAKE
291	13441	APACHE PK					MONARCH LAKE
314	13409	NAVAJO PK		APACHE PK	309	0.4	MONARCH LAKE
	13397	SOUTH ARAPAHO PK		NORTH ARAPAHO PK	97	0.5	MONARCH LAKE
522	13150	ARIKAREE PK		KIOWA PK	570	0.8	MONARCH LAKE
578	13088	PAIUTE PK		AUDUBON, MT	468	0.9	MONARCH LAKE
615	13038	UN 13038		SOUTH ARAPAHO PK	338	0.7	MONARCH LAKE
	13023	NIWOT RIDGE		NAVAJO PK	163	0.6	MONARCH LAKE
111	13794	SQUARE TOP MTN		EDWARDS, MT	814	3.4	MONTEZUMA
129	13738	ARGENTINE PK		EDWARDS, MT	638	1.9	MONTEZUMA
315	13408	WILCOX, MT		ARGENTINE PK	548	1.1	MONTEZUMA
418	13277	RUBY MTN		GRAYS PK	439	1.2	MONTEZUMA
424	13266	GENEVA PK		ARGENTINE PK	926	4.7	MONTEZUMA
	13238	LANDSLIDE PK		GENEVA PK	138	0.4	MONTEZUMA
498	13180	SANTA FE PK		GENEVA PK	480	1.3	MONTEZUMA
	13134	SULLIVAN MTN		SANTA FE PK	274	0.6	MONTEZUMA
10	14269	ANTERO, MT					MT ANTERO
20	14197	PRINCETON, MT					MT ANTERO
140	13712	UN 13712		SHAVANO, MT	332	0.9	MT ANTERO
164	13667	WHITE, MT		ANTERO, MT	847	1.3	MT ANTERO
	13604	JONES PK		UN 13712	144	0.7	MT ANTERO
85	13845	OKLAHOMA, MT		MASSIVE, MT	745	1.8	MT CHAMPION
123	13761	DEER MTN		OKLAHOMA, MT	941	1.7	MT CHAMPION
133	13736	UN 13736		DEER MTN	676	1.2	MT CHAMPION
141	13711	TWINING PK					MT CHAMPION
173	13646	CHAMPION, MT		UN 13736	306	0.6	MT CHAMPION
231	13535	UN 13535 A		DEER MTN	555	1.2	MT CHAMPION
330	13382	WILLIAMS MTN					MT CHAMPION
331	13380	GEISSLER MTN EAST	M	TWINING PK	560	1.1	MT CHAMPION
390	13301	GEISSLER MTN WEST	M	GEISSLER MTN EAST	481	0.6	MT CHAMPION
397	13300	UN 13300 B		TWINING PK	600	2.7	MT CHAMPION
410	13284	UN 13284		UN 13300 B	424	2.7	MT CHAMPION
472	13212	UN 13212		UN 13284	312	0.7	MT CHAMPION
486	13203	WILLIAMS MTN SOUTH B	M	WILLIAMS MTN	423	0.5	MT CHAMPION
487	13202	UN 13202		TWINING PK	422	2.0	MT CHAMPION
561	13108	WILLIAMS MTN NORTH	M	WILLIAMS MTN	408	0.8	MT CHAMPION
621	13026	UN 13026		UN 13202	326	1.7	MT CHAMPION
635	13003	UN 13003		UN 13026	503	1.9	MT CHAMPION
636	13001	UN 13001		UN 13202	501	0.9	MT CHAMPION
1	14433	ELBERT, MT					MT ELBERT
5	14336	LA PLATA PK					MT ELBERT

210

Listed by Topographic Map

RANK	HT	NAME	FN	NEIGHBOR	DROP	MI	QUAD
64	13933	HOPE, MT		LA PLATA PK	873	2.9	MT ELBERT
69	13908	CASCO PK		FRENCH MTN	648	1.2	MT ELBERT
114	13783	RINKER PK		LA PLATA PK	923	1.8	MT ELBERT
122	13761	BULL HILL		ELBERT, MT	421	1.6	MT ELBERT
132	13738	SAYRES BM		LA PLATA PK	958	1.9	MT ELBERT
186	13616	UN 13616		LA PLATA PK	436	1.6	MT ELBERT
233	13531	UN 13531		HOPE, MT	431	1.5	MT ELBERT
281	13461	QUAIL MTN		HOPE, MT	921	1.4	MT ELBERT
	13333	TWIN PKS B		RINKER PK	233	0.9	MT ELBERT
	13220	ELLINGWOOD RIDGE		LA PLATA PK	280	1.5	MT ELBERT
14	14264	EVANS A, MT					MT EVANS
38	14060	BIERSTADT, MT		EVANS A, MT	720	1.4	MT EVANS
	13842	SPAULDING, MT		EVANS A, MT	262	1.1	MT EVANS
190	13602	GRAY WOLF MTN		SPAULDING, MT	582	1.2	MT EVANS
388	13307	WARREN, MT		ROGERS PK	367	1.1	MT EVANS
3	14420	HARVARD, MT					MT HARVARD
18	14197	BELFORD, MT					MT HARVARD
26	14153	OXFORD, MT		BELFORD, MT	653	1.2	MT HARVARD
35	14073	COLUMBIA, MT		HARVARD, MT	893	1.9	MT HARVARD
121	13762	UN 13762		HARVARD, MT	822	2.8	MT HARVARD
340	13374	UN 13374		HARVARD, MT	394	1.9	MT HARVARD
	13292	WAVERLY MTN		OXFORD, MT	152	1.1	MT HARVARD
	13270	PECKS PK		BELFORD, MT	50	1.0	MT HARVARD
163	13670	JACKSON, MT					MT JACKSON
297	13433	UN 13433		JACKSON, MT	413	0.6	MT JACKSON
329	13382	GOLD DUST PK		JACKSON, MT	922	3.1	MT JACKSON
354	13346	UN 13346		GOLD DUST PK	806	1.3	MT JACKSON
493	13192	UN 13192		UN 13768	372	2.2	MT JACKSON
537	13139	SAVAGE PK					MT JACKSON
546	13126	PIKA PK		GOLD DUST PK	506	0.7	MT JACKSON
568	13100	UN 13100 B		PIKA PK	600	2.1	MT JACKSON
581	13085	UN 13085 A		UN 13100 B	625	1.0	MT JACKSON
	13043	EAGLE PK B		UN 13100 B	223	0.4	MT JACKSON
2	14421	MASSIVE, MT					MT MASSIVE
63	13940	FRENCH MTN					MT MASSIVE
	13876	FRASCO BM		FRENCH MTN	256	0.5	MT MASSIVE
51	14005	HOLY CROSS, MT OF THE					MT OF THE HOLY CROSS
91	13831	HOLY CROSS RIDGE		HOLY CROSS, MT OF THE	331	0.6	MT OF THE HOLY CROSS
118	13768	UN 13768		HOLY CROSS RIDGE	388	0.8	MT OF THE HOLY CROSS
421	13271	WHITNEY PK		UN 13768	691	1.4	MT OF THE HOLY CROSS
440	13248	UN 13248		HOLY CROSS RIDGE	308	1.3	MT OF THE HOLY CROSS
	13237	NOTCH MTN		UN 13248	217	0.9	MT OF THE HOLY CROSS
58	13971	OURAY, MT					MT OURAY
273	13472	UN 13472					MT OURAY
199	13580	POWELL, MT					MT POWELL
306	13420	EAGLES NEST		POWELL, MT	640	1.2	MT POWELL

211

Listed by Topographic Map (continued)

RANK	HT	NAME	FN	NEIGHBOR	DROP	MI	QUAD
	13140	GUYSELMAN MTN		UN 13213	240	0.6	MT POWELL
552	13121	UN 13121 B		GUYSELMAN MTN	421	0.6	MT POWELL
45	14036	SHERMAN, MT					MT SHERMAN
	13951	GEMINI PK		SHERMAN, MT	171	0.7	MT SHERMAN
72	13898	HORSESHOE MTN		SHERMAN, MT	758	2.8	MT SHERMAN
81	13855	DYER MTN		GEMINI PK	475	0.9	MT SHERMAN
126	13748	SHERIDAN, MT		SHERMAN, MT	608	1.3	MT SHERMAN
	13739	PTARMIGAN PK		HORSESHOE MTN	279	2.5	MT SHERMAN
	13684	WHITE RIDGE		SHERMAN, MT	184	1.2	MT SHERMAN
	13572	WESTON PK		PTARMIGAN PK	272	1.1	MT SHERMAN
	13409	FINNBACK KNOB		HORSESHOE MTN	149	0.6	MT SHERMAN
	13348	PEERLESS MTN		HORSESHOE MTN	168	0.9	MT SHERMAN
	13047	WEST DYER MTN		DYER MTN	267	0.7	MT SHERMAN
27	14150	SNEFFELS, MT					MT SNEFFELS
98	13819	TEAKETTLE MTN		SNEFFELS, MT	759	1.7	MT SNEFFELS
155	13686	CIRQUE MTN		TEAKETTLE MTN	546	0.6	MT SNEFFELS
259	13496	MEARS PK		T 0	556	1.3	MT SNEFFELS
275	13468	RIDGWAY, MT		TEAKETTLE MTN	448	1.0	MT SNEFFELS
292	13441	S 6	Z	T 0	381	1.0	MT SNEFFELS
444	13242	S 4	Z	S 6	302	0.8	MT SNEFFELS
	13041	WOLCOTT MTN		S 6	181	0.6	MT SNEFFELS
16	14246	WILSON, MT					MT WILSON
48	14017	WILSON PK		WILSON, MT	877	1.5	MT WILSON
67	13913	GLADSTONE PK		WILSON, MT	733	0.6	MT WILSON
	13188	SHEEP MTN B		SAN MIGUEL PK	128	1.3	MT WILSON
555	13113	LIZARD HEAD					MT WILSON
21	14196	YALE, MT					MT YALE
183	13626	UN 13626		PRINCETON, MT	486	1.4	MT YALE
295	13435	UN 13435		YALE, MT	375	0.8	MT YALE
473	13209	GLADSTONE RIDGE		JONES MTN B	949	2.6	MT YALE
	13125	KENNEDY, MT		AZTEC MTN	265	0.6	MTN VIEW CREST
179	13631	UN 13631 A		GARFIELD PK	971	2.2	NEW YORK PK
252	13505	UN 13505		UN 13631 A	525	1.3	NEW YORK PK
396	13300	UN 13300 A		UN 13505	520	1.4	NEW YORK PK
412	13282	TRURO PK		UN 13300 A	822	1.3	NEW YORK PK
413	13282	UN 13282		UN 13300 A	822	1.1	NEW YORK PK
535	13140	UN 13140 C		TRURO PK	320	0.4	NEW YORK PK
576	13090	UN 13090 A		UN 13140 C	350	1.1	NEW YORK PK
591	13074	UN 13074		UN 13300 A	454	1.0	NEW YORK PK
602	13058	OWEN B, MT					OH BE JOYFUL
74	13894	VERMILLION PK					OPHIR
117	13780	GOLDEN HORN		VERMILLION PK	400	0.4	OPHIR
119	13767	U S GRANT PK		GOLDEN HORN	747	1.7	OPHIR
	13761	FULLER PK		VERMILLION PK	261	0.5	OPHIR
124	13752	SAN MIGUEL PK					OPHIR
130	13738	GRIZZLY PK B		SAN MIGUEL PK	758	1.6	OPHIR

Listed by Topographic Map (continued)

RANK	HT	NAME	FN	NEIGHBOR	DROP	MI	QUAD
131	13738	PILOT KNOB		GOLDEN HORN	398	0.5	OPHIR
150	13693	ROLLING MTN		SAN MIGUEL PK	913	2.3	OPHIR
166	13661	LOOKOUT PK		GILPIN PK	841	8.6	OPHIR
227	13540	V 4	Z	U S GRANT PK	320	0.4	OPHIR
238	13528	V 3	Z	U S GRANT PK	388	0.4	OPHIR
271	13475	V 10	Z	GRIZZLY PK B	375	0.7	OPHIR
299	13432	TWIN SISTER EAST	M				OPHIR
334	13380	SOUTH LOOKOUT PK		U S GRANT PK	520	1.2	OPHIR
339	13374	TWIN SISTER WEST	M	TWIN SISTER EAST	394	0.4	OPHIR
356	13342	BEATTIE PK		FULLER PK	322	0.4	OPHIR
386	13309	V 2	Z	U S GRANT PK	409	0.8	OPHIR
400	13300	UN 13300 E		BEATTIE PK	320	0.6	OPHIR
434	13260	V 9	Z	ROLLING MTN	397	1.0	OPHIR
	13177	YELLOW MTN		PILOT KNOB	197	0.6	OPHIR
512	13159	UN 13159		LOOKOUT PK	379	1.3	OPHIR
516	13156	V 5	Z	SOUTH LOOKOUT PK	616	1.3	OPHIR
260	13492	WHITEHOUSE MTN		TEAKETTLE MTN	592	1.9	OURAY
569	13100	UN 13100 C		WHITEHOUSE MTN	320	0.5	OURAY
242	13521	STAR PK		CASTLE PK	816	4.1	PEARL PASS
294	13435	TAYLOR PK A		STAR PK	015	1.3	PEARL PASS
336	13378	ITALIAN MTN					PEARL PASS
348	13362	PEARL MTN		CASTLE PK	582	2.5	PEARL PASS
380	13312	UN 13312 B		PEARL MTN	412	0.6	PEARL PASS
	13051	LAMBERTSON PK		ITALIAN MTN	231	1.1	PEARL PASS
298	13432	JENKINS MTN		SAYRES BM	692	4.0	PIEPLANT
326	13384	PRIZE BM		UN 13631 A	604	1.6	PIEPLANT
373	13322	UN 13322		JENKINS MTN	902	2.4	PIEPLANT
381	13312	UN 13312 C		UN 13463	452	1.0	PIEPLANT
402	13295	UN 13295		SAYRES BM	435	2.7	PIEPLANT
414	13281	GRIZZLY PK E		JENKINS MTN	581	1.9	PIEPLANT
446	13235	UN 13235		UN 13253	375	0.9	PIEPLANT
451	13232	UN 13232 A		SAYRES BM	332	1.7	PIEPLANT
534	13140	UN 13140 B		JENKINS MTN	320	1.1	PIEPLANT
30	14109	PIKES PK					PIKES PK
503	13172	CONEJOS PK					PLATORO
87	13841	HALF PK					POLE CREEK MTN
138	13716	POLE CREEK MTN					POLE CREEK MTN
168	13660	UN 13660 B		POLE CREEK MTN	840	1.5	POLE CREEK MTN
170	13657	CARSON PK					POLE CREEK MTN
197	13581	UN 13581		CARSON PK	681	1.5	POLE CREEK MTN
201	13580	UN 13580 A		UN 13581	360	1.2	POLE CREEK MTN
239	13524	UN 13524 A		CARSON PK	464	1.4	POLE CREEK MTN
290	13450	UN 13450		CARSON PK	350	1.2	POLE CREEK MTN
322	13393	BENT PK		CARSON PK	373	1.2	POLE CREEK MTN
509	13164	UN 13164		HALF PK	384	1.3	POLE CREEK MTN
46	14034	REDCLOUD PK					REDCLOUD PK

Listed by Topographic Map (continued)

RANK	HT	NAME	FN	NEIGHBOR	DROP	MI	QUAD
53	14001	SUNSHINE PK		REDCLOUD PK	501	1.3	REDCLOUD PK
90	13832	UN 13832		REDCLOUD PK	812	1.4	REDCLOUD PK
99	13811	UN 13811		UN 13832	551	1.2	REDCLOUD PK
109	13795	UN 13795		HANDIES PK	495	1.3	REDCLOUD PK
151	13691	UN 13691		UN 13832	471	2.7	REDCLOUD PK
153	13688	UN 13688 A		UN 13832	428	1.6	REDCLOUD PK
161	13674	UN 13674		HALF PK	734	1.3	REDCLOUD PK
211	13566	UN 13566		UN 13691	746	1.9	REDCLOUD PK
222	13542	WHITECROSS MTN		HANDIES PK	562	1.4	REDCLOUD PK
226	13540	UN 13540 B		WOOD MTN	520	2.6	REDCLOUD PK
287	13454	UN 13454		UN 13795	394	1.0	REDCLOUD PK
300	13432	UN 13432		SUNSHINE PK	332	0.9	REDCLOUD PK
379	13312	UN 13312 A		UN 13566	452	0.8	REDCLOUD PK
500	13180	UN 13180 B		UN 13691	524	2.1	REDCLOUD PK
97	13821	RIO GRANDE PYRAMID					RIO GRANDE PYRAMID
285	13455	UTE RIDGE		WHITE DOME	962	4.9	RIO GRANDE PYRAMID
357	13342	UN 13342		UTE RIDGE	726	1.4	RIO GRANDE PYRAMID
387	13308	UN 13308		UN 13342	606	0.8	RIO GRANDE PYRAMID
453	13230	UN 13230 A		UN 13308	770	1.9	RIO GRANDE PYRAMID
504	13169	UN 13169		UN 13230 A	989	1.2	RIO GRANDE PYRAMID
515	13157	UN 13157		RIO GRANDE PYRAMID	300	0.9	RIO GRANDE PYRAMID
627	13017	UN 13017		UN 13157	400	1.0	RIO GRANDE PYRAMID
110	13794	RITO ALTO PK					RITO ALTO PK
240	13524	UN 13524 B		GIBBS PK	624	3.3	RITO ALTO PK
251	13507	EUREKA MTN		RITO ALTO PK	807	2.0	RITO ALTO PK
262	13490	UN 13490		UN 13513	990	1.0	RITO ALTO PK
352	13350	HERMIT PK		RITO ALTO PK	330	0.9	RITO ALTO PK
366	13334	VENABLE PK		FLUTED PK	634	2.7	RITO ALTO PK
550	13122	UN 13122		UN 13490	302	1.2	RITO ALTO PK
598	13062	UN 13062 B		HERMIT PK	842	1.9	RITO ALTO PK
601	13060	UN 13060 B		UN 13062 B	360	0.4	RITO ALTO PK
605	13054	UN 13054		EUREKA MTN	594	1.6	RITO ALTO PK
620	13028	UN 13028		UN 13060 B	328	0.7	RITO ALTO PK
25	14155	TABEGUACHE PK		SHAVANO, MT	455	0.7	SAINT ELMO
75	13870	UN 13870					SAINT ELMO
142	13708	GRIZZLY MTN		UN 13870	568	1.7	SAINT ELMO
165	13663	CARBONATE MTN		UN 13870	434	2.0	SAINT ELMO
174	13646	MAMMA, MT		GRIZZLY MTN	546	1.7	SAINT ELMO
192	13596	CYCLONE MTN		CARBONATE MTN	336	0.5	SAINT ELMO
235	13528	BOULDER MTN		MAMMA, MT	588	1.6	SAINT ELMO
376	13317	UN 13317		UN 13626	737	2.3	SAINT ELMO
521	13151	POMEROY MTN		GRIZZLY MTN	611	2.1	SAINT ELMO
585	13078	UN 13078		UN 13317	738	1.4	SAINT ELMO
595	13070	UN 13070		POMEROY MTN	330	0.6	SAINT ELMO
439	13252	S 8	Z	MEARS PK	552	1.6	SAMS
462	13220	S 7	Z	MEARS PK	400	1.0	SAMS

Listed by Topographic Map (continued)

RANK	HT	NAME	FN	NEIGHBOR	DROP	MI	QUAD
541	13134	S 9	Z	S 8	354	0.7	SAMS
623	13020	S 10	Z	S 9	360	0.8	SAMS
	13003	RUFFNER MTN		S 7	23	0.4	SAMS
50	14014	SAN LUIS PK					SAN LUIS PK
106	13801	ORGAN MTN A		SAN LUIS PK	694	2.0	SAN LUIS PK
409	13285	UN 13285		SAN LUIS PK	665	2.5	SAN LUIS PK
517	13155	UN 13155		UN 13285	415	1.7	SAN LUIS PK
558	13111	UN 13111		UN 13510 A	811	4.6	SAN LUIS PK
505	13168	SHEEP MTN C		UN 13681	592	2.7	SHEEP MTN
567	13100	UN 13100 A		UN 13681	480	1.8	SHEEP MTN
265	13487	STORM PK A		TOWER MTN	627	1.4	SILVERTON
345	13368	SULTAN MTN					SILVERTON
363	13338	KENDALL MTN		KENDALL PK	318	0.7	SILVERTON
372	13325	UN 13325		STORM PK A	465	0.5	SILVERTON
497	13180	GRAND TURK		SULTAN MTN	404	0.6	SILVERTON
	13066	KENDALL BM		KENDALL MTN	286	0.7	SILVERTON
611	13042	UN 13042		TWIN SISTER EAST	942	2.1	SILVERTON
57	13972	PIGEON PK					SNOWDON PK
89	13835	TURRET PK		PIGEON PK	735	0.5	SNOWDON PK
112	13786	ANIMAS MTN					SNOWDON PK
145	13700	FIFTEEN, PK		TURRET PK	320	0.2	SNOWDON PK
	13500	SIXTEEN, PK		FIFTEEN, PK	80	0.1	SNOWDON PK
	13420	INDEX, THE		ANIMAS MTN	240	0.2	SNOWDON PK
	13220	LITTLE FINGER		SIXTEEN, PK	120	0.1	SNOWDON PK
	13180	POINT PUN		GRAYSTONE PK	200	0.6	SNOWDON PK
513	13158	TWILIGHT PK					SNOWDON PK
	13100	SOUTH TWILIGHT PK		TWILIGHT PK	200	0.3	SNOWDON PK
587	13077	SNOWDON PK					SNOWDON PK
588	13075	NORTH TWILIGHT PK		TWILIGHT PK	335	0.4	SNOWDON PK
590	13074	GARFIELD, MT		POINT PUN	374	0.6	SNOWDON PK
599	13062	WEST NEEDLE MTN		SOUTH TWILIGHT PK	562	0.7	SNOWDON PK
610	13046	UN 13046		SNOWDON PK	386	0.6	SNOWDON PK
31	14092	SNOWMASS MTN					SNOWMASS MTN
86	13841	HAGERMAN PK		SNOWMASS MTN	341	0.6	SNOWMASS MTN
	13620	SNOWMASS PK		HAGERMAN PK	120	0.2	SNOWMASS MTN
237	13528	TREASURE MTN					SNOWMASS MTN
278	13462	TREASURY MTN		TREASURE MTN	522	1.4	SNOWMASS MTN
307	13420	UN 13420		SNOWMASS MTN	760	1.2	SNOWMASS MTN
597	13062	UN 13062 A		SNOWMASS PK	642	1.8	SNOWMASS MTN
525	13148	SOUTH RIVER PK					SOUTH RIVER PK
184	13626	WEST SPANISH PK					SPANISH PKS
55	13983	STEWART PK		SAN LUIS PK	883	2.5	STEWART PK
147	13698	BALDY ALTO		SAN LUIS PK	518	1.4	STEWART PK
	13401	BALDY CHATO		STEWART PK	181	1.5	STEWART PK
39	14059	SUNLIGHT PK		WINDOM PK	399	0.5	STORM KING PK
	14039	NORTH EOLUS		EOLUS, MT	179	0.2	STORM KING PK

215

Listed by Topographic Map (continued)

RANK	HT	NAME	FN	NEIGHBOR	DROP	MI	QUAD
77	13864	VESTAL PK					STORM KING PK
94	13824	JAGGED MTN		SUNLIGHT PK	964	1.4	STORM KING PK
103	13805	TRINITY PK		VESTAL PK	945	1.2	STORM KING PK
104	13803	ARROW PK		VESTAL PK	943	0.5	STORM KING PK
120	13765	TRINITY PK WEST	M	TRINITY PK	385	0.4	STORM KING PK
125	13752	STORM KING PK		TRINITY PK	612	1.3	STORM KING PK
128	13745	TRINITY PK EAST	M	TRINITY PK	405	0.2	STORM KING PK
144	13705	SIX, PK		JAGGED MTN	685	1.0	STORM KING PK
	13705	THIRTEEN, PK		ANIMAS MTN	245	0.3	STORM KING PK
	13704	GLACIER PT		NORTH EOLUS	284	0.4	STORM KING PK
148	13695	MONITOR PK		THIRTEEN, PK	315	0.2	STORM KING PK
158	13682	SEVEN, PK		SIX, PK	422	0.8	STORM KING PK
181	13628	SILEX, MT		STORM KING PK	808	0.8	STORM KING PK
182	13627	WHITE DOME		TRINITY PK EAST	967	2.2	STORM KING PK
185	13617	GUARDIAN, THE		SILEX, MT	557	0.6	STORM KING PK
194	13589	ONE, PK		WHITE DOME	409	0.8	STORM KING PK
224	13540	ELEVEN, PK		SUNLIGHT PK	400	0.6	STORM KING PK
236	13528	LEVIATHAN PK		JAGGED MTN	588	0.7	STORM KING PK
	13500	NEEDLE RIDGE		SUNLIGHT PK	200	0.4	STORM KING PK
263	13489	GRAYSTONE PK		ARROW PK	509	0.6	STORM KING PK
268	13478	THREE, PK		TRINITY PK EAST	498	0.9	STORM KING PK
270	13475	TWO, PK		THREE, PK	535	0.8	STORM KING PK
	13430	GRAY NEEDLE		JAGGED MTN	130	0.3	STORM KING PK
301	13428	VALLECITO MTN		LEVIATHAN PK	568	0.5	STORM KING PK
	13420	TEN, PK		JAGGED MTN	280	0.3	STORM KING PK
	13420	TWIN THUMBS		ELEVEN, PK	120	0.2	STORM KING PK
312	13410	FOUR, PK		SIX, PK	510	1.2	STORM KING PK
317	13402	NINE, PK		STORM KING PK	582	0.5	STORM KING PK
389	13302	UN 13302		OSO, MT	722	1.7	STORM KING PK
405	13292	ELECTRIC PK B		ARROW PK	832	0.6	STORM KING PK
411	13283	FIVE, PK		FOUR, PK	303	0.6	STORM KING PK
427	13265	KNIFE PT		SUNLIGHT PK	325	0.8	STORM KING PK
428	13262	HEISSPITZ, THE		FOUR, PK	362	0.9	STORM KING PK
	13228	EIGHT, PK		NINE, PK	288	0.4	STORM KING PK
481	13205	NEBO, MT		UN 13230 A	505	0.6	STORM KING PK
532	13140	TWELVE, PK	Z	NORTH EOLUS	320	0.5	STORM KING PK
539	13136	HUNCHBACK MTN		WHITE DOME	356	0.8	STORM KING PK
559	13110	UN 13110		UN 13308	450	1.2	STORM KING PK
395	13300	SUMMIT PK					SUMMIT PK
523	13150	MONTEZUMA PK		SUMMIT PK	690	1.6	SUMMIT PK
626	13020	UN 13020 C		MONTEZUMA PK	440	0.6	SUMMIT PK
100	13809	DALLAS PK		SNEFFELS, MT	869	2.0	TELLURIDE
134	13735	T 0	Z	DALLAS PK	395	1.4	TELLURIDE
149	13694	GILPIN PK		DALLAS PK	720	1.7	TELLURIDE
196	13581	EMMA, MT		GILPIN PK	561	0.8	TELLURIDE
214	13555	WASATCH MTN		LOOKOUT PK	495	2.1	TELLURIDE

216

Listed by Topographic Map (continued)

RANK	HT	NAME	FN	NEIGHBOR	DROP	MI	QUAD
248	13510	T 11	Z	LOOKOUT PK	452	1.3	TELLURIDE
266	13481	THREE NEEDLES		T 11	421	1.0	TELLURIDE
272	13472	LA JUNTA PK		WASATCH MTN	612	0.7	TELLURIDE
274	13470	SILVER MTN B		WASATCH MTN	410	2.2	TELLURIDE
282	13460	SAN JOAQUIN RIDGE		SILVER MTN B	360	1.3	TELLURIDE
293	13436	T 5	Z	TELLURIDE PK	416	2.8	TELLURIDE
	13319	PALMYRA PK		SILVER MTN B	179	0.5	TELLURIDE
	13275	MENDOTA PK		T 5	175	0.8	TELLURIDE
	13213	CAMPBELL PK		T 0	233	0.5	TELLURIDE
528	13145	UN 13145		LA JUNTA PK	325	0.6	TELLURIDE
573	13095	UN 13095		CHICAGO PK	315	0.5	TELLURIDE
	13060	SAINT SOPHIA RIDGE		EMMA, MT	160	0.5	TELLURIDE
382	13312	WILLIAMS MTN SOUTH A	M	WILLIAMS MTN	572	1.5	THIMBLE ROCK
618	13033	WILLIAMS MTN SOUTH C	M	WILLIAMS MTN SOUTH A	493	1.4	THIMBLE ROCK
449	13233	TURNER PK					TINCUP
467	13218	JONES MTN B		EMMA BURR MTN	638	3.0	TINCUP
572	13095	KREUTZER, MT		EMMA BURR MTN	355	1.6	TINCUP
604	13055	UN 13055		KREUTZER, MT	315	1.6	TINCUP
213	13560	HAGUES PK					TRAIL RIDGE
246	13514	YPSILON MTN					TRAIL RIDGE
253	13502	FAIRCHILD MTN		YPSILON MTN	922	1.2	TRAIL RIDGE
	13420	ROWE PK		HAGUES PK	200	0.4	TRAIL RIDGE
	13184	ROWE MTN		ROWE PK	44	0.5	TRAIL RIDGE
	13069	CHIQUITA, MT		YPSILON MTN	283	1.0	TRAIL RIDGE
243	13517	TRINCHERA PK					TRINCHERA PK
264	13487	CUATRO PK		TRINCHERA PK	707	2.2	TRINCHERA PK
485	13203	UN 13203		CUATRO PK	303	1.1	TRINCHERA PK
167	13660	UN 13660 A		CALIFORNIA PK	400	1.1	TWIN PKS
200	13580	TWIN PKS A		ELLINGWOOD PT	640	1.6	TWIN PKS
6	14309	UNCOMPAHGRE PK					UNCOMPAHGRE PK
139	13714	SILVER MTN A					UNCOMPAHGRE PK
159	13681	UN 13681		SILVER MTN A	501	1.0	UNCOMPAHGRE PK
193	13590	MATTERHORN PK		WETTERHORN PK	570	0.9	UNCOMPAHGRE PK
361	13340	UN 13340 B		UN 13411	745	1.7	UNCOMPAHGRE PK
401	13300	UN 13300 F		UN 13340 B	320	0.6	UNCOMPAHGRE PK
435	13256	BROKEN HILL		MATTERHORN PK	798	2.0	UNCOMPAHGRE PK
458	13222	UN 13222 A		UN 13340 B	322	0.6	UNCOMPAHGRE PK
514	13158	UN 13158		UNCOMPAHGRE PK	378	1.8	UNCOMPAHGRE PK
562	13106	UN 13106		UNCOMPAHGRE PK	726	2.2	UNCOMPAHGRE PK
575	13091	UN 13091		UN 13106 A	591	1.8	UNCOMPAHGRE PK
607	13051	UN 13051		SILVER MTN A	351	1.1	UNCOMPAHGRE PK
628	13016	UN 13016		UN 13051	676	1.5	UNCOMPAHGRE PK
432	13260	UN 13260 C					VAIL EAST
454	13230	UN 13230 B		UN 13260 C	730	2.0	VAIL EAST
464	13220	UN 13220 B		UN 13260 C	520	1.6	VAIL EAST
471	13213	UN 13213		UN 13230 B	753	1.5	VAIL EAST

217

Listed by Topographic Map (continued)

RANK	HT	NAME	FN	NEIGHBOR	DROP	MI	QUAD
	13129	BLACK BM		UN 13260 C	29	0.2	VAIL EAST
577	13090	UN 13090 B		UN 13245	710	2.0	VAIL EAST
582	13085	UN 13085 B		UN 13245	465	0.8	VAIL EAST
603	13057	UN 13057		UN 13085 B	557	1.0	VAIL EAST
612	13041	UN 13041 A		UN 13057	581	0.9	VAIL EAST
195	13588	COTTONWOOD PK					VALLEY VIEW HOT SPRG
419	13276	KIOWA PK		NAVAJO PK	736	1.3	WARD
457	13223	AUDUBON, MT		APACHE PK	843	3.4	WARD
593	13071	HUNTS PK		BUSHNELL PK	891	4.3	WELLSVILLE
416	13278	UN 13278		RIO GRANDE PYRAMID	633	1.1	WEMINUCHE PASS
429	13261	UN 13261		UN 13278	321	0.7	WEMINUCHE PASS
616	13035	WEST ELK PK					WEST ELK PK
49	14015	WETTERHORN PK					WETTERHORN PK
171	13656	COXCOMB PK		WETTERHORN PK	796	1.8	WETTERHORN PK
175	13642	REDCLIFF		COXCOMB PK	502	0.5	WETTERHORN PK
311	13411	UN 13411		WETTERHORN PK	471	1.2	WETTERHORN PK
337	13377	UN 13377		UN 13411	357	0.5	WETTERHORN PK
398	13300	UN 13300 C		WETTERHORN PK	440	0.7	WETTERHORN PK
426	13266	WILDHORSE PK		SEIGAL MTN	966	4.0	WETTERHORN PK
445	13241	U 3	Z	REDCLIFF	461	0.7	WETTERHORN PK
478	13206	UN 13206		UN 13377	306	0.6	WETTERHORN PK
488	13201	UN 13201		UN 13300 C	661	1.3	WETTERHORN PK
529	13144	PRECIPICE PK		U 3	484	1.5	WETTERHORN PK
557	13111	COW BM		UN 13132	531	2.3	WETTERHORN PK
592	13073	BLACKWALL MTN		WILDHORSE PK	453	1.3	WETTERHORN PK
350	13357	WILLOW BM					WILLOW LAKES
441	13245	UN 13245		UN 13260 C	785	4.0	WILLOW LAKES
494	13189	RED PK B	·	WILLOW BM	929	1.6	WILLOW LAKES
501	13180	UN 13180 C		WILLOW BM	760	1.6	WILLOW LAKES
580	13085	KELLER MTN		UN 13180 C	745	2.1	WILLOW LAKES
584	13079	UN 13079		UN 13180 C	659	1.3	WILLOW LAKES
613	13041	UN 13041 B		UN 13079	301	0.7	WILLOW LAKES
622	13024	UN 13024		UN 13180 C	484	0.8	WILLOW LAKES
36	14067	MISSOURI MTN		BELFORD, MT	847	1.3	WINFIELD
52	14003	HURON PK					WINFIELD
60	13951	ICE MTN					WINFIELD
71	13904	EMERALD PK		MISSOURI MTN	564	1.3	WINFIELD
78	13860	APOSTLE NORTH	M	ICE MTN	400	0.4	WINFIELD
	13831	IOWA PK		MISSOURI MTN	291	0.6	WINFIELD
210	13568	APOSTLE WEST	M	ICE MTN	508	0.6	WINFIELD
	13523	BROWNS PK		HURON PK	183	0.7	WINFIELD
244	13517	UN 13517		HURON PK	457	1.5	WINFIELD
279	13462	UN 13462 A		BROWNS PK	322	0.6	WINFIELD
280	13462	UN 13462 B		UN 13517	562	1.6	WINFIELD
436	13255	UN 13255		GRIZZLY PK E	555	1.6	WINFIELD
438	13253	UN 13253		UN 13255	433	2.0	WINFIELD

218

Listed by Topographic Map (continued)

RANK	HT	NAME	FN	NEIGHBOR	DROP	MI	QUAD
533	13140	UN 13140 A		UN 13255	320	0.6	WINFIELD
579	13088	VIRGINIA PK		UN 13140 A	428	0.8	WINFIELD
	13077	WINFIELD PK		VIRGINIA PK	177	0.7	WINFIELD
	13060	MIDDLE MTN B		UN 13462 A	120	0.6	WINFIELD

Colorado Summits 13,000 Feet and Above — Listed Alphabetically

RANK	HT	NAME	FN	NEIGHBOR	DROP	MI	QUAD
66	13931	ADAMS, MT		KIT CARSON MTN	871	1.9	HORN PK
127	13745	AETNA, MT					GARFIELD
383	13310	ALICE, MT		CHIEFS HEAD PK	850	1.4	ISOLATION PK
506	13165	AMHERST MTN					COLUMBINE PASS
112	13786	ANIMAS MTN					SNOWDON PK
10	14269	ANTERO, MT					MT ANTERO
423	13269	ANTORA PK					BONANZA
291	13441	APACHE PK					MONARCH LAKE
78	13860	APOSTLE NORTH	M	ICE MTN	400	0.4	WINFIELD
210	13568	APOSTLE WEST	M	ICE MTN	508	0.6	WINFIELD
129	13738	ARGENTINE PK		EDWARDS, MT	638	1.9	MONTEZUMA
522	13150	ARIKAREE PK		KIOWA PK	570	0.8	MONARCH LAKE
108	13795	ARKANSAS, MT		BUCKSKIN, MT	575	1.9	CLIMAX
104	13803	ARROW PK		VESTAL PK	943	0.5	STORM KING PK
457	13223	AUDUBON, MT		APACHE PK	843	3.4	WARD
384	13310	AZTEC MTN		JUPITER MTN	610	1.9	COLUMBINE PASS
524	13149	BABCOCK PK		MOSS, MT	529	0.7	LA PLATA
156	13684	BALD MTN					BOREAS PASS
147	13698	BALDY ALTO		SAN LUIS PK	518	1.4	STEWART PK
	13401	BALDY CHATO		STEWART PK	181	1.5	STEWART PK
328	13383	BALDY CINCO		UN 13510 A	843	1.9	BALDY CINCO
	13155	BALDY MTN		UN 13244	175	0.6	HIGHLAND PK
	13250	BANCROFT, MT		PARRY PK	253	0.7	EMPIRE
176	13641	BARD PK					GRAYS PK
356	13342	BEATTIE PK		FULLER PK	322	0.4	OPHIR
496	13184	BEAUBIEN PK		MIRANDA PK	604	3.1	EL VALLE CREEK
18	14197	BELFORD, MT					MT HARVARD
448	13233	BELLEVIEW MTN		MAROON PK	693	1.9	MAROON BELLS
483	13203	BENNETT PK					JASPER
322	13393	BENT PK		CARSON PK	373	1.2	POLE CREEK MTN
38	14060	BIERSTADT, MT		EVANS A, MT	720	1.4	MT EVANS
	13129	BLACK BM		UN 13260 C	29	0.2	VAIL EAST
592	13073	BLACKWALL MTN		WILDHORSE PK	453	1.3	WETTERHORN PK
4	14345	BLANCA PK					BLANCA PK
408	13286	BONITA PK		EMERY PK	506	0.6	HANDIES PK
583	13082	BOREAS MTN		BALD MTN	923	2.9	BOREAS PASS
235	13528	BOULDER MTN		MAMMA, MT	588	1.6	SAINT ELMO
209	13573	BROKEN HAND PK		CRESTONE NEEDLE	673	0.8	CRESTONE PK
435	13256	BROKEN HILL		MATTERHORN PK	798	2.0	UNCOMPAHGRE PK
22	14172	BROSS, MT		CAMERON, MT	312	1.0	ALMA
362	13339	BROWN MTN		HURRICANE PK	639	1.0	IRONTON
	13523	BROWNS PK		HURON PK	183	0.7	WINFIELD
341	13370	BUCKSKIN BM		SLEEPING SEXTON	908	2.0	MAROON BELLS
76	13865	BUCKSKIN, MT		DEMOCRAT, MT	725	1.5	CLIMAX
122	13761	BULL HILL		ELBERT, MT	421	1.6	MT ELBERT
	13182	BULLION MTN		AZTEC MTN	202	0.8	COLUMBINE PASS

220

Listed Alphabetically (continued)

RANK	HT	NAME	FN	NEIGHBOR	DROP	MI	QUAD
563	13105	BUSHNELL PK					BUSHNELL PK
	13220	CALIFORNIA MTN		HANSON PK	280	0.6	HANDIES PK
84	13849	CALIFORNIA PK		ELLINGWOOD PT	629	2.2	BLANCA PK
	14238	CAMERON, MT		LINCOLN, MT	138	0.5	ALMA
	13213	CAMPBELL PK		T 0	233	0.5	TELLURIDE
267	13478	CANBY MTN		CROWN MTN	938	5.6	HOWARDSVILLE
29	14130	CAPITOL PK					CAPITOL PK
165	13663	CARBONATE MTN		UN 13870	434	2.0	SAINT ELMO
170	13657	CARSON PK					POLE CREEK MTN
69	13908	CASCO PK		FRENCH MTN	648	1.2	MT ELBERT
12	14265	CASTLE PK					HAYDEN PK
62	13943	CATHEDRAL PK		CONUNDRUM PK	523	1.4	HAYDEN PK
	13062	CENTENNIAL PK		LAVENDER PK	282	0.5	LA PLATA
34	14081	CHALLENGER POINT		KIT CARSON MTN	301	0.2	CRESTONE PK
173	13646	CHAMPION, MT		UN 13736	306	0.6	MT CHAMPION
325	13385	CHICAGO PK		TELLURIDE PK	365	1.3	IRONTON
630	13014	CHIEF MTN					LITTLE SQUAW CREEK
203	13579	CHIEFS HEAD PK		LONGS PK	719	1.4	ISOLATION PK
	13069	CHIQUITA, MT		YPSILON MTN	283	1.0	TRAIL RIDGE
369	13328	CINNAMON MTN		UN 13535 B	308	1.1	HANDIES PK
155	13686	CIRQUE MTN		TEAKETTLE MTN	546	0.6	MT SNEFFELS
198	13580	CLARK PK		CAPITOL PK	440	1.2	CAPITOL PK
310	13414	CLEVELAND PK		TIJERAS PK	434	1.4	CRESTONE PK
80	13857	CLINTON PK		FLETCHER MTN	517	2.7	CLIMAX
143	13705	COLONY BALDY		HUMBOLDT PK	925	1.4	CRESTONE PK
35	14073	COLUMBIA, MT		HARVARD, MT	893	1.9	MT HARVARD
417	13277	COMANCHE PK		FLUTED PK	497	1.5	HORN PK
503	13172	CONEJOS PK					PLATORO
365	13334	CONEY BM		BENT PK	994	1.9	FINGER MESA
	14060	CONUNDRUM PK		CASTLE PK	240	0.4	HAYDEN PK
502	13176	COPELAND MTN					ISOLATION PK
195	13588	COTTONWOOD PK					VALLEY VIEW HOT SPRG
557	13111	COW BM		UN 13132	531	2.3	WETTERHORN PK
171	13656	COXCOMB PK		WETTERHORN PK	796	1.8	WETTERHORN PK
19	14197	CRESTONE NEEDLE		CRESTONE PK	457	0.5	CRESTONE PK
7	14294	CRESTONE PK					CRESTONE PK
	13569	CROWN MTN		NIAGARA PK	229	0.6	HANDIES PK
82	13852	CRYSTAL PK		PACIFIC PK	632	0.9	BRECKENRIDGE
264	13487	CUATRO PK		TRINCHERA PK	707	2.2	TRINCHERA PK
	13019	CUBA BM		CROWN MTN	119	2.7	HOWARDSVILLE
41	14047	CULEBRA PK					CULEBRA PK
192	13596	CYCLONE MTN		CARBONATE MTN	336	0.5	SAINT ELMO
100	13809	DALLAS PK		SNEFFELS, MT	869	2.0	TELLURIDE
391	13300	DALY, MT		CLARK PK	800	1.4	CAPITOL PK
346	13362	DE ANZA PK A		GIBBS PK	622	1.1	ELECTRIC PK
367	13333	DE ANZA PK B		MARIQUITA PK	473	1.0	EL VALLE CREEK

221

Listed Alphabetically (continued)

RANK	HT	NAME	FN	NEIGHBOR	DROP	MI	QUAD
123	13761	DEER MTN		OKLAHOMA, MT	941	1.7	MT CHAMPION
28	14148	DEMOCRAT, MT		CAMERON, MT	768	1.3	CLIMAX
407	13290	DOLORES PK		MIDDLE PK	710	1.1	DOLORES PK
342	13370	DOME MTN		TOWER MTN	670	1.3	HOWARDSVILLE
81	13855	DYER MTN		GEMINI PK	475	0.9	MT SHERMAN
479	13205	EAGLE PK A		THIRSTY PK	545	1.6	ELECTRIC PK
	13043	EAGLE PK B		UN 13100 B	223	0.4	MT JACKSON
306	13420	EAGLES NEST		POWELL, MT	640	1.2	MT POWELL
392	13300	EAST BUFFALO PK		WEST BUFFALO PK	480	0.9	MARMOT PK
	13309	ECHO MTN		MCCAULEY PK	209	0.5	COLUMBINE PASS
83	13850	EDWARDS, MT		GRAYS PK	470	1.3	GRAYS PK
	13228	EIGHT, PK		NINE, PK	288	0.4	STORM KING PK
	14159	EL DIENTE		WILSON, MT	259	0.8	DOLORES PK
1	14433	ELBERT, MT					MT ELBERT
191	13598	ELECTRIC PK A		RITO ALTO PK	938	6.1	ELECTRIC PK
405	13292	ELECTRIC PK B		ARROW PK	832	0.6	STORM KING PK
224	13540	ELEVEN, PK		SUNLIGHT PK	400	0.6	STORM KING PK
42	14042	ELLINGWOOD PT		BLANCA PK	342	0.5	BLANCA PK
	13220	ELLINGWOOD RIDGE		LA PLATA PK	280	1.5	MT ELBERT
71	13904	EMERALD PK		MISSOURI MTN	564	1.3	WINFIELD
	13140	EMERSON MTN		AMHERST MTN	280	0.5	COLUMBINE PASS
	13310	EMERY PK		UN 13330	130	0.4	HANDIES PK
229	13538	EMMA BURR MTN					CUMBERLAND PASS
196	13581	EMMA, MT		GILPIN PK	561	0.8	TELLURIDE
347	13362	ENGELMANN PK		BARD PK	542	1.8	GRAYS PK
465	13218	ENGINEER MTN		UN 13260 A	438	0.9	HANDIES PK
32	14083	EOLUS, MT					COLUMBINE PASS
234	13530	EPAULET MTN		EVANS A, MT	350	1.9	HARRIS PARK
251	13507	EUREKA MTN		RITO ALTO PK	807	2.0	RITO ALTO PK
543	13130	EVA, MT		PARRY PK	430	0.8	EMPIRE
14	14264	EVANS A, MT					MT EVANS
204	13577	EVANS B, MT		DYER MTN	317	1.2	CLIMAX
253	13502	FAIRCHILD MTN		YPSILON MTN	922	1.2	TRAIL RIDGE
470	13214	FAIRVIEW PK					FAIRVIEW PK
	13615	FATHER DYER PK		CRYSTAL PK	115	0.6	BRECKENRIDGE
145	13700	FIFTEEN, PK		TURRET PK	320	0.2	SNOWDON PK
	13409	FINNBACK KNOB		HORSESHOE MTN	149	0.6	MT SHERMAN
556	13112	FITZPATRICK PK		UN 13345	958	2.1	CUMBERLAND PASS
411	13283	FIVE, PK		FOUR, PK	303	0.6	STORM KING PK
59	13951	FLETCHER MTN		QUANDARY PK	611	1.2	COPPER MTN
527	13146	FLORA, MT		PARRY PK	686	2.4	EMPIRE
	13076	FLORIDA MTN		VALOIS, MT	176	0.8	COLUMBINE PASS
215	13554	FLUTED PK		ADAMS, MT	734	1.2	HORN PK
312	13410	FOUR, PK		SIX, PK	510	1.2	STORM KING PK
540	13135	FRANCISCO PK		BEAUBIEN PK	435	1.0	EL VALLE CREEK
	13876	FRASCO BM		FRENCH MTN	256	0.5	MT MASSIVE

222

Listed Alphabetically (continued)

RANK	HT	NAME	FN	NEIGHBOR	DROP	MI	QUAD
63	13940	FRENCH MTN					MT MASSIVE
	13761	FULLER PK		VERMILLION PK	261	0.5	OPHIR
393	13300	GALENA MTN		CANBY MTN	360	2.1	HOWARDSVILLE
116	13780	GARFIELD PK		GRIZZLY PK A	360	0.8	INDEPENDENCE PASS
590	13074	GARFIELD, MT		POINT PUN	374	0.6	SNOWDON PK
331	13380	GEISSLER MTN EAST	M	TWINING PK	560	1.1	MT CHAMPION
390	13301	GEISSLER MTN WEST	M	GEISSLER MTN EAST	481	0.6	MT CHAMPION
	13951	GEMINI PK		SHERMAN, MT	171	0.7	MT SHERMAN
424	13266	GENEVA PK		ARGENTINE PK	926	4.7	MONTEZUMA
217	13553	GIBBS PK		RITO ALTO PK	693	4.2	ELECTRIC PK
149	13694	GILPIN PK		DALLAS PK	720	1.7	TELLURIDE
	13704	GLACIER PT		NORTH EOLUS	284	0.4	STORM KING PK
67	13913	GLADSTONE PK		WILSON, MT	733	0.6	MT WILSON
473	13209	GLADSTONE RIDGE		JONES MTN B	949	2.6	MT YALE
329	13382	GOLD DUST PK		JACKSON, MT	922	3.1	MT JACKSON
117	13780	GOLDEN HORN		VERMILLION PK	400	0.4	OPHIR
497	13180	GRAND TURK		SULTAN MTN	404	0.6	SILVERTON
	13577	GRAVEL MTN		UN 13688 B	157	0.4	HANDIES PK
	13430	GRAY NEEDLE		JAGGED MTN	130	0.3	STORM KING PK
190	13602	GRAY WOLF MTN		SPAULDING, MT	502	1.2	MT EVANS
9	14270	GRAYS PK					GRAYS PK
263	13489	GRAYSTONE PK		ARROW PK	509	0.6	STORM KING PK
	13049	GREEN MTN		UN 13165	69	0.6	HOWARDSVILLE
460	13220	GREENHALGH MTN		SHEEP MTN A	400	0.8	HOWARDSVILLE
206	13575	GREYLOCK MTN		WINDOM PK	555	1.2	COLUMBINE PASS
142	13708	GRIZZLY MTN		UN 13870	568	1.7	SAINT ELMO
54	13988	GRIZZLY PK A					INDEPENDENCE PASS
130	13738	GRIZZLY PK B		SAN MIGUEL PK	758	1.6	OPHIR
146	13700	GRIZZLY PK C		JUPITER MTN	440	0.7	COLUMBINE PASS
302	13427	GRIZZLY PK D		TORREYS PK	847	1.5	GRAYS PK
414	13281	GRIZZLY PK E		JENKINS MTN	581	1.9	PIEPLANT
185	13617	GUARDIAN, THE		SILEX, MT	557	0.6	STORM KING PK
343	13370	GUYOT, MT					BOREAS PASS
	13140	GUYSELMAN MT		UN 13213	240	0.6	MT POWELL
461	13220	HAGAR MTN		UN 13294	320	0.5	LOVELAND PASS
86	13841	HAGERMAN PK		SNOWMASS MTN	341	0.6	SNOWMASS MTN
213	13560	HAGUES PK					TRAIL RIDGE
87	13841	HALF PK					POLE CREEK MTN
	13658	HAMILTON PK		BLANCA PK	278	1.5	BLANCA PK
40	14048	HANDIES PK					HANDIES PK
286	13454	HANSON PK		TOWER MTN	914	3.6	HANDIES PK
3	14420	HARVARD, MT					MT HARVARD
536	13139	HAYDEN MTN NORTH	M	HAYDEN MTN SOUTH	519	1.2	IRONTON
477	13206	HAYDEN MTN SOUTH	M	T 8	549	1.1	IRONTON
	13561	HAYDEN PK		UN 13635	181	0.8	HAYDEN PK
428	13262	HEISSPITZ, THE		FOUR, PK	362	0.9	STORM KING PK

Listed Alphabetically (continued)

RANK	HT	NAME	FN	NEIGHBOR	DROP	MI	QUAD
	13164	HELEN, MT		FATHER DYER PK	264	1.0	BRECKENRIDGE
437	13254	HENRY MTN					FAIRVIEW PK
358	13340	HERARD, MT					MEDANO PASS
352	13350	HERMIT PK		RITO ALTO PK	330	0.9	RITO ALTO PK
450	13232	HESPERUS MTN					LA PLATA
313	13409	HILLIARD PK		KEEFE PK	309	0.6	MAROON BELLS
91	13831	HOLY CROSS RIDGE		HOLY CROSS, MT OF THE	331	0.6	MT OF THE HOLY CROSS
51	14005	HOLY CROSS, MT OF THE					MT OF THE HOLY CROSS
474	13209	HOMESTAKE PK					HOMESTAKE RESERVIOR
351	13352	HOOSIER RIDGE		SILVERHEELS, MT	932	3.3	BRECKENRIDGE
	13012	HOPE MTN		JUPITER MTN	232	0.9	COLUMBINE PASS
64	13933	HOPE, MT		LA PLATA PK	873	2.9	MT ELBERT
289	13450	HORN PK		FLUTED PK	710	1.3	HORN PK
72	13898	HORSESHOE MTN		SHERMAN, MT	758	2.8	MT SHERMAN
606	13052	HOUGHTON MTN		TUTTLE MTN	472	1.5	HANDIES PK
37	14064	HUMBOLDT PK					CRESTONE PK
539	13136	HUNCHBACK MTN		WHITE DOME	356	0.8	STORM KING PK
257	13497	HUNTER PK		KEEFE PK	477	1.4	MAROON BELLS
593	13071	HUNTS PK		BUSHNELL PK	891	4.3	WELLSVILLE
52	14003	HURON PK					WINFIELD
	13447	HURRICANE PK		HANSON PK	267	0.8	HANDIES PK
60	13951	ICE MTN					WINFIELD
	13420	INDEX, THE		ANIMAS MTN	240	0.2	SNOWDON PK
	13831	IOWA PK		MISSOURI MTN	291	0.6	WINFIELD
	13500	IRON NIPPLE		UN 13828	200	0.6	BLANCA PK
466	13218	IRVING PK		OSO, MT	638	1.2	COLUMBINE PASS
553	13118	ISOLATION PK		COPELAND MTN	938	2.2	ISOLATION PK
336	13378	ITALIAN MTN					PEARL PASS
163	13670	JACKSON, MT					MT JACKSON
480	13205	JACQUE PK					COPPER MTN
94	13824	JAGGED MTN		SUNLIGHT PK	964	1.4	STORM KING PK
403	13294	JAMES PK		PARRY PK	714	1.5	EMPIRE
298	13432	JENKINS MTN		SAYRES BM	692	4.0	PIEPLANT
79	13860	JONES MTN A		HANDIES PK	520	1.7	HANDIES PK
467	13218	JONES MTN B		EMMA BURR MTN	638	3.0	TINCUP
	13604	JONES PK		UN 13712	144	0.7	MT ANTERO
92	13830	JUPITER MTN		WINDOM PK	370	0.6	COLUMBINE PASS
245	13516	KEEFE PK		UN 13537	496	1.3	MAROON BELLS
580	13085	KELLER MTN		UN 13180 C	745	2.1	WILLOW LAKES
508	13164	KELSO MTN		TORREYS PK	784	1.6	GRAYS PK
	13066	KENDALL BM		KENDALL MTN	286	0.7	SILVERTON
363	13338	KENDALL MTN		KENDALL PK	318	0.7	SILVERTON
288	13451	KENDALL PK					HOWARDSVILLE
	13125	KENNEDY, MT		AZTEC MTN	265	0.6	MTN VIEW CREST
	13220	KING SOLOMON MTN		LITTLE GIANT PK	280	0.5	HOWARDSVILLE
419	13276	KIOWA PK		NAVAJO PK	736	1.3	WARD

224

Listed Alphabetically (continued)

RANK	HT	NAME	FN	NEIGHBOR	DROP	MI	QUAD
23	14165	KIT CARSON MTN					CRESTONE PK
427	13265	KNIFE PT		SUNLIGHT PK	325	0.8	STORM KING PK
572	13095	KREUTZER, MT		EMMA BURR MTN	355	1.6	TINCUP
	13710	LA GARITA PK		UN 13895	232	1.9	HALFMOON PASS
272	13472	LA JUNTA PK		WASATCH MTN	612	0.7	TELLURIDE
5	14336	LA PLATA PK					MT ELBERT
415	13281	LADY WASHINGTON, MT		LONGS PK	301	0.7	LONGS PK
338	13375	LAKES PK		COTTONWOOD PK	675	2.1	ELECTRIC PK
	13051	LAMBERTSON PK		ITALIAN MTN	231	1.1	PEARL PASS
	13238	LANDSLIDE PK		GENEVA PK	138	0.4	MONTEZUMA
	13180	LAVENDER PK		MOSS, MT	280	0.2	LA PLATA
	13322	LEAHY PK		UN 13635	142	0.9	HAYDEN PK
482	13204	LENAWEE MTN		GRIZZLY PK D	344	1.0	GRAYS PK
236	13528	LEVIATHAN PK		JAGGED MTN	588	0.7	STORM KING PK
8	14286	LINCOLN, MT					ALMA
43	14042	LINDSEY, MT					BLANCA PK
44	14037	LITTLE BEAR PK		BLANCA PK	377	1.0	BLANCA PK
	13220	LITTLE FINGER		SIXTEEN, PK	120	0.1	SNOWDON PK
309	13416	LITTLE GIANT PK		KENDALL PK	556	1.3	HOWARDSVILLE
530	13143	LITTLE HORN PK		FLUTED PK	323	0.0	HORN PK
555	13113	LIZARD HEAD					MT WILSON
545	13128	LOMO LISO MTN		FRANCISCO PK	308	0.8	EL VALLE CREEK
491	13194	LONDON MTN		MOSQUITO PK	534	1.7	CLIMAX
15	14255	LONGS PK					LONGS PK
166	13661	LOOKOUT PK		GILPIN PK	841	8.6	OPHIR
	13692	LOVELAND MTN		BUCKSKIN, MT	192	0.8	CLIMAX
	13222	MACOMBER PK		TOWER MTN	122	0.7	HOWARDSVILLE
353	13348	MALEMUTE PK		CONUNDRUM PK	368	1.1	HAYDEN PK
174	13646	MAMMA, MT		GRIZZLY MTN	546	1.7	SAINT ELMO
425	13266	MARBLE MTN		MILWAUKEE PK	526	1.1	CRESTONE PK
261	13490	MARCY, MT		UN 13513	430	1.2	ELECTRIC PK
316	13405	MARIQUITA PK		CUATRO PK	385	1.4	EL VALLE CREEK
24	14156	MAROON PK					MAROON BELLS
2	14421	MASSIVE, MT					MT MASSIVE
193	13590	MATTERHORN PK		WETTERHORN PK	570	0.9	UNCOMPAHGRE PK
	13335	MAXWELL, MT		MARIQUITA PK	275	0.8	EL VALLE CREEK
216	13554	MCCAULEY PK		GRIZZLY PK C	454	0.7	COLUMBINE PASS
	13587	MCCLELLAN MTN		EDWARDS, MT	167	0.8	GRAYS PK
370	13327	MCHENRYS PK		CHIEFS HEAD PK	907	1.2	MCHENRYS PK
	13780	MCNAMEE PK		CLINTON PK	80	0.5	CLIMAX
259	13496	MEARS PK		T 0	556	1.3	MT SNEFFELS
68	13911	MEEKER, MT		LONGS PK	451	0.7	ALLENS PARK
	13275	MENDOTA PK		T 5	175	0.8	TELLURIDE
566	13100	MIDDLE MTN A		UN 13463	520	1.1	INDEPENDENCE PASS
	13060	MIDDLE MTN B		UN 13462 A	120	0.6	WINFIELD
394	13300	MIDDLE PK					DOLORES PK

225

Listed Alphabetically (continued)

RANK	HT	NAME	FN	NEIGHBOR	DROP	MI	QUAD
241	13522	MILWAUKEE PK		PICO ASILADO	302	0.5	CRESTONE PK
	13468	MIRANDA PK		UN 13565	288	0.9	EL VALLE CREEK
36	14067	MISSOURI MTN		BELFORD, MT	847	1.3	WINFIELD
148	13695	MONITOR PK		THIRTEEN, PK	315	0.2	STORM KING PK
523	13150	MONTEZUMA PK		SUMMIT PK	690	1.6	SUMMIT PK
344	13369	MONUMENTAL PK					GARFIELD
115	13781	MOSQUITO PK		BUCKSKIN, MT	561	2.3	CLIMAX
492	13192	MOSS, MT		HESPERUS MTN	372	0.7	LA PLATA
304	13425	MUMMY MTN		HAGUES PK	485	1.4	ESTES PARK
332	13380	MUSIC MTN		MILWAUKEE PK	400	0.9	CRESTONE PK
314	13409	NAVAJO PK		APACHE PK	309	0.4	MONARCH LAKE
481	13205	NEBO, MT		UN 13230 A	505	0.6	STORM KING PK
	13500	NEEDLE RIDGE		SUNLIGHT PK	200	0.4	STORM KING PK
101	13807	NIAGARA PK		JONES MTN A	587	0.6	HANDIES PK
317	13402	NINE, PK		STORM KING PK	582	0.5	STORM KING PK
	13023	NIWOT RIDGE		NAVAJO PK	163	0.6	MONARCH LAKE
254	13502	NORTH ARAPAHO PK					MONARCH LAKE
	14039	NORTH EOLUS		EOLUS, MT	179	0.2	STORM KING PK
	14014	NORTH MAROON PK		MAROON PK	234	0.4	MAROON BELLS
187	13614	NORTH STAR MTN		WHEELER MTN	434	0.9	BRECKENRIDGE
588	13075	NORTH TWILIGHT PK		TWILIGHT PK	335	0.4	SNOWDON PK
	13237	NOTCH MTN		UN 13248	217	0.9	MT OF THE HOLY CROSS
538	13138	OGALALLA PK		COPELAND MTN	718	1.4	ISOLATION PK
85	13845	OKLAHOMA, MT		MASSIVE, MT	745	1.8	MT CHAMPION
194	13589	ONE, PK		WHITE DOME	409	0.8	STORM KING PK
106	13801	ORGAN MTN A		SAN LUIS PK	694	2.0	SAN LUIS PK
619	13032	ORGAN MTN B		AMHERST MTN	452	0.4	COLUMBINE PASS
157	13684	OSO, MT					EMERALD LAKE
58	13971	OURAY, MT					MT OURAY
359	13340	OWEN A, MT		UN 13490	600	2.0	ELECTRIC PK
602	13058	OWEN B, MT					OH BE JOYFUL
26	14153	OXFORD, MT		BELFORD, MT	653	1.2	MT HARVARD
61	13950	PACIFIC PK		FLETCHER MTN	570	1.4	BRECKENRIDGE
258	13497	PAGODA MTN		LONGS PK	397	0.7	ISOLATION PK
578	13088	PAIUTE PK		AUDUBON, MT	468	0.9	MONARCH LAKE
	13319	PALMYRA PK		SILVER MTN B	179	0.5	TELLURIDE
208	13574	PARNASSUS, MT		BARD PK	537	1.0	GRAYS PK
323	13391	PARRY PK					EMPIRE
178	13633	PEAK 10		CRYSTAL PK	373	0.9	BRECKENRIDGE
490	13195	PEAK 9		PEAK 10	415	0.6	BRECKENRIDGE
348	13362	PEARL MTN		CASTLE PK	582	2.5	PEARL PASS
	13270	PECKS PK		BELFORD, MT	50	1.0	MT HARVARD
	13348	PEERLESS MTN		HORSESHOE MTN	168	0.9	MT SHERMAN
634	13006	PENNSYLVANIA MTN		EVANS B, MT	699	2.2	CLIMAX
549	13122	PETERS PK		UN 13222 B	342	0.4	EMERALD LAKE
218	13553	PETTINGELL PK					LOVELAND PASS

Listed Alphabetically (continued)

RANK	HT	NAME	FN	NEIGHBOR	DROP	MI	QUAD
188	13611	PICO ASILADO		CRESTONE NEEDLE	831	1.7	CRESTONE PK
57	13972	PIGEON PK					SNOWDON PK
546	13126	PIKA PK		GOLD DUST PK	506	0.7	MT JACKSON
30	14109	PIKES PK					PIKES PK
131	13738	PILOT KNOB		GOLDEN HORN	398	0.5	OPHIR
	13180	POINT PUN		GRAYSTONE PK	200	0.6	SNOWDON PK
138	13716	POLE CREEK MTN					POLE CREEK MTN
521	13151	POMEROY MTN		GRIZZLY MTN	611	2.1	SAINT ELMO
113	13786	POTOSI PK		TEAKETTLE MTN	806	1.0	IRONTON
475	13208	POWELL PK		MCHENRYS PK	388	0.4	MCHENRYS PK
199	13580	POWELL, MT					MT POWELL
333	13380	PRECARIOUS PK		UN 13631 B	640	2.1	MAROON BELLS
529	13144	PRECIPICE PK		U 3	484	1.5	WETTERHORN PK
20	14197	PRINCETON, MT					MT ANTERO
326	13384	PRIZE BM		UN 13631 A	604	1.6	PIEPLANT
	13739	PTARMIGAN PK		HORSESHOE MTN	279	2.5	MT SHERMAN
160	13676	PURGATOIRE PK		VERMEJO PK	849	1.8	CULEBRA PK
47	14018	PYRAMID PK					MAROON BELLS
281	13461	QUAIL MTN		HOPE, MT	921	1.4	MT ELBERT
13	14265	QUANDARY PK					BRECKENRIDGE
70	13908	RED MTN A		CULEBRA PK	448	0.7	CULEBRA PK
	13500	RED MTN B		GARFIELD PK	120	0.4	INDEPENDENCE PASS
455	13229	RED MTN C		HOOSIER RIDGE	369	0.7	BRECKENRIDGE
	13215	RED PK A		HOOSIER RIDGE	115	0.7	BRECKENRIDGE
494	13189	RED PK B		WILLOW BM	929	1.6	WILLOW LAKES
175	13642	REDCLIFF		COXCOMB PK	502	0.5	WETTERHORN PK
46	14034	REDCLOUD PK					REDCLOUD PK
318	13402	RHODA, MT		UN 13434	302	0.4	HOWARDSVILLE
275	13468	RIDGWAY, MT		TEAKETTLE MTN	448	1.0	MT SNEFFELS
114	13783	RINKER PK		LA PLATA PK	923	1.8	MT ELBERT
97	13821	RIO GRANDE PYRAMID					RIO GRANDE PYRAMID
110	13794	RITO ALTO PK					RITO ALTO PK
	13140	ROBESON PK		BARD PK	200	0.9	GRAYS PK
324	13391	ROGERS PK		EVANS A, MT	515	2.4	HARRIS PARK
150	13693	ROLLING MTN		SAN MIGUEL PK	913	2.3	OPHIR
207	13575	ROSALIE PK		EVANS A, MT	675	3.0	HARRIS PARK
	13184	ROWE MTN		ROWE PK	44	0.5	TRAIL RIDGE
	13420	ROWE PK		HAGUES PK	200	0.4	TRAIL RIDGE
418	13277	RUBY MTN		GRAYS PK	439	1.2	MONTEZUMA
	13003	RUFFNER MTN		S 7	23	0.4	SAMS
623	13020	S 10	Z	S 9	360	0.8	SAMS
444	13242	S 4	Z	S 6	302	0.8	MT SNEFFELS
292	13441	S 6	Z	T 0	381	1.0	MT SNEFFELS
462	13220	S 7	Z	MEARS PK	400	1.0	SAMS
439	13252	S 8	Z	MEARS PK	552	1.6	SAMS
541	13134	S 9	Z	S 8	354	0.7	SAMS

227

Listed Alphabetically (continued)

RANK	HT	NAME	FN	NEIGHBOR	DROP	MI	QUAD
	13060	SAINT SOPHIA RIDGE		EMMA, MT	160	0.5	TELLURIDE
282	13460	SAN JOAQUIN RIDGE		SILVER MTN B	360	1.3	TELLURIDE
50	14014	SAN LUIS PK					SAN LUIS PK
124	13752	SAN MIGUEL PK					OPHIR
498	13180	SANTA FE PK		GENEVA PK	480	1.3	MONTEZUMA
537	13139	SAVAGE PK					MT JACKSON
132	13738	SAYRES BM		LA PLATA PK	958	1.9	MT ELBERT
420	13274	SEIGAL MTN		UN 13722 B	374	1.0	HANDIES PK
158	13682	SEVEN, PK		SIX, PK	422	0.8	STORM KING PK
	13132	SEWANEE PK		UN 13147	232	0.6	GARFIELD
17	14229	SHAVANO, MT					MAYSVILLE
406	13292	SHEEP MTN A		CANBY MTN	632	1.9	HOWARDSVILLE
	13188	SHEEP MTN B		SAN MIGUEL PK	128	1.3	MT WILSON
505	13168	SHEEP MTN C		UN 13681	592	2.7	SHEEP MTN
594	13070	SHEEP MTN D		UN 13105	370	0.4	COLUMBINE PASS
126	13748	SHERIDAN, MT		SHERMAN, MT	608	1.3	MT SHERMAN
45	14036	SHERMAN, MT					MT SHERMAN
181	13628	SILEX, MT		STORM KING PK	808	0.8	STORM KING PK
139	13714	SILVER MTN A					UNCOMPAHGRE PK
274	13470	SILVER MTN B		WASATCH MTN	410	2.2	TELLURIDE
96	13822	SILVERHEELS, MT					ALMA
144	13705	SIX, PK		JAGGED MTN	685	1.0	STORM KING PK
	13500	SIXTEEN, PK		FIFTEEN, PK	80	0.1	SNOWDON PK
283	13460	SLEEPING SEXTON		NORTH MAROON PK	440	0.6	MAROON BELLS
27	14150	SNEFFELS, MT					MT SNEFFELS
447	13234	SNIKTAU, MT		GRIZZLY PK D	520	2.4	GRAYS PK
587	13077	SNOWDON PK					SNOWDON PK
31	14092	SNOWMASS MTN					SNOWMASS MTN
	13620	SNOWMASS PK		HAGERMAN PK	120	0.2	SNOWMASS MTN
	13397	SOUTH ARAPAHO PK		NORTH ARAPAHO PK	97	0.5	MONARCH LAKE
334	13380	SOUTH LOOKOUT PK		U S GRANT PK	520	1.2	OPHIR
525	13148	SOUTH RIVER PK					SOUTH RIVER PK
	13100	SOUTH TWILIGHT PK		TWILIGHT PK	200	0.3	SNOWDON PK
	13842	SPAULDING, MT		EVANS A, MT	262	1.1	MT EVANS
	13123	SPILLER PK		BABCOCK PK	183	0.5	LA PLATA
305	13423	SPREAD EAGLE PK		UN 13524 B	443	0.9	ELECTRIC PK
442	13244	SPRING MTN		VENABLE PK	464	0.7	HORN PK
111	13794	SQUARE TOP MTN		EDWARDS, MT	814	3.4	MONTEZUMA
242	13521	STAR PK		CASTLE PK	816	4.1	PEARL PASS
55	13983	STEWART PK		SAN LUIS PK	883	2.5	STEWART PK
125	13752	STORM KING PK		TRINITY PK	612	1.3	STORM KING PK
265	13487	STORM PK A		TOWER MTN	627	1.4	SILVERTON
	13326	STORM PK B		LONGS PK	186	0.8	LONGS PK
	13134	SULLIVAN MTN		SANTA FE PK	274	0.6	MONTEZUMA
345	13368	SULTAN MTN					SILVERTON
395	13300	SUMMIT PK					SUMMIT PK

228

Listed Alphabetically (continued)

RANK	HT	NAME	FN	NEIGHBOR	DROP	MI	QUAD
39	14059	SUNLIGHT PK		WINDOM PK	399	0.5	STORM KING PK
374	13321	SUNSHINE MTN					HANDIES PK
53	14001	SUNSHINE PK		REDCLOUD PK	501	1.3	REDCLOUD PK
134	13735	T 0	Z	DALLAS PK	395	1.4	TELLURIDE
269	13477	T 10	Z	THREE NEEDLES	537	0.6	IRONTON
248	13510	T 11	Z	LOOKOUT PK	452	1.3	TELLURIDE
293	13436	T 5	Z	TELLURIDE PK	416	2.8	TELLURIDE
349	13359	T 7	Z	TELLURIDE PK	499	1.0	IRONTON
377	13315	T 8	Z	T 7	495	0.7	IRONTON
25	14155	TABEGUACHE PK		SHAVANO, MT	455	0.7	SAINT ELMO
172	13651	TAYLOR MTN		AETNA, MT	631	1.2	GARFIELD
294	13435	TAYLOR PK A		STAR PK	815	1.3	PEARL PASS
518	13153	TAYLOR PK B		POWELL PK	413	1.0	MCHENRYS PK
98	13819	TEAKETTLE MTN		SNEFFELS, MT	759	1.7	MT SNEFFELS
	13509	TELLURIDE PK		UN 13510 B	289	0.5	IRONTON
	13420	TEN, PK		JAGGED MTN	280	0.3	STORM KING PK
476	13208	TEOCALLI MTN		UN 13550	788	2.4	GOTHIC
	13213	THIRSTY PK		LAKES PK	233	0.8	ELECTRIC PK
	13705	THIRTEEN, PK		ANIMAS MTN	245	0.3	STORM KING PK
266	13481	THREE NEEDLES		T 11	421	1.0	TELLURIDE
268	13478	THREE, PK		TRINITY PK EAST	498	0.9	STORM KING PK
	13108	THUNDER MTN		GREYLOCK MTN	248	1.0	COLUMBINE PASS
189	13604	TIJERAS PK		PICO ASILADO	744	1.7	CRESTONE PK
11	14267	TORREYS PK		GRAYS PK	560	0.6	GRAYS PK
219	13552	TOWER MTN					HOWARDSVILLE
	13852	TRAVER PK		CLINTON PK	232	0.7	CLIMAX
237	13528	TREASURE MTN					SNOWMASS MTN
	13701	TREASUREVAULT MTN		MOSQUITO PK	281	0.4	CLIMAX
278	13462	TREASURY MTN		TREASURE MTN	522	1.4	SNOWMASS MTN
375	13321	TRICO PK		UN 13510 B	461	0.9	IRONTON
243	13517	TRINCHERA PK					TRINCHERA PK
103	13805	TRINITY PK		VESTAL PK	945	1.2	STORM KING PK
128	13745	TRINITY PK EAST	M	TRINITY PK	405	0.2	STORM KING PK
120	13765	TRINITY PK WEST	M	TRINITY PK	385	0.4	STORM KING PK
412	13282	TRURO PK		UN 13300 A	822	1.3	NEW YORK PK
449	13233	TURNER PK					TINCUP
89	13835	TURRET PK		PIGEON PK	735	0.5	SNOWDON PK
484	13203	TUTTLE MTN		CALIFORNIA MTN	503	1.3	HANDIES PK
532	13140	TWELVE, PK	Z	NORTH EOLUS	320	0.5	STORM KING PK
162	13672	TWETO, MT		BUCKSKIN, MT	412	1.2	CLIMAX
513	13158	TWILIGHT PK					SNOWDON PK
200	13580	TWIN PKS A		ELLINGWOOD PT	640	1.6	TWIN PKS
	13333	TWIN PKS B		RINKER PK	233	0.9	MT ELBERT
299	13432	TWIN SISTER EAST	M				OPHIR
339	13374	TWIN SISTER WEST	M	TWIN SISTER EAST	394	0.4	OPHIR
631	13012	TWIN SISTERS		BUSHNELL PK	552	1.0	BUSHNELL PK

229

Listed Alphabetically (continued)

RANK	HT	NAME	FN	NEIGHBOR	DROP	MI	QUAD
	13420	TWIN THUMBS		ELEVEN, PK	120	0.2	STORM KING PK
141	13711	TWINING PK					MT CHAMPION
270	13475	TWO, PK		THREE, PK	535	0.8	STORM KING PK
445	13241	U 3	Z	REDCLIFF	461	0.7	WETTERHORN PK
119	13767	U S GRANT PK		GOLDEN HORN	747	1.7	OPHIR
636	13001	UN 13001		UN 13202	501	0.9	MT CHAMPION
635	13003	UN 13003		UN 13026	503	1.9	MT CHAMPION
632	13010	UN 13010 A		HAGAR MTN	350	1.2	LOVELAND PASS
633	13010	UN 13010 B					CIMARRONA PK
629	13015	UN 13015		UN 13402	315	1.2	HALFMOON PASS
628	13016	UN 13016		UN 13051	676	1.5	UNCOMPAHGRE PK
627	13017	UN 13017		UN 13157	400	1.0	RIO GRANDE PYRAMID
624	13020	UN 13020 A		UN 13336	320	0.5	MAROON BELLS
625	13020	UN 13020 B		PICO ASILADO	360	0.7	CRESTONE PK
626	13020	UN 13020 C		MONTEZUMA PK	440	0.6	SUMMIT PK
622	13024	UN 13024		UN 13180 C	484	0.8	WILLOW LAKES
621	13026	UN 13026		UN 13202	326	1.7	MT CHAMPION
620	13028	UN 13028		UN 13060 B	328	0.7	RITO ALTO PK
617	13034	UN 13034		UN 13111	654	2.0	BALDY CINCO
615	13038	UN 13038		SOUTH ARAPAHO PK	338	0.7	MONARCH LAKE
614	13039	UN 13039		SLEEPING SEXTON	419	0.9	MAROON BELLS
612	13041	UN 13041 A		UN 13057	581	0.9	VAIL EAST
613	13041	UN 13041 B		UN 13079	301	0.7	WILLOW LAKES
611	13042	UN 13042		TWIN SISTER EAST	942	2.1	SILVERTON
610	13046	UN 13046		SNOWDON PK	386	0.6	SNOWDON PK
608	13050	UN 13050 A		UN 13384	390	0.8	CRESTONE PK
609	13050	UN 13050 B		UN 13345	550	1.5	CUMBERLAND PASS
607	13051	UN 13051		SILVER MTN A	351	1.1	UNCOMPAHGRE PK
605	13054	UN 13054		EUREKA MTN	594	1.6	RITO ALTO PK
604	13055	UN 13055		KREUTZER, MT	315	1.6	TINCUP
603	13057	UN 13057		UN 13085 B	557	1.0	VAIL EAST
600	13060	UN 13060 A		CLARK PK	320	0.5	CAPITOL PK
601	13060	UN 13060 B		UN 13062 B	360	0.4	RITO ALTO PK
597	13062	UN 13062 A		SNOWMASS PK	642	1.8	SNOWMASS MTN
598	13062	UN 13062 B		HERMIT PK	842	1.9	RITO ALTO PK
596	13069	UN 13069		CROWN MTN	329	3.4	HOWARDSVILLE
595	13070	UN 13070		POMEROY MTN	330	0.6	SAINT ELMO
591	13074	UN 13074		UN 13300 A	454	1.0	NEW YORK PK
589	13075	UN 13075		HANSON PK	415	1.0	HANDIES PK
585	13078	UN 13078		UN 13317	738	1.4	SAINT ELMO
584	13079	UN 13079		UN 13180 C	659	1.3	WILLOW LAKES
581	13085	UN 13085 A		UN 13100 B	625	1.0	MT JACKSON
582	13085	UN 13085 B		UN 13245	465	0.8	VAIL EAST
576	13090	UN 13090 A		UN 13140 C	350	1.1	NEW YORK PK
577	13090	UN 13090 B		UN 13245	710	2.0	VAIL EAST
575	13091	UN 13091		UN 13106 A	591	1.8	UNCOMPAHGRE PK

Listed Alphabetically (continued)

RANK	HT	NAME	FN	NEIGHBOR	DROP	MI	QUAD
574	13093	UN 13093		SUNSHINE MTN	353	1.4	HANDIES PK
573	13095	UN 13095		CHICAGO PK	315	0.5	TELLURIDE
567	13100	UN 13100 A		UN 13681	480	1.8	SHEEP MTN
568	13100	UN 13100 B		PIKA PK	600	2.1	MT JACKSON
569	13100	UN 13100 C		WHITEHOUSE MTN	320	0.5	OURAY
570	13100	UN 13100 D		BLANCA PK	520	1.3	BLANCA PK
571	13100	UN 13100 E		UN 13111	400	1.9	BALDY CINCO
565	13102	UN 13102		MONUMENTAL PK	482	1.7	GARFIELD
564	13105	UN 13105		EMERSON MTN	325	0.4	COLUMBINE PASS
562	13106	UN 13106		UNCOMPAHGRE PK	726	2.2	UNCOMPAHGRE PK
560	13109	UN 13109		WHITEHEAD PK	329	0.6	HOWARDSVILLE
559	13110	UN 13110		UN 13308	450	1.2	STORM KING PK
558	13111	UN 13111		UN 13510 A	811	4.6	SAN LUIS PK
554	13117	UN 13117		GRIZZLY PK D	377	1.0	GRAYS PK
551	13121	UN 13121 A		GREYLOCK MTN	341	0.5	COLUMBINE PASS
552	13121	UN 13121 B		GUYSELMAN MTN	421	0.6	MT POWELL
550	13122	UN 13122		UN 13490	302	1.2	RITO ALTO PK
547	13123	UN 13123 A		UN 13498	463	1.1	DOLORES PK
548	13123	UN 13123 B		COTTONWOOD PK	303	0.8	ELECTRIC PK
544	13130	UN 13130		UN 13180 A	350	0.0	MAROON BELLS
542	13132	UN 13132		UN 13260 A	512	0.9	HANDIES PK
533	13140	UN 13140 A		UN 13255	320	0.6	WINFIELD
534	13140	UN 13140 B		JENKINS MTN	320	1.1	PIEPLANT
535	13140	UN 13140 C		TRURO PK	320	0.4	NEW YORK PK
528	13145	UN 13145		LA JUNTA PK	325	0.6	TELLURIDE
526	13147	UN 13147		AETNA, MT	527	1.6	GARFIELD
519	13153	UN 13153 A		HERARD, MT	653	0.9	MEDANO PASS
520	13153	UN 13153 B		ADAMS, MT	373	0.7	HORN PK
517	13155	UN 13155		UN 13285	415	1.7	SAN LUIS PK
515	13157	UN 13157		RIO GRANDE PYRAMID	300	0.9	RIO GRANDE PYRAMID
514	13158	UN 13158		UNCOMPAHGRE PK	378	1.8	UNCOMPAHGRE PK
512	13159	UN 13159		LOOKOUT PK	379	1.3	OPHIR
510	13162	UN 13162 A		BALDY CINCO	493	1.3	BALDY CINCO
511	13162	UN 13162 B		UN 13550	382	0.9	GOTHIC
509	13164	UN 13164		HALF PK	384	1.3	POLE CREEK MTN
507	13165	UN 13165		CANBY MTN	577	0.7	HOWARDSVILLE
504	13169	UN 13169		UN 13230 A	989	1.2	RIO GRANDE PYRAMID
499	13180	UN 13180 A		UN 13631 B	320	0.5	MAROON BELLS
500	13180	UN 13180 B		UN 13691	524	2.1	REDCLOUD PK
501	13180	UN 13180 C		WILLOW BM	760	1.6	WILLOW LAKES
493	13192	UN 13192		UN 13768	372	2.2	MT JACKSON
489	13198	UN 13198		GRIZZLY PK A	658	2.8	INDEPENDENCE PASS
488	13201	UN 13201		UN 13300 C	661	1.3	WETTERHORN PK
487	13202	UN 13202		TWINING PK	422	2.0	MT CHAMPION
485	13203	UN 13203		CUATRO PK	303	1.1	TRINCHERA PK
478	13206	UN 13206		UN 13377	306	0.6	WETTERHORN PK

231

Listed Alphabetically (continued)

RANK	HT	NAME	FN	NEIGHBOR	DROP	MI	QUAD
472	13212	UN 13212		UN 13284	312	0.7	MT CHAMPION
471	13213	UN 13213		UN 13230 B	753	1.5	VAIL EAST
469	13215	UN 13215		PETTINGELL PK	395	1.5	LOVELAND PASS
468	13216	UN 13216		UN 13380	316	0.7	MAROON BELLS
463	13220	UN 13220 A		UN 13417	800	1.8	EMERALD LAKE
464	13220	UN 13220 B		UN 13260 C	520	1.6	VAIL EAST
458	13222	UN 13222 A		UN 13340 B	322	0.6	UNCOMPAHGRE PK
459	13222	UN 13222 B		UN 13300 D	402	0.8	EMERALD LAKE
456	13229	UN 13229		UN 13565	329	0.6	EL VALLE CREEK
453	13230	UN 13230 A		UN 13308	770	1.9	RIO GRANDE PYRAMID
454	13230	UN 13230 B		UN 13260 C	730	2.0	VAIL EAST
451	13232	UN 13232 A		SAYRES BM	332	1.7	PIEPLANT
452	13232	UN 13232 B		UN 13260 B	412	0.4	MAROON BELLS
446	13235	UN 13235		UN 13253	375	0.9	PIEPLANT
443	13244	UN 13244		UN 13336	424	1.1	HIGHLAND PK
441	13245	UN 13245		UN 13260 C	785	4.0	WILLOW LAKES
440	13248	UN 13248		HOLY CROSS RIDGE	308	1.3	MT OF THE HOLY CROSS
438	13253	UN 13253		UN 13255	433	2.0	WINFIELD
436	13255	UN 13255		GRIZZLY PK E	555	1.6	WINFIELD
430	13260	UN 13260 A		SEIGAL MTN	520	2.2	HANDIES PK
431	13260	UN 13260 B		PRECARIOUS PK	440	0.8	MAROON BELLS
432	13260	UN 13260 C					VAIL EAST
433	13260	UN 13260 D		CONEY BM	400	1.2	FINGER MESA
429	13261	UN 13261		UN 13278	321	0.7	WEMINUCHE PASS
422	13270	UN 13270		BROKEN HAND PK	490	0.5	CRESTONE PK
416	13278	UN 13278		RIO GRANDE PYRAMID	633	1.1	WEMINUCHE PASS
413	13282	UN 13282		UN 13300 A	822	1.1	NEW YORK PK
410	13284	UN 13284		UN 13300 B	424	2.7	MT CHAMPION
409	13285	UN 13285		SAN LUIS PK	665	2.5	SAN LUIS PK
404	13294	UN 13294		PETTINGELL PK	314	1.0	LOVELAND PASS
402	13295	UN 13295		SAYRES BM	435	2.7	PIEPLANT
396	13300	UN 13300 A		UN 13505	520	1.4	NEW YORK PK
397	13300	UN 13300 B		TWINING PK	600	2.7	MT CHAMPION
398	13300	UN 13300 C		WETTERHORN PK	440	0.7	WETTERHORN PK
399	13300	UN 13300 D		UN 13302	560	0.6	COLUMBINE PASS
400	13300	UN 13300 E		BEATTIE PK	320	0.6	OPHIR
401	13300	UN 13300 F		UN 13340 B	320	0.6	UNCOMPAHGRE PK
389	13302	UN 13302		OSO, MT	722	1.7	STORM KING PK
387	13308	UN 13308		UN 13342	606	0.8	RIO GRANDE PYRAMID
385	13310	UN 13310		UN 13340 A	330	0.6	EMERALD LAKE
379	13312	UN 13312 A		UN 13566	452	0.8	REDCLOUD PK
380	13312	UN 13312 B		PEARL MTN	412	0.6	PEARL PASS
381	13312	UN 13312 C		UN 13463	452	1.0	PIEPLANT
378	13313	UN 13313		BALDY CINCO	413	0.7	BALDY CINCO
376	13317	UN 13317		UN 13626	737	2.3	SAINT ELMO
373	13322	UN 13322		JENKINS MTN	902	2.4	PIEPLANT

Listed Alphabetically (continued)

RANK	HT	NAME	FN	NEIGHBOR	DROP	MI	QUAD
372	13325	UN 13325		STORM PK A	465	0.5	SILVERTON
368	13330	UN 13330		HANSON PK	550	1.9	HANDIES PK
364	13336	UN 13336		BUCKSKIN BM	636	1.1	MAROON BELLS
360	13340	UN 13340 A		UN 13417	440	1.2	EMERALD LAKE
361	13340	UN 13340 B		UN 13411	745	1.7	UNCOMPAHGRE PK
357	13342	UN 13342		UTE RIDGE	726	1.4	RIO GRANDE PYRAMID
355	13345	UN 13345		EMMA BURR MTN	445	1.1	CUMBERLAND PASS
354	13346	UN 13346		GOLD DUST PK	806	1.3	MT JACKSON
340	13374	UN 13374		HARVARD, MT	394	1.9	MT HARVARD
337	13377	UN 13377		UN 13411	357	0.5	WETTERHORN PK
335	13380	UN 13380		WHITE ROCK MTN	480	1.3	GOTHIC
327	13384	UN 13384		CLEVELAND PK	364	0.9	CRESTONE PK
320	13401	UN 13401		TIJERAS PK	301	0.9	CRESTONE PK
319	13402	UN 13402		UN 13895	422	1.7	HALFMOON PASS
311	13411	UN 13411		WETTERHORN PK	471	1.2	WETTERHORN PK
308	13417	UN 13417		OSO, MT	677	0.8	EMERALD LAKE
307	13420	UN 13420		SNOWMASS MTN	760	1.2	SNOWMASS MTN
303	13427	UN 13427		WOOD MTN	407	1.4	HANDIES PK
300	13432	UN 13432		SUNSHINE PK	332	0.9	REDCLOUD PK
297	13433	UN 13433		JACKSON, MT	413	0.6	MT JACKSON
296	13434	UN 13434		KENDALL PK	534	1.2	HOWARDSVILLE
295	13435	UN 13435		YALE, MT	375	0.8	MT YALE
290	13450	UN 13450		CARSON PK	350	1.2	POLE CREEK MTN
287	13454	UN 13454		UN 13795	394	1.0	REDCLOUD PK
284	13460	UN 13460		SAYRES BM	440	1.4	INDEPENDENCE PASS
279	13462	UN 13462 A		BROWNS PK	322	0.6	WINFIELD
280	13462	UN 13462 B		UN 13517	562	1.6	WINFIELD
277	13463	UN 13463		RED MTN B	563	1.3	INDEPENDENCE PASS
276	13466	UN 13466		VERMEJO PK	557	1.2	CULEBRA PK
273	13472	UN 13472					MT OURAY
262	13490	UN 13490		UN 13513	990	1.0	RITO ALTO PK
256	13498	UN 13498		UN 13540 A	358	0.6	DOLORES PK
255	13500	UN 13500		TWINING PK	360	0.7	INDEPENDENCE PASS
252	13505	UN 13505		UN 13631 A	525	1.3	NEW YORK PK
249	13510	UN 13510 A					BALDY CINCO
250	13510	UN 13510 B		EMMA, MT	610	5.0	IRONTON
247	13513	UN 13513		GIBBS PK	453	2.4	ELECTRIC PK
244	13517	UN 13517		HURON PK	457	1.5	WINFIELD
239	13524	UN 13524 A		CARSON PK	464	1.4	POLE CREEK MTN
240	13524	UN 13524 B		GIBBS PK	624	3.3	RITO ALTO PK
233	13531	UN 13531		HOPE, MT	431	1.5	MT ELBERT
231	13535	UN 13535 A		DEER MTN	555	1.2	MT CHAMPION
232	13535	UN 13535 B		JONES MTN A	515	1.5	HANDIES PK
230	13537	UN 13537		WHITE ROCK MTN	757	2.5	MAROON BELLS
225	13540	UN 13540 A		WILSON PK	520	1.0	DOLORES PK
226	13540	UN 13540 B		WOOD MTN	520	2.6	REDCLOUD PK

Listed Alphabetically (continued)

RANK	HT	NAME	FN	NEIGHBOR	DROP	MI	QUAD
223	13541	UN 13541		UN 13580 B	361	0.8	CRESTONE PK
221	13546	UN 13546		ADAMS, MT	646	0.8	HORN PK
220	13550	UN 13550		UN 13803	530	0.9	GOTHIC
212	13565	UN 13565		CULEBRA PK	545	1.4	EL VALLE CREEK
211	13566	UN 13566		UN 13691	746	1.9	REDCLOUD PK
205	13577	UN 13577		UN 13660 A	317	0.5	BLANCA PK
201	13580	UN 13580 A		UN 13581	360	1.2	POLE CREEK MTN
202	13580	UN 13580 B		ADAMS, MT	440	0.5	HORN PK
197	13581	UN 13581		CARSON PK	681	1.5	POLE CREEK MTN
186	13616	UN 13616		LA PLATA PK	436	1.6	MT ELBERT
183	13626	UN 13626		PRINCETON, MT	486	1.4	MT YALE
179	13631	UN 13631 A		GARFIELD PK	971	2.2	NEW YORK PK
180	13631	UN 13631 B		UN 13722 A	331	0.7	MAROON BELLS
177	13635	UN 13635		CATHEDRAL PK	335	0.9	HAYDEN PK
167	13660	UN 13660 A		CALIFORNIA PK	400	1.1	TWIN PKS
168	13660	UN 13660 B		POLE CREEK MTN	840	1.5	POLE CREEK MTN
161	13674	UN 13674		HALF PK	734	1.3	REDCLOUD PK
159	13681	UN 13681		SILVER MTN A	501	1.0	UNCOMPAHGRE PK
153	13688	UN 13688 A		UN 13832	428	1.6	REDCLOUD PK
154	13688	UN 13688 B		UN 13722 B	388	1.1	HANDIES PK
151	13691	UN 13691		UN 13832	471	2.7	REDCLOUD PK
140	13712	UN 13712		SHAVANO, MT	332	0.9	MT ANTERO
136	13722	UN 13722 A		UN 13932	302	0.4	MAROON BELLS
137	13722	UN 13722 B					HANDIES PK
133	13736	UN 13736		DEER MTN	676	1.2	MT CHAMPION
121	13762	UN 13762		HARVARD, MT	822	2.8	MT HARVARD
118	13768	UN 13768		HOLY CROSS RIDGE	388	0.8	MT OF THE HOLY CROSS
109	13795	UN 13795		HANDIES PK	495	1.3	REDCLOUD PK
107	13799	UN 13799		UN 13980	339	0.5	CRESTONE PK
105	13803	UN 13803		CASTLE PK	423	0.9	MAROON BELLS
102	13806	UN 13806		JONES MTN A	466	0.8	HANDIES PK
99	13811	UN 13811		UN 13832	551	1.2	REDCLOUD PK
95	13823	UN 13823		CASCO PK	883	1.8	INDEPENDENCE PASS
93	13828	UN 13828		LINDSEY, MT	688	1.2	BLANCA PK
90	13832	UN 13832		REDCLOUD PK	812	1.4	REDCLOUD PK
88	13841	UN 13841		FLETCHER MTN	421	0.7	COPPER MTN
75	13870	UN 13870					SAINT ELMO
73	13895	UN 13895					HALFMOON PASS
65	13932	UN 13932		PYRAMID PK	312	0.6	MAROON BELLS
56	13980	UN 13980		KIT CARSON MTN	360	0.2	CRESTONE PK
6	14309	UNCOMPAHGRE PK					UNCOMPAHGRE PK
	13036	UNITED STATES MTN		CHICAGO PK	176	1.0	IRONTON
285	13455	UTE RIDGE		WHITE DOME	962	4.9	RIO GRANDE PYRAMID
271	13475	V 10	Z	GRIZZLY PK B	375	0.7	OPHIR
386	13309	V 2	Z	U S GRANT PK	409	0.8	OPHIR
238	13528	V 3	Z	U S GRANT PK	388	0.4	OPHIR

234

Listed Alphabetically (continued)

RANK	HT	NAME	FN	NEIGHBOR	DROP	MI	QUAD
227	13540	V 4	Z	U S GRANT PK	320	0.4	OPHIR
516	13156	V 5	Z	SOUTH LOOKOUT PK	616	1.3	OPHIR
434	13260	V 9	Z	ROLLING MTN	397	1.0	OPHIR
301	13428	VALLECITO MTN		LEVIATHAN PK	568	0.5	STORM KING PK
495	13185	VALOIS, MT		AZTEC MTN	325	2.1	COLUMBINE PASS
	13024	VAN WIRT MTN		UN 13102	284	0.7	GARFIELD
366	13334	VENABLE PK		FLUTED PK	634	2.7	RITO ALTO PK
135	13723	VERMEJO PK		RED MTN A	761	1.3	CULEBRA PK
74	13894	VERMILLION PK					OPHIR
77	13864	VESTAL PK					STORM KING PK
579	13088	VIRGINIA PK		UN 13140 A	428	0.8	WINFIELD
388	13307	WARREN, MT		ROGERS PK	367	1.1	MT EVANS
214	13555	WASATCH MTN		LOOKOUT PK	495	2.1	TELLURIDE
	13292	WAVERLY MTN		OXFORD, MT	152	1.1	MT HARVARD
371	13326	WEST BUFFALO PK					MARMOT PK
	13047	WEST DYER MTN		DYER MTN	267	0.7	MT SHERMAN
616	13035	WEST ELK PK					WEST ELK PK
599	13062	WEST NEEDLE MTN		SOUTH TWILIGHT PK	562	0.7	SNOWDON PK
184	13626	WEST SPANISH PK					SPANISH PKS
	13572	WESTON PK		PTARMIGAN PK	272	1.1	MT SHERMAN
49	14015	WETTERHORN PK					WETTERHORN PK
586	13078	WHALE PK		LANDSLIDE PK	982	4.8	JEFFERSON
152	13690	WHEELER MTN		FLETCHER MTN	310	1.6	COPPER MTN
321	13401	WHITE BM		WHITE ROCK MTN	381	0.5	GOTHIC
182	13627	WHITE DOME		TRINITY PK EAST	967	2.2	STORM KING PK
	13684	WHITE RIDGE		SHERMAN, MT	184	1.2	MT SHERMAN
228	13540	WHITE ROCK MTN		UN 13550	800	2.8	GOTHIC
164	13667	WHITE, MT		ANTERO, MT	847	1.3	MT ANTERO
222	13542	WHITECROSS MTN		HANDIES PK	562	1.4	REDCLOUD PK
	13259	WHITEHEAD PK		RHODA, MT	119	0.4	HOWARDSVILLE
260	13492	WHITEHOUSE MTN		TEAKETTLE MTN	592	1.9	OURAY
421	13271	WHITNEY PK		UN 13768	691	1.4	MT OF THE HOLY CROSS
315	13408	WILCOX, MT		ARGENTINE PK	548	1.1	MONTEZUMA
426	13266	WILDHORSE PK		SEIGAL MTN	966	4.0	WETTERHORN PK
330	13382	WILLIAMS MTN					MT CHAMPION
561	13108	WILLIAMS MTN NORTH	M	WILLIAMS MTN	408	0.8	MT CHAMPION
382	13312	WILLIAMS MTN SOUTH A	M	WILLIAMS MTN	572	1.5	THIMBLE ROCK
486	13203	WILLIAMS MTN SOUTH B	M	WILLIAMS MTN	423	0.5	MT CHAMPION
618	13033	WILLIAMS MTN SOUTH C	M	WILLIAMS MTN SOUTH A	493	1.4	THIMBLE ROCK
531	13142	WILLOUGHBY MTN		UN 13336	442	1.8	HIGHLAND PK
350	13357	WILLOW BM					WILLOW LAKES
48	14017	WILSON PK		WILSON, MT	877	1.5	MT WILSON
16	14246	WILSON, MT					MT WILSON
33	14082	WINDOM PK					COLUMBINE PASS
	13077	WINFIELD PK		VIRGINIA PK	177	0.7	WINFIELD
	13041	WOLCOTT MTN		S 6	181	0.6	MT SNEFFELS

235

Listed Alphabetically (continued)

RANK	HT	NAME	FN	NEIGHBOR	DROP	MI	QUAD
169	13660	WOOD MTN		UN 13688 B	320	0.5	HANDIES PK
21	14196	YALE, MT					MT YALE
	13177	YELLOW MTN		PILOT KNOB	197	0.6	OPHIR
246	13514	YPSILON MTN					TRAIL RIDGE

Index

238

244

Related Titles from Johnson Books

ARIZONA'S MOUNTAINS
A Hiking and Climbing Guide
Bob and Dotty Martin

EXPLORING THE BLACK HILLS AND BADLANDS
A Guide for Hikers, Cross-country Skiers, and Mountain Bikers
Hiram Rogers

MEXICO'S COPPER CANYON COUNTRY
A Hiking and Backpacking Guide
Revised Edition
M. John Fayhee

THE OUTDOOR ATHLETE
Total Training for Outdoor Performance
Steve Ilg

ROADSIDE HISTORY OF COLORADO
Revised Edition
James McTighe

THE SAN JUAN MOUNTAINS
A Climbing and Hiking Guide
Robert F. Rosebrough

TAKE 'EM ALONG
Sharing the Wilderness with your Children
Barbara J. Euser